The British Monarchy

The British Monarchy
in the twentieth century

Philip Howard

Hamish Hamilton
London

This book was designed and produced by
George Rainbird Ltd
36 Park Street
London WIY 4DE

Published in Great Britain in 1977 by
Hamish Hamilton Ltd
90 Great Russell Street
London WC1B 3PT

Text set by Jolly & Barber Ltd, Rugby.
Printed and bound by Dai Nippon Printing Co. Ltd,
Tokyo, Japan.

ISBN 0 241 89564 2

Frontispiece The Coronation of Her Majesty
Queen Elizabeth II in Westminster Abbey 1953

For Juliette and Jock

Acknowledgments

The author's grateful thanks are due to:

Hugo Vickers, who did the research and allowed access to his comprehensive
files and library on royalty;
Joy Law, the most punctilious and creative of editors, for help with the text and
illustrations;
Irene Clephane for editorial help and the index;
Patrick Yapp for designing the book;
the Buckingham Palace press office, for its customary efficiency and helpfulness
in answering questions;
Mrs Doë Howard, for research;
Sir Alan Lascelles, for wise advice and access to his library.

*The author and publishers gratefully acknowledge permission to quote short extracts from
the following books:*

The Second World War, Volume I, *The Gathering Storm,* by Winston S. Churchill,
Cassell, 1948
King George V by Harold Nicolson, Constable, 1952
As It Happened by Clement Attlee, Heinemann, 1954
King George VI by John Wheeler-Bennett, Macmillan, 1958
A Dictionary of Modern English Usage by H. W. Fowler, second edition revised
by Sir Ernest Gowers, Oxford University Press, 1965
A Wreath to Clio by Sir John Wheeler-Bennett, Macmillan, 1967
The Art of the Possible by Lord Butler, copyright © Thomson Newspapers
Limited, Hamish Hamilton, 1971
The Labour Government 1964–70 by Harold Wilson, Weidenfeld and Nicolson,
1971
Memoirs by Harold Macmillan, Volume IV, *Riding the Storm,* 1971, and
Volume V, *Pointing the Way,* 1972, Macmillan

Contents

List of Colour Plates

NOTE: *The page numbers given are those opposite the colour plates, or, in the case of a double-page spread, those either side of the plate*

Select Family Tree

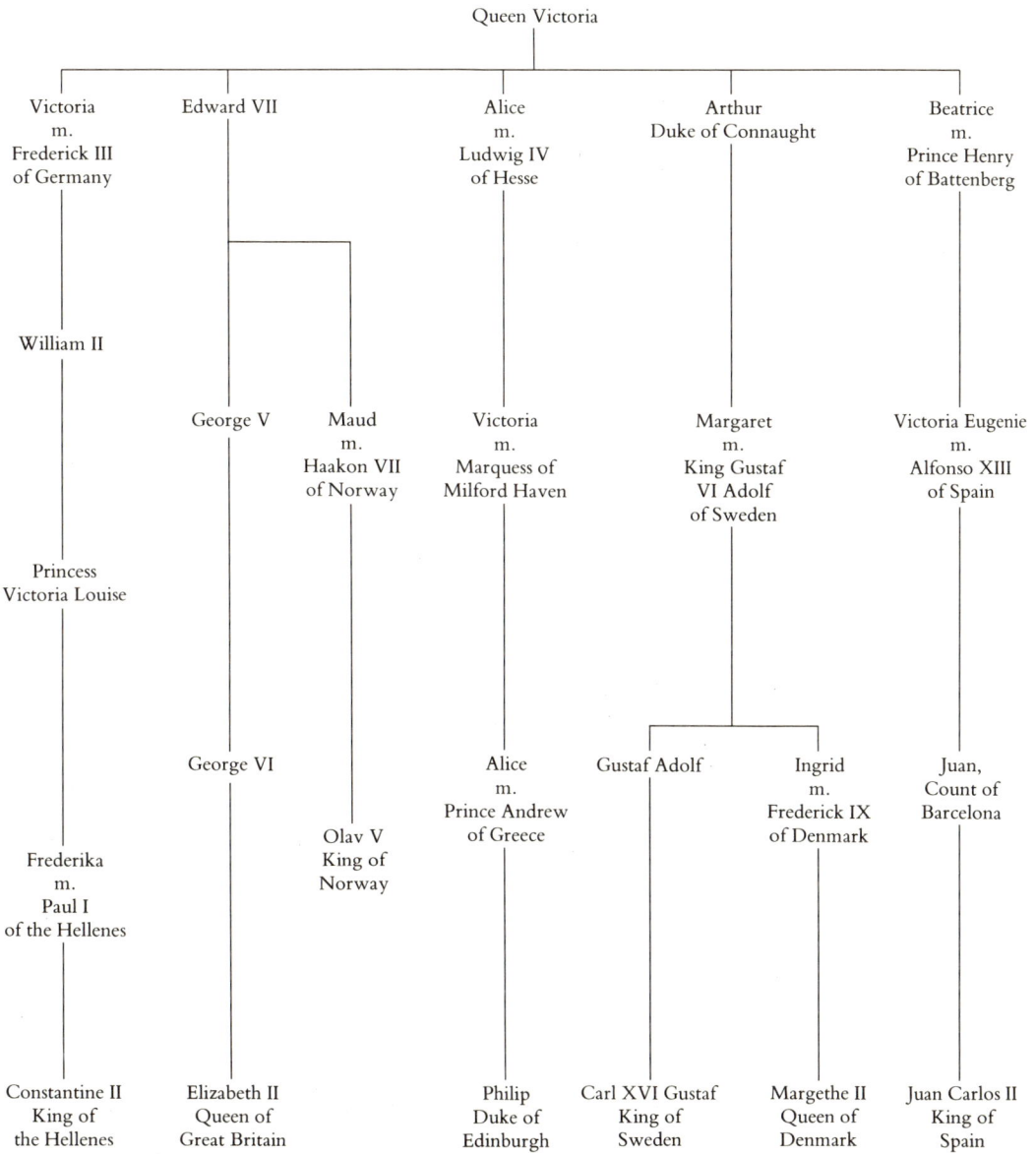

Queen Victoria

- Victoria
m.
Frederick III
of Germany
- Edward VII
- Alice
m.
Ludwig IV
of Hesse
- Arthur
Duke of Connaught
- Beatrice
m.
Prince Henry
of Battenberg

William II

George V

Maud
m.
Haakon VII
of Norway

Victoria
m.
Marquess of
Milford Haven

Margaret
m.
King Gustaf
VI Adolf
of Sweden

Victoria Eugenie
m.
Alfonso XIII
of Spain

Princess
Victoria Louise

George VI

Alice
m.
Prince Andrew
of Greece

Gustaf Adolf

Ingrid
m.
Frederick IX
of Denmark

Juan,
Count of
Barcelona

Olav V
King of
Norway

Frederika
m.
Paul I
of the Hellenes

Constantine II
King of
the Hellenes

Elizabeth II
Queen of
Great Britain

Philip
Duke of
Edinburgh

Carl XVI Gustaf
King of
Sweden

Margethe II
Queen of
Denmark

Juan Carlos II
King of
Spain

1 Introduction

Throughout 1977 the United Kingdom and the Commonwealth countries of which she is sovereign celebrated the silver jubilee of the Queen's accession. She is only the thirteenth of the forty English monarchs since the Norman conquest to have earned a silver jubilee by having reigned for twenty-five years or more. The life of a monarch was hard and a poor risk, especially in the Middle Ages: only twenty-four English sovereigns since 1066 have attained the age of fifty.

Jubilees and other significant dates in the monarch's life are still seen as climacterics in a nation's history, in the same way that birthdays and other anniversaries are waymarks in an individual's life. They help ordinary people to impose a pattern on the confused and frightening flux of time. So British schoolchildren still study history in the anachronistic framework of their kings and queens, not just because kings and queens used to be powerful, and at times all-powerful, makers of history; but also because their lives and deaths symbolize and personalize the passage of time, making it easier to comprehend. Recently we have started to use decades as yardsticks for the passing years, making tidy historical generalizations about the 'Fifties and the 'Sixties. But royal anniversaries still appeal to deep tribal instincts, and remain convenient signposts for marking history.

Thus Queen Victoria's diamond jubilee in 1897 is a convenient marker of the zenith and splendid isolation of the old British Empire. She touched an electric button that telegraphed her jubilee message around the Empire of which she was Great White Mother and on which the pink sunset never set around the globe: 'From my heart I thank my beloved people. May God bless them'. Sir George Trevelyan captured the feeling of occasion felicitously: 'As the little grey figure passed in her open carriage through the shouting streets, there was a sense that we had come into port after a long voyage. But in human affairs there is no permanent haven and we are forever setting out afresh across new and stormy seas'. Similarly contemporaries saw the death of Victoria as the end of an era; and so it still seems today, though eras, like other measurements of time, are artificial and arbitrary.

Queen Victoria, 'the little grey figure in her open carriage', leaves Buckingham Palace for St Paul's Cathedral during the diamond jubilee celebrations, 1897.

George V's silver jubilee in 1935 was by all accounts an occasion of extraordinarily spontaneous national rejoicing. When he returned from a triumphant and hilarious drive through the East End the King said with his customary frankness: 'I had no idea they felt like that about me; I am beginning to think they must really like me for myself'. It was partly national recognition of the modest, decent man who had made the monarchy democratic, who wanted social justice more than most of the ruling class, and who had made himself and the monarchy models of constitutional rectitude. It was also a national celebration of the nation's survival of the storms of the previous twenty-five years, a brief fanfare between movements of the music of time. The monarch is both person and national representative, and his anniversaries are national as well as personal. This is one reason why monarchy has such an ancient and potent subconscious appeal. A person is an easily intelligible symbol for the awesome abstractions of fleeting history.

The British are a traditional people, especially about their monarchy, which is so grey with antiquity that time has consecrated it into a religion. So there are traditions for celebrating a jubilee. There is a thanksgiving service, not in Westminster Abbey, the central shrine of the monarchy, but in St Paul's Cathedral, the central shrine of the capital and the kingdom. The Queen's grandfather drove there for his silver jubilee; and his grandmother for her diamond jubilee. Like them the Queen drives in procession through streets lined with cheering crowds, to personify another stage in the long march of national history. At jubilees the Royal Navy is traditionally reviewed at Spithead, and the other armed services on their appropriate parade grounds. The Royal Mint

customarily strikes a commemorative jubilee medal or coin; in 1977, the currency having been decimalized since the last such occasion, it will strike a crown piece with a face value of 25p. In 1977 there will be a royal progress on the Thames, reviving a custom of Elizabeth I, who used the London river as her familiar main road. Television and radio make it possible for Elizabeth II to address her subjects at the round earth's imagined corners more directly than by pressing a telegraph button; and aircraft and other fast modern means of transport will make it possible for her to celebrate her silver jubilee in person in all the component countries of the United Kingdom and the dozen Commonwealth countries of which she is sovereign.

We are too close to events to be able to tell whether history will select 1977 as a significant turning-point, in the way that 1897 has been made the high noon of Empire, and 1935 the breathing-space between two world earthquakes. But the Queen conformed to the national economic decline and impoverishment by asking that her government and local government should not mark her silver jubilee with undue expenditure.

Even if it is not selected in the future as a historical turning-point, 1977 is significant because it marks the continuing survival and vigour of that ancient English institution, the monarchy. It might be surprising to a logical outsider to find a modern social democratic state in the last quarter of the twentieth century still masquerading as a monarchy. When the Queen acceded to the throne in 1952, her accession was hailed by a fulsome press and a sentimental public as the dawn of a new Elizabethan Age to be presided over by a new Gloriana. What has in fact happened in the twenty-five years since then is that British society has changed more drastically, and Britain's political and economic status as a great power has declined more precipitately than in any previous quarter of a century. Although most other national institutions are blamed for the change and associated with the decline, the monarchy carries serenely on, unchanged and generally uncriticized, above the ferment and the recrimination. What is this small, conscientious, sensible woman, officially and archaically styled Elizabeth II by The Grace of God, of The United Kingdom of Great Britain, and Northern Ireland and of Her other Realms and Territories Queen, Head of the Commonwealth, Defender of the Faith, doing as a nominal head of a formerly great power?

Cynics and republicans answer that her function is an otiose or even socially harmful charade. They have described the monarchy as a soporific for a geriatric society, and comic relief to the death rattle of a nation. But such clever superficialities do not explain why the monarchy, if it really is an obsolete anachronism, survives and flourishes and remains widely popular.

Edward Gibbon got closer to the usefulness of the monarchy two centuries ago, with characteristic classical elegance: 'Of the various forms of government which have prevailed in the world, an hereditary monarchy seems to present the fairest scope for ridicule. But our more serious thoughts will respect a useful prejudice that establishes a rule of succession, independent of the passions of mankind: and we shall cheerfully acquiesce in any expedient which deprives the multitude of the dangerous, and indeed the ideal, power of giving themselves a master'. The passage echoes Tacitus on the discovery by the legions of the dangerous secret power of making an emperor. Gibbon spent his life describing the calamities that happened to Rome when that secret got out. One of the most useful mechanisms in any constitution is some method for securing orderly changes of government, when the governed want them. There is great advantage in having your official head of state above competition, and so above party contention. Constitutional monarchy is, paradoxically, a democratic institution: by giving the official head of state no power, it makes her a representative of all her subjects, particularly the weaker and the powerless.

The practical powers and prerogatives of the monarchy are dead or dormant. When James Callaghan became Prime Minister in 1976, the Queen sent for him, in the traditional formula, and requested him to form an administration. But behind the traditional procedure the Queen had no choice in the matter. What had actually happened behind the customary ritual was an interesting and unprecedented constitutional innovation. Harold Wilson announced that he intended to resign, and that his formal resignation would take effect when Labour Members of Parliament had elected a new leader. It took a series of three exciting elections and four weeks to select James Callaghan. Harold Wilson then went through the formality of resigning and advising the Queen to accept the choice of the parliamentary Labour Party. In nice constitutional theory the Queen could have disregarded his advice and sent for somebody else to form a government. She is not bound to consult a retiring Prime Minister about his successor. In practice nobody except James Callaghan would have been able to form a government; and the practical power of the royal prerogative of choosing the Prime Minister appeared to have atrophied to formality.

By a curious irony this latest erosion of the royal prerogative had been started by that staunch royalist and constitutionalist, Harold Macmillan. When ill health forced Macmillan to resign in 1963 he set the precedent of announcing his resignation in advance and stage-managing what he called 'the customary processes of consultation' to choose his successor.

These processes produced Lord Home, soon to be alias Sir Alec Douglas-Home, like a white rabbit out of a hat. In his memoirs Macmillan recorded his motive for this constitutional innovation: 'She [the Queen] feels the great importance of maintaining the prerogative intact. I was determined at all costs to preserve the prerogative, which had been so useful in the past and which might be so valuable in the future'.

There was no previous obligation on the monarch to seek or to follow the advice of an outgoing Prime Minister about who should succeed him. By going along with this innovation, adopted by Harold Wilson, the Queen gave up one of her last remaining practical powers.

The change of Prime Ministers in 1976 illustrated conveniently not only the erosion of this royal prerogative, but also the enduring strength of royal political influence behind the scenes, as opposed to practical power on the stage. Harold Wilson's resignation came as an unexpected shock to his Cabinet colleagues, who were theoretically his political intimates and collaborators, and to the country at large. But he had told the Queen of his intention to resign four months before he broke the news to his colleagues. If in day-to-day politics the Queen has become for practical purposes a figurehead, she remains an enormously well-informed and influential one.

There is more to the durability of the monarchy, however, than its vestigial and ornamental political powers. It has a hermetic role as a symbol of continuity and national unity in a pluralist democracy. It is the most ancient secular institution in the United Kingdom. Its continuity has been broken only once, by Oliver Cromwell, in more than a thousand years. The direct line of succession has occasionally been interrupted or bypassed, but the hereditary principle upon which the monarchy was founded has never been abandoned. There are elements of religion, hieratic authority, and tribal totem, potent because of its antiquity, in the monarchy of the United Kingdom. Enoch Powell put this well: 'Our monarch is not a crowned president. She is anointed. She represents a supernatural element in the nation'. It is three hundred years since the British, in their only major civil war, managed to get rid of the notion of the divine right of kings. But a recent public opinion poll indicated that a third of the Queen's United Kingdom subjects still say that they believe that she was chosen by God. It is probable that an even larger part of them believe in a hazy way that she is ultimately responsible for their government. The monarchy is embedded in very old and very deep beliefs, not all of them rational.

One of the deepest is the hereditary basis, which links the Queen directly with the Anglo-Saxon founding fathers of the monarchy.

Heredity is an unfashionable principle in an egalitarian age that disapproves of elitism. Neither of the two main political parties, which have become the efficient pumping machinery of the fount of hereditary honour, has created any new hereditary titles since 1964. It seems unlikely that any will ever be created again. Death duties and capital transfer taxes are intended to abolish inherited wealth and privilege. The hereditary monarchy is becoming an increasingly singular and isolated institution.

The Queen's family tree has been explored higher up its remote and curious branches than any other genealogy in the world. Genealogy is an English enthusiasm that goes with English antiquarianism and conservatism. Bernard Shaw observed, with customary sharpness, that Englishmen hate liberty and equality too much to understand them; but every Englishman loves a pedigree. The Queen is the fortieth monarch since the Norman conquest. She is fourth in descent from Queen Victoria, and tenth from the Electress Sophia of Hanover, who is the root of title to the throne under the Act of Settlement of 1701. She is twelfth from James I of England and VI of Scotland, who united the crowns of England and Scotland; she is thirty-first in line from William the Conqueror, tracing her ancestors through the senior Yorkist line, though she is also descended from John of Gaunt, the patriarch of the Lancastrian kings.

With happy impartiality, since the monarch must be all things to all subjects, she is also a descendant of Harold II, the last of the Anglo-Saxon kings, whom William conquered and killed at Hastings; so is the Duke of Edinburgh. She is thirty-eighth in line from Alfred the Great, from whom *The Anglo-Saxon Chronicle*, with divine self-assurance, takes her pedigree in direct male line to the god Woden, in Norse Odin, from whom our Wednesday or Woden's Day is derived. In the Scottish monarchy she is thirteenth in descent from Mary Queen of Scots, and, through her, twenty-second from Robert the Bruce, and twenty-seventh from Saint Margaret, Queen of Scotland in the eleventh century. Or, if you examine her Welsh roots, through Henry Tudor she is twenty-third in line from Llewellyn-ap-Gruffyd, Prince of all Wales, the leader of Welsh resistance against the English kings in the twelfth and thirteenth centuries.

Carried away by the exuberance of their own virtuosity the curious genealogists have traced the Queen's pedigree back to the remotest shores of history and romance: to Charlemagne, Barbarossa, Rodrigo the Cid, Egbert King of Wessex and all England, and Saint Louis King of France; to Neill of the Nine Hostages and the High Kings of Erin; to Cadwallader and Vortigern; to Musa ibn Naseir, an Arab sheikh who was born in Mecca in AD 660, and to Mahomet himself. Sir Anthony Wagner, Garter King of Arms, has demonstrated that she is George Washington's sixth cousin twice removed, which in effect means that she is one of his closest living relations. No institution based on heredity could grow from a more impressive or more wonderfully comprehensive family tree.

The Queen's title to the Crown derives partly from statute, and partly from common law rules of descent. Statute confines the succession to lineal Protestant descendants of Princess Sophia, the Electress of Hanover, granddaughter of James I of England. Although the succession is not bound to continue in its present line, it cannot now be altered except by the common consent of all the Commonwealth nations of which the Queen is sovereign. Common law rules of descent provide that the sons of the sovereign succeed to the throne in order of seniority. If there are no sons, daughters succeed in their order of seniority, as the Queen herself did.

When a daughter succeeds, there is no sexual discrimination in this aspect of the monarchy. She becomes a queen regnant, with all the powers and prerogatives of the Crown as though she were a king. However there is discrimination about consorts. By a peculiar convention the consort of a king takes the rank and style of her husband. But the male chauvinist constitution allows the husband of a queen regnant no special rank or privileges.

There is no interregnum between the death of one sovereign and the accession of his successor: the king is dead, long live the king is a succinct expression of the continuity of the monarchy. The sovereign never dies, only changes. As soon as a king or queen dies, the next in line is proclaimed at an accession council, to which all members of the Privy Council are summoned, along with the Lords Spiritual and Temporal, the Lord Mayor of London, his aldermen and other leading citizens, and the High Commissioners in London of the members of the Commonwealth. About a year after his accession the new monarch is crowned at Westminster Abbey in a coronation ceremony whose ritual and tribal elements have remained substantially unchanged for more than a thousand years from the crownings of the pristine Anglo-Saxon kings.

Hereditary monarchy is not a peculiarly British survival. Most societies at some time have used a system of government that consorts with some deep instinct in human nature. John Selden, the republican lawyer and orientalist who took an active part against the Crown in the Civil War, defined part of the universal appeal of the institution: 'A king is a thing men have made for their own sakes, for quietness' sake. Just as if in a family one man is appointed to buy the meat'. Whatever the reasons, monarchy is still a surprisingly widespread form of government in the second half of the twentieth century. About sixty hereditary monarchs are still in business around the world, not counting chiefs of small tribes.

Their powers range from the old-fashioned autocracies of, for example, some of the sheikhs of the Persian Gulf, to the exotic constitututional monarchy substituted in Japan after the last war for the feudal and divine powers of the Mikado. Europe still has no fewer than ten reigning sovereigns. These consists of three queens regnant: of the United Kingdom, the Netherlands, and Denmark; and four kings: of the Belgians, Norway, Sweden, and Spain. In addition there are the hereditary rulers of Europe's three pocket principalities: Prince Rainier of Monaco; Grand Duke Jean of Luxemburg; and Prince Franz Joseph II of Liechtenstein, whose principality on the upper Rhine covers only sixty-five square miles, but boasts seventy-two princes and princesses. There are proportionately more royalties to the common population and the square metre in Liechtenstein than in any other country under the sun. Consequently there is also the highest proportion of snobs, title worshippers, royalty fetishists, and assorted flunkeys.

Royalty is an endogamous profession. The Queen of Denmark and the Kings of Norway, Sweden, and Spain are cousins of the Queen and descendants of Queen Victoria. The remainder of the European royalties are related to the Duke of Edinburgh. All of them to some extent perform the useful and almost magical function of supplying the sense of identity, continuity, and history that helps to make diverse peoples and pluralist societies one nation. But there is no doubt that the oldest, most durable, and most efficient of the surviving monarchies is that of the United Kingdom and the countries of the Commonwealth that have adopted constitutional monarchy as their system of government.

There are a number of reasons why the British have more of a taste and a talent for monarchy than other nations: deference and love of class distinction; English pragmatism and dislike of violent change; the accidents of history; traditionalism; propensity to emotion and distrust of logic; above all, the native genius for preserving old institutions while adapting them to perform new functions. The monarchy of the United Kingdom today is the descendant of a very old, very long, very peculiar story. For a number of reasons, for a thousand years the English have been better than other people at regulating the rule of their monarchs, partly by force, once by the axe, but particularly by the bridle and curb of the purse. The early constitutional history of England is largely the history of a process of pruning the monarchy to keep it in step with the evolution of political civilization.

The process of whittling away the supreme power of the monarchy began in the power struggles between King, Church, magnates, and stubborn citizens almost immediately after the Norman conquest. It was carried forward by Magna Carta and by the Parliament summoned by Simon de Montfort seven centuries ago, which gave the English a legacy of practice and a legacy of interest. The struggle eventually led to the pruning of a king's head; and was continued more civilly by the Bill of Rights and then the Act of Settlement of 1701, by Dunning's motion in the House of Commons in 1780, by the Reform Bills of the nineteenth century, and by centuries of laboriously and dangerously established precedents, built up as gradually as the common law. John Dunning, the first Baron Ashburnham, an eminent lawyer and statesman, moved two historic resolutions in Parliament, that 'the influence of the Crown has increased, is increasing, and ought to be diminished', and that 'it is competent to this house to examine into and correct abuses in the expenditure of the Civil List revenues [the public income of the monarchy], as well as in every other branch of the public revenue, whenever it shall appear expedient to the wisdom of the house so to do'. In the teeth of the opposition of Lord North, George III's calamitous Prime Minister, the first resolution was just carried, and the second agreed to without a division. Both were important constitutional precedents in the long process of civilizing the rude monarchy.

The sudden abolition of the venerable structure of the English monarchy was tried only once, and it was generally agreed after a while that it did not work. There was no provision for continuity and an orderly and secure succession of the head of state. There is little reason to suppose that abolition of the monarchy at a stroke would be any more satisfactory now, though the process of pruning and adapting the monarchy will no doubt continue.

The idea of monarchy was introduced into England from their Germanic homelands by the successive waves of tribes that invaded the island after the Romans had left in what historians have come to call the Age of Settlement. The name king or *cyning* wears its Teutonic origins on its sleeve; and it is explained either as scion of the kin or tribe, or scion of a noble kin, or son of one of noble birth. These primitive, inchoate kings were petty tribal warleaders, and ruled over nomadic tribes rather than territories. They seem to have been elected rather than hereditary. Some of the archaeology suggests that they had pagan hieratic attributes. They enforced their tribal law and exacted tribute from their own folk, or, better still, on behalf of their folk from the neighbouring tribes.

During the seventh century England was converted to Christianity; and the kings of the converted tribes and the bishops of the new religion supported and legitimated each other's authority in the first appearance of what much later came to be termed colloquially the Establishment.

Gradually the tribes settled and amalgamated into wider and wider regional confederations. The external threat from the Danish invaders in the ninth century forced the tribes to coalesce,

Magna Carta, 'the great charter of the liberties of England'. One of the four surviving original copies of Magna Carta was loaned to the United States Government by the Government of Great Britain for one year during the Bicentennial celebrations in 1976, and is seen here on display at the Capitol, Washington. A golden copy was handed over as a permanent gift.

and out of their coalition Alfred emerged as the King, warlord, and defender of Christian England. Edgar the Peaceful, however, who reigned from 959 to 975 is generally taken as the first King of England in recognizable modern form. He was consecrated and crowned King; he swore a coronation oath; he was effective King of all the Christian peoples of England, and was recognized fitfully as overlord by many of the Celtic rulers in Britain.

The Norman conquest crudely imposed the feudal system and a hereditary and autocratic monarchy on the religious and political foundations of the Anglo-Saxon monarchy. It also gradually imposed stronger legal, financial, and administrative government on the kingdom. The continual power struggles between the magnates of the kingdom and the monarch, and uncertainties about rights and the hereditary succession, not only of the monarchy but also of the baronial estates carved out as rewards for the Norman conquerors, led eventually to crisis and the first great curb on the power of the king.

Magna Carta, the great charter of the liberties of England, was granted by King John under pressure from his barons at Runnymede in the Thames on 15 June 1215. Its principal provisions were that no freeman should be imprisoned, banished, or in any way destroyed except by the law of the land; and that supplies (except aids imposed on tenants-in-chief on certain specified occasions) should not be demanded without the consent of the Common Council of the realm. It was the first major cut in the autocratic powers of arbitrary justice and taxation of the Norman kings. The condition that no supplies, that is no money, should be demanded without the consent of the Common Council forged a potent weapon, the palladium of an Englishman's liberty, which would gradually be used to make Parliament master and kings servants of the constitution. It made the king subject to the law of the land, and established the rights and powers of the landed magnates. From it after seven centuries of evolution every man and woman derive their rights and powers under the law, and the principle of Magna Carta became the basis for other constitutions.

The next great traditional landmark in the pruning of monarchical autocracy was Simon de Montfort's Parliament of 1265. Simon was the Earl of Leicester and husband of Eleanor, the sister of the King, Henry III. He emerged as leader of the barons in their nationalist quarrel with the King over his dependence on Poitevin favourites. In 1264 Simon defeated the royal forces at Lewes and captured the King. He summoned a Parliament in the name of the captive King, sending writs not just to the ecclesiastical and secular magnates of the realm, but also to four knights to be elected from each shire. This Parliament of 1264 tried to substitute government by council for arbitrary royal rule. It imposed the beginnings of parliamentary control on the government, though it also served as a veil to cover Simon's autocracy. For the ordinary citizen of England the choice of being ruled by the King or the council of Simon de Montfort and his barons was a choice between being fleeced by wolves or shorn by lions. But the precedent of summoning a Parliament was established, which was eventually to bring power to the people.

Further civil disorders forced de Montfort to turn again to Parliament to strengthen his position in the following year. This Parliament summoned representatives of the middle classes, knights from the shires, burgesses from the towns, and representatives from the Cinque Ports, to a central assembly of the realm. This seminal Parliament of 1265 reconciled the King and his barons; secured the release of the King's son, Edward, who later succeeded to the throne as Edward I; and confirmed the 1264 constitution, with its drastic limits to the power of the monarchy. Simon de Montfort did not create the House of Commons. But quite unintentionally, as a selfish move in a sabre-toothed feudal power struggle, he sowed parliamentary innovations from which popular social democracy would eventually grow.

Although the Tudors were authoritarian, talented, and often successful, or at any rate lucky, they made their revolutionary changes through Parliament, and regarded themselves as subject to the law. The seating plan for the Blackfriars Parliament of 1523 shows the King and the Lords Spiritual and Temporal.

After the medieval monarchy had shipwrecked in the blood and constitutional chaos of the Wars of the Roses, the Tudors became the bridge between the medieval and the modern monarchy, the transition from power monarchy to popular monarchy. The Tudors are popularly thought of as the most despotic of English monarchs, the nearest we came to having Renaissance princes according to the prescription of Machiavelli. But this impression is a caricature, drawn by the larger than life personalities and personality cults of Henry VIII (still, significantly, regarded by erroneous folklore as England's most impressive monarch) and his daughter Elizabeth.

The Tudors were authoritarian, talented, and often successful, or at any rate lucky. But they made their revolutionary changes through Parliament, and, unlike their autocratic medieval predecessors, regarded themselves as subject to the law. Parliament was acquiescent partly because of the external threats to the state, and partly because the finances of the monarchy did not necessitate frequent calls on Parliament for supply.

The Stuarts were chronically hard-up, and they took a different side to most of their people in the great religious schism of their age. They also attempted to revive the atrophied and atavistic justification for the monarchy, invented by the bishops in the Dark Ages, that kings ruled by divine right. James I, as usual, put it exactly: 'Kings are justly called gods, because they exercise a manner of resemblance to divine power on earth. They have power to exalt low things and abase high things and to make of their subjects like men at chess'.

The English Civil War, like all major historical events, was a complex matter with many interlocking causes and results, political, religious, financial, and constitutional. But its simple and fundamental cause was the struggle to determine who should govern, King or Parliament. Parliament won. Since then monarchy in the United Kingdom has no longer seriously tried to use divine right as its justification, and kings have reigned under licence from Parliament, not ruled. The licence could be revoked. The heroic stubbornness of the Stuarts for a foolish ideal cost the head of Charles I, the throne of his son, James II, and the eventual exile of their incorrigible dynasty. The government had finally ceased even to pretend to be the personal affair of an absolute king; and the king had started to evolve into his modern role as constitutional monarch, servant and ceremonial head of the constitution, and symbolic representative of the people.

The Glorious Revolution of 1688, bloodless compared with most revolutions to get rid of kings, formalized these changes. William III of Orange was invited from Holland with his wife Mary to replace his father-in-law under licence from Parliament. The terms of his contract with his people, an idea quite as unhistorical as divine right but less dangerous, were set out in the Declaration and Bill of Rights.

These instruments tied the royal prerogative, which was the basis of Stuart absolutism, in constitutional chains. They denied the king the power of suspending the laws of the land, except with the permission of parliamentary statute. They deprived the king of his purse: the authority to levy taxes without the consent of Parliament. They deprived him of his sword: the right to raise and maintain a standing army in time of peace without the consent of Parliament. The rights to trial by jury and to petition the sovereign were confirmed. Parliamentary elections were to be free, and parliamentary debate was to be free from the threat of subsequent impeachment. Parliaments had to be summoned at least every three years, and could not continue for longer than three years. Above all the Bill of Rights established as the basis of the constitution that the king reigned solely with and by the consent of Parliament, and under strict constitutional limitations. The principal provisions of the Bill of Rights are echoed or adapted in many subsequent democratic constitutions, including that of the United States.

The Act of Settlement of 1701, which settled the succession to the thrones of the United Kingdom on Sophia, wife of the Elector of Hanover and her heirs so long as they remained Protestants, added the important new idea that ministers should be responsible for the acts of the monarch. This is the origin of the concepts of responsible government and Cabinet responsibility.

Henceforth the great political and constitutional struggles were fought between politicians and parties in Parliament. Some monarchs, like George III, tried to play the party game. Some, like Victoria, who did not really understand constitutional monarchy, used unconstitutional pressures and influences on her ministers behind the scenes. But most of the royal prerogative was dead. And monarchs were increasingly reluctant to exercise the prerogatives that were left to them, in case Parliament took those way also. If a monarch reigns under contract, there is no need for a revolution to get rid of him. The way that he reigns can be modified by the popular will. If he refuses to bend, as James II refused, Parliament can take away his contract and send for somebody else to do the job. Rather than risk such a conflict, Edward VIII surrendered his licence by abdicating.

Before 1832 voting was restricted to about a twentieth of the population. Since then the progress from parliamentary oligarchy to mass democracy has been complete, even though it took a century and a half and six Representation of the People Acts to achieve it. The franchise has been extended to cover almost the whole population, the latest group to be enfranchised being those who have reached the age of eighteen. Even citizens of the Irish Republic can vote in United Kingdom elections. The only exceptions to universal democracy remaining are such minorities as the Queen, peers, felons, persons convicted of corrupt or illegal practices in connexion with elections, and persons of unsound mind, who may, however, vote 'during lucid intervals', if voting and lucidity are not a contradiction in terms.

The general principle of the monarchy during the past century of transition to social democracy has been to swim along with this democratic tide, while trying to preserve as far as possible what is left of the royal prerogative by not using it. Monarchs have been concerned to mitigate political conflict; to avoid even the appearance of resisting what seems to be the popular will; to keep their heads down and their conduct out of hot water; to avoid being forced into constitutional corners. In the overriding interest of preserving the monarchy, monarchs have refrained whenever possible from exercising even their residual constitutional powers. This has not been pure self-interest of a threatened species; monarchs like everybody else have been affected by the democratic spirit of the age. They want to preserve their constitutional function and prerogative, but are embarrassed to use them. Therefore in some respects the prerogative has rusted in disuse, though Parliament has taken no major new measures to curb or abolish it.

There has been a trend over the past hundred years towards assigning powers directly to ministers without the necessity for royal intervention. But in constitutional theory the royal prerogative powers remain very large, and there are still many important acts of government that are invalid without the participation of the Queen. As head of state the Queen has the constitutional power to declare war and make peace, to recognize foreign states and governments, to conclude treaties, and to annexe or cede territory. In practice, of course, she does none of these things except on the advice of her ministers, who are responsible to Parliament and can be questioned about a particular policy. There is no law that Parliament has to authorize the exercise of these powers, but Parliament is now sovereign, and can pass laws to restrict or abolish these prerogative powers.

The Queen is the personification of the state, the symbol of the national identity. In law she is the head of the executive, an integral part of the legislature, the head of the judiciary, the commander-in-chief of all the armed forces of the Crown, and the temporal governor of the established Church of England. The Queen's participation is necessary to perform such vital acts of state as the summoning, prorogation, and dissolution of Parliament. Her ancient prerogative to perform any of these important acts on her own initiative, or, as the old lawyers put it, by her mere motion, has withered from disuse, and is so unlikely ever to be tested again that to consider her exercising it is fantasy. But in theory the prerogative subsists.

No Bill can become law, after it has been passed by both Houses of Parliament, until the Queen has given it her Royal Assent. In practice the Queen assents to legislation automatically. She makes the formal appointments to all important offices of state, such as those of government ministers, judges, officers in the armed forces, and all the leading positions in the Church of England. Behind the formality such appointments are in practice made by the Prime Minister, other ministers, and other public or Church servants, and formally confirmed by the Queen.

In constitutional theory the Queen is the fount of honour, conferring peerages, knighthoods, and other honours and distinguishing gewgaws in which English snobbery has taken pleasure from time immemorial. In efficient practice the Prime Minister pumps the fount of honour and wields the dubbing sword by advising the Queen whom to honour, after himself having been given honorific advice by other party leaders, institutions, and individuals. The British system is open to criticism because of the great volume and nicely complicated hierarchy of honours that is spewed out at least twice a year. It is also criticized for the inappropriate selection by party politicians of those for the Queen to honour. A Prime Minister can make a nobleman, but he cannot make a gentleman, and he does not often seem able to recognize gentleness or unselfish merit.

The system reached one of its periodic crises of disrepute with Sir Harold Wilson's resignation honours list in the summer of

The awarder of honours honoured. Sir Harold Wilson and the Duke of Grafton, as the newest recruits to the Most Honourable and Noble Order of the Garter, lead the Knights down the hill to St George's Chapel, Windsor, for the installation service in June 1976.

1976. Retiring Prime Ministers have invented a right for themselves to distribute honours among their faithful friends, followers, hangers-on, and servants. It is a right usually exercised with decent restraint. Clement Attlee in his resignation list abstemiously distributed modest honours to a handful of loyal associates such as his Parliamentary Private Secretary and the doorman at Number Ten Downing Street. Sir Anthony Eden, now Lord Avon, abstained altogether from a resignation honours list.

Sir Harold's list was an extraordinary one for a Socialist Prime Minister to draw up, distributing life peerages and knighthoods capriciously among a selection of business tycoons from the wilder shores of capitalism, New Elizabethan buccaneers, and show business impresarios not notable either for their public service or their devotion to Socialism. In the main those honoured appeared to have little in common other than appropriate qualifications to form a panel to judge the Miss World beauty contest. They were described by more than a hundred Labour Members of Parliament as representatives of the unpleasant face of capitalism. It was a list to bring a blush to the mulberry cheeks of Sir Robert Walpole or Lloyd George, both of whom sold honours shamelessly, and used them openly as bribes.

Mischievous cynics suggested that Sir Harold had done it deliberately to destroy the honours system with ridicule. In fact, probably quite unintentionally, he brought nearer the desirable reform of the honours system, which needs to have its size reduced and its elaborate and snobbish differentiations simplified. It would clearly be an improvement to remove honours from the hands of the Prime Minister and entrust them to someone above politics like the monarch, with checks and safeguards to ensure impartiality. In the nature of the prime ministerial beast this useful improvement is unlikely to commend itself to any Prime Minister.

A less radical improvement would be to increase the powers of the Political Honours Scrutiny Committee, the body that was formed to examine recommendations for political honours after the scandal of Lloyd George's openly venal attitude to the honours system. The Committee consists of three elderly and senior Privy Councillors, one from each of the three principal political parties. Until Sir Harold's resignation list the watchdogs had never, so far as can be ascertained, barked or even whimpered at any nomination for a political honour. The Committee should be given power to scrutinize the whole of each honours list, not just the political section, and it should be emboldened to scrutinize more rigorously. The Queen could be made umpire over any nominations about which the Committee was unhappy.

The Queen is hostess and guest on behalf of the nation. She entertains Commonwealth and foreign heads of state who make state visits to Britain; and, always accompanied by the Duke of Edinburgh, she pays state visits on behalf of Great Britain to foreign governments. They both make regular and lengthy tours of the other countries of the Commonwealth of which the Queen is head. Other members of the royal family make official and private visits overseas to help the Queen in her function as national representative. This ceremonial role is one that is particularly suited to a monarch. A Queen is a far more glamorous and popular hostess and guest than a president, who is usually indistinguishable from other elderly retired statesmen.

The ceremonial aspects of monarchy survive in home as well as foreign affairs, though the mood of the times and of the monarchy is for informality rather than the hieratic royal theatre of a generation ago. The most regular employment of the Queen and her family is to make visits all over the United Kingdom to open factories, schools, and other enterprises; to inaugurate, to commemorate, to congratulate, to approve, to meet the people. A royal visit gives the cachet of national importance to a local occasion, and attracts the attention of press and television.

The changing of the guard in the forecourt of Buckingham Palace is the most popular free spectacle for tourists to London. There are state banquets for official tourists, frequent investitures to confer the honours that have been awarded by politicians, and royal processions to divert the public and congest the traffic on such occasions as the state opening of Parliament, usually in November, when the Queen drives in cavalcade from Buckingham Palace to her palace of Westminster. Royal marriages and funerals are publicly marked by stately tribal ceremonies. The Queen's birthday is celebrated officially early in June for the benefit of the weather and the tourists (although she was in fact born on 21 April 1926) by the Queen's Birthday Parade, known as Trooping the Colour, on Horse Guards Parade. The same day is also celebrated as Commonwealth Day.

Although she has no efficient power, the Queen is an essential formal part of the machinery of government and national life. She sees the Prime Minister at least once a week; holds regular meetings of the Privy Council for official business; gives audiences to ministers, ambassadors, and other holders of office at home and overseas; receives accounts of Cabinet decisions and daily bulletins of business in Parliament; reads a great many dispatches every day; and every day signs a great many state papers, which are invalid without her signature. She has a right to be informed and consulted about every aspect of government and national life, and a duty to advise when she thinks advice is necessary. She must be impartial, disinterested, above party politics and other factional interests. As far as any person can do, she must represent the whole nation.

The Queen as hostess. Here she entertains Canadian Indian Chiefs in traditional dress at Buckingham Palace in June 1976. They had come to Britain to commemorate the signing of two treaties with 'the Great White Mother', Queen Victoria, in 1876 and 1877.

Because the royal element is still essential to the constitutional machinery, the constitution makes provision for a regent to be appointed to perform the royal functions if the sovereign is totally incapacitated, or is under the age of eighteen on accession to the throne. The last regent to be so appointed was the Prince of Wales, later George IV, during the final period of madness of his father. But Queen Victoria avoided a regency on account of her youth by less than a month, having only just had her eighteenth birthday when her uncle, William IV, died, and she succeeded him. The constitution provides that the regent would be the Prince of Wales, and, failing him, those nearest in line to the succession who are of age.

The monarchy today is the result of more than a thousand years of constitutional evolution. There have been great changes in it over the past hundred years. An oligarchical form of government based on traditional British deference and class conformity has

State visitors at Buckingham Palace. The Queen and the Duke of Edinburgh welcome President and Senhora Geisel of Brazil to Buckingham Palace in 1976 after the procession from Victoria Station. In the background stands the Master of the Horse, the Duke of Beaufort.

been replaced by mass democracy. The Empire has vanished, and the Commonwealth has dwindled to an ornamental but still interesting and potentially useful vestige. Britain has joined the European Economic Community. The old constitutional bonds of the United Kingdom itself are showing signs of strain, and the industrial economy that was the wonder of the industrial revolution is showing signs of collapse. The mood of the age is undeferential and egalitarian. Britain is no longer a great power, and is going through a crisis of national morale and political and economic weakness. There is more dissatisfaction with government and the quality of life in the country than has been felt for a century. There are even doubts about the way that the bedrock of the United Kingdom, its ancient constitution, is working. And yet, in spite of the knocking and ominous noises in the constitutional machinery, the monarchy, the old ghost in the machine, survives, and flourishes, and performs its ordained functions smoothly.

2 Politics

The British constitution owes its success in practice to its inconsistencies in principle. Surprisingly for such a prolific and proficient constitution-framer, it was Napoleon Bonaparte, of all people, who recommended that a constitution should be short and obscure. He was not very good at practising what he preached, since his constitutions tended to be long and detailed, and to be written with a magnificent Gallic clarity. The British constitution, however, follows his recommendations exactly. It is built up, like common law, on ancient precedents. The written part of it is so short that it is virtually unwritten. It is so obscure that parliamentary lawyers and constitutional theorists can wrangle for years over its minutiae without coming to any firm conclusion. It is notoriously flexible and adaptive. During its long evolution it has enabled us to unmake kings constitutionally, and then to remake them equally constitutionally, and to perform hundreds of other U-turns hardly less sharp. For a thousand years and more it has been able to bend to the winds of change where more rigid Napoleonic instruments would have broken under the strain. It works wonderfully, not least in bringing overmighty subjects under control for the common good. But there is no doubt that its machinery moves in a mysterious way its wonders to perform.

An intelligent observer from outer space would certainly at first conclude that the British constitution is what it nominally pretends to be: a monarchy under the rule of an autocrat. Every Act of Parliament begins with this impressive recital: 'Be it enacted therefore by the Queen's most Excellent Majesty, by and with the advice and consent of the Lords Spiritual and Temporal, and Commons in this present Parliament assembled, and by the authority of the same as follows . . .'

It is the Queen who rides in a state coach to open each new session of Parliament, and announces the programme of forthcoming legislation as if it is her programme and has her personal approval. This can lead to such ironic paradoxes as the Queen announcing in November 1967 that legislation would be introduced to reduce the powers of the House of Lords and eliminate its present hereditary basis, thereby enabling it to develop within

The Queen and the Duke of Edinburgh leaving Buckingham Palace for the state opening of Parliament.

the framework of a modern parliamentary system. It never happened, of course. An elected second chamber, whose findings could no longer be dismissed as the unrepresentative views of undemocratic old stumblebums and reactionary backwoodsmen, would curb the almost unlimited powers of the modern Prime Minister. But the real rulers find it convenient to conform to the theatre that the Queen's Speech is really the Queen's. Out of courtesy to her, the address in reply to it is agreed to without a division, and 'Her Majesty's most dutiful and loyal subjects in the Commons' always 'beg leave to offer our humble thanks to Your Majesty for the Gracious Speech which Your Majesty has addressed to both Houses of Parliament'. When that motion has been carried, the House turns to amendments, which begin with the word 'but' and try to add or delete something that would destroy the government's programme.

If he was a perceptive and quick-witted spaceman, our vistor might notice after a session or two that the Queen and other important people dignified by those honorific capital letters in the recital to an Act have almost no say in its contents or in the contents of the Queen's Speech. And if he persevered further, he might arrive at the half-truth that the supreme power of the constitution today is vested in the Cabinet. This would take some perseverance since the Cabinet owes its existence to no statute; it has no independent legal authority; it has no fixed rules for its own procedure. If he searched the statute books diligently, the spaceman would discover only two Acts that mention the Cabinet: the Minister of the Crown Act 1937, and the Parliamentary Commissioner Act 1969 refer to it in passing. Every Act mentions the Queen in the place of honour at the beginning, and many refer to her repeatedly. And yet it is the Cabinet not the Queen that has the power. While it enjoys the confidence of a majority in the House of Commons, the Cabinet acts as the supreme coordinator of national policy; its decisions are accepted without question throughout the government machine; and legal or executive form is given to those decisions by or on behalf of the appropriate minister, who accepts responsibility for them to Parliament.

The Cabinet's supremacy emerged by a gradual, haphazard, and nebulous process entirely characteristic of the British constitution. Some attribute the origin of Cabinet government to the Cabal, the junta of Charles II's five ministers who had names whose initials could be arranged to form the word 'cabal', and who signed the treaty of alliance with France for war against Holland in 1672. Whether that is the correct view of its origin or not, the Cabinet system emerged into prominence under the first two Hanoverian kings, who took little interest in their political duties. Senior Crown ministers met as a group during the kings' long absences

The Queen reading the Speech from the throne in the Chamber of the House of Lords.

abroad, offered advice to the king collectively, and were then individually responsible for the execution of policies of which he had approved. During his long term as First Lord of the Treasury Sir Robert Walpole assumed a dominant role, drove out those who would not accept his leadership, and established himself in the position that his successors have learned to call that of Prime Minister.

If our inquisitive visitor from outer space had the nose of a journalist, the instincts of a historian, and a taste for constitutional theory, he might conclude that the balance of the constitution has been shifting again in the past thirty years. Two great party oligarchies now dominate the political scene, having usurped and divided between themselves most of the sovereign powers that used to be ascribed by constitutional theorists to the Commons. Power is increasingly concentrated in the single person of the Prime Minister, who is at the apex not only of his own highly centralized political machine, but also of an equally centralized and vastly more powerful administrative machine.

Supremacy has gradually been ebbing from Cabinet government ever since Sir Winston Churchill's individual dominance over the war coalition Cabinet. Today, behind the customary ambiguities and impressions of the constitution, we have prime ministerial or presidential government. The outsider would find it as hard to discern the constitutional basis for this as it was hard to discern the constitutional basis for Cabinet government. The very term 'Prime Minister' is a nineteenth-century innovation. In the eighteenth century, when used at all, it was used in a derogatory sense. The term only appears in three Acts of Parliament, notably in the Chequers Estate Act of 1917. It occurs in only two official documents, namely: the Treaty of Berlin in 1878, when Disraeli signed himself 'Prime Minister of England'; and when Edward VII in 1905 assigned the Prime Minister place and precedence next after the Archbishop of York.

The dogged little man from outer space who had persevered thus far, no doubt turning even greener in complexion in the process than his monocular face was by nature, would conclude that there was more to the British constitution than meets the eye. He would be right. There is an element of illusion and prestigious conjuring trick about the constitution. On the stage in the spotlights dignified and gorgeous persons led by the monarch enact legislation, open Parliament, and pull other constitutional rabbits out of their top hats and the Imperial State Crown. In the wings and behind the scenes the Prime Minister, the Cabinet, and the inconspicuous top bureaucrats of Whitehall pull the strings and ventriloquize the script for those on stage.

George Orwell, that eloquent and passionate democrat, put it

Walter Bagehot: one of the greatest lobby journalists, who kept his ears and eyes open and his mouth shut in the corridors of power.

well: 'In a dictatorship the power and the glory belong to the same person. In England the real power belongs to unprepossessing men in bowler hats: the creature who rides in a gilded coach behind soldiers in steel breast-plates is really a waxwork. It is at any rate possible that while this division of functions exists a Hitler or a Stalin cannot come to power'.

The man who first systematically observed this crucial division between appearance and reality in the British constitution was Walter Bagehot, the eminent Victorian editor of *The Economist*, and one of the greatest lobby journalists who ever kept his ears and eyes open and his mouth shut in the corridors of power.

Before Bagehot the theory had been that the constitution was based on a balance of power between the three limbs of a triune Parliament: Monarch, Commons, and Lords. This ancient doctrine was formally described by Edward Coke's *Report* of the Prince's Case in 1606: this established the principle that nothing can become a valid Act of Parliament unless it has been passed by all three elements of the legislature. Its importance in the seventeenth century was to prevent the monarch and the upper house combining to bypass the Commons.

Bagehot noticed what he called 'the efficient secret' of the constitution: that is, the difference between its appearance and reality. He called the appearance the 'dignified' part of the constitution; made necessary because ordinary voters cannot understand or be bothered with abstract political questions, but need a theatrical show to satisfy their sense of deference and concrete view of the world. The real political power resided in the efficient part of the constitution out of the spotlight and behind the gilded scenes.

Bagehot described this secret with an elegant simplicity that is still irresistible: 'The characteristic merit of the English constitution is that its dignified parts are very complicated and somewhat imposing, very old and rather venerable; while its efficient part, at least when in great and critical action, is decidedly simple and rather modern. Its essence is strong with the strength of modern simplicity; its exterior is august with the Gothic grandeur of a more imposing age'.

According to Bagehot this august or dignified aspect of the constitution, personified by the monarch, disguises the fact that we really have a republic in the United Kingdom. Real power resides in the Cabinet, with the Prime Minister at its apex. The House of Commons has the function of an electoral college to choose the Prime Minister, who then selects his Cabinet; and the function of dismissing him by withholding a vote of confidence. In practice these functions have been greatly eroded by the discipline of the party system, which has divided the Commons into two armies of automata for mock battle in the lobbies; and by the Prime

Minister's right of dissolution, which hangs like the sword of Damocles over the back benches to restrain independently minded members.

Yet in a paradoxical way the monarch, this dignified and impotent figurehead for the constitutional mechanism, is in some respects the hero of Bagehot's narrative. In a limited or constitutional monarchy the monarch reigns, but does not rule. The Queen now has only reserve powers, but great influence. She has accumulated a larger store of day-to-day political experience than anybody else in her kingdom. She has been on the throne for twenty-five years, and worked with no less than seven Prime Ministers. This advantage will augment from year to year, and gives the monarch the advantage that a Permanent Secretary in one of the departments of Whitehall has over his superior, the Parliamentary Secretary, 'that of having shared in the proceedings of the previous parliamentary secretaries'. Above all, Bagehot enunciated the constitutional rights of the monarch in the English system as: 'the right to be consulted, the right to encourage, the right to warn'. A king of great sense and sagacity, argued Bagehot, would want no others. He would find that his having no other rights would enable him to use these three with singular effect. A wise king would gradually acquire a fund of knowledge and experience that few ministers could rival.

Bagehot took a characteristically cynical (or realistic) view of the probability of our regularly getting such an ideal king to make the wheels of the constitution run smoothly. A constitutional sovereign must, he maintained, in the common course of government be a man of but common ability: 'I am afraid, looking to the early acquired feebleness of hereditary dynasties, that we must expect him to be a man of inferior ability. Theory and experience both teach that the education of a prince can be but a poor education, and that a royal family will generally have less ability than other families. What right have we then to expect the perpetual entail on any family of an exquisite discretion, which if it be not a sort of genius, is at least as rare as genius?'

Bagehot took an equally disparaging view of the capacities of the electorate: 'The masses of Englishmen are not fit for an elective government; if they knew how near they were to it, they would be surprised, and almost tremble'. The ordinary voter could understand a monarchy because it consisted of an individual, or better still a family, doing interesting things that appealed to the imagination and emotions. 'The women – one half the human race at least – care fifty times more for a marriage than a ministry'. Bagehot's conclusion in favour of a republic disguised as a monarchy clearly earns the vogue epithet of elitist: 'Accordingly, so long as the human heart is strong and the human reason weak, royalty will be strong because it appeals to diffused feeling, and republics weak because they appeal to the understanding'.

One must not be so dazzled by the epigrammatic brilliance of his prose as to lose sight of what Bagehot is up to. Is his description of the system as he saw it as a journalist in the years just before the publication of *The English Constitution* in the 1860s accurate? Queen Victoria's letters show that she played a more active part in politics, usually against reform, than Bagehot allowed her in his system. The mass adulation of the royal family, whose utility he commended, did not begin until after the jubilee. Bagehot, like many contemporary Liberals, was frightened of the masses taking the levers of his constitutional machine out of the hands of safe, middle-class Liberals like himself, who understood the arcane mystery of the constitution. Once that secret got out, the machine might go out of control. His writings are accordingly split between objective description and Machiavellian prescription for using the monarchy to dupe 'the bovine stupidity' of the people and keep them deferential.

By an ironic coincidence in the very year of publication of Bagehot's masterpiece Disraeli's Parliamentary Act extended the vote to artisans in towns, and so introduced the present era of mass democracy, whose advent so terrified good elitists like Bagehot. Bagehot's description of the system is the classic definition of the classic period of Cabinet government from the first Reform Act of 1832 to 1867. But it has been made obsolete in some respects by the introduction of universal suffrage at eighteen. And the growth of huge, almost autonomous satrapies of the Civil Service to administer our vast welfare state; the creation of the party machines; and the growth of the presidential power of the Prime Minister have all combined to modify the workings of Bagehot's machine.

How have these changes affected the role of the monarchy? Are ordinary people still duped by the dignified myth of the monarchy into believing that the Queen actually rules; that she could, if she wanted, compose her own Queen's Speech? Recent public opinion polls, for what such meters of hot air are worth, have indicated that a frightening percentage of the population really believes that the Queen governs. But Richard Crossman was surely right when he pointed out that the myths and legends of the monarchy are only credible to the masses so long as those who propagate them believe their own propaganda.

It is instructive to start with Bagehot's description of the role of the monarchy and examine how it has altered in the subsequent century. In an amusing passage Bagehot listed some of the many things that Queen Victoria, by exercising her prerogative, was legally entitled to do without consulting Parliament: 'She could disband the army; she could dismiss all the officers, from the general commanding-in-chief downwards; she could dismiss all the sailors too; she could sell off all our ships of war and all our naval stores; she could make a peace by the sacrifice of Cornwall or begin a war for the conquest of Brittany. She could make every citizen in the United Kingdom, male or female, a peer; she could make every parish in the United Kingdom a university; she could dismiss most of the civil servants; she could pardon all offenders. In a word, the Queen could, by prerogative, upset all the action of civil government, could disgrace the nation by a bad war or peace, and could, by disbanding our forces, whether land or sea, leave us defenceless against foreign nations'.

Queen Victoria did not, of course, attempt any of these entertaining suggestions, because she knew very well that as soon as she tried one of them the government would have resigned; a general election would have followed; the Crown would have become involved in party controversy; and the Queen might have discovered, as her uncle William IV did to his discomfiture, that the country was against her. The overriding principle of British constitutional monarchy is that the monarch does not act except on the advice of the Prime Minister of the day. The Queen still can and in fact does vigilantly exercise her triple rights to influence decisions behind the scenes: the right to be consulted, the right to encourage, and the right to warn.

In addition Bagehot allowed the monarch certain executive powers, acting as a long stop or safety-net in such times of constitutional crisis as changes of government. The most important of these residual independent functions is the choice of whom to send for as the successor of a Prime Minister who has resigned his office or died. The choice is limited because the new Prime Minister must command the support of his own party and the confidence of the House of Commons. In particular the monarch has to act as the fly-wheel of state in this function in circumstances where the majority party in the House of Commons has no recognized leader, or where no party in the Commons commands a clear majority. The former circumstance can probably no longer arise, because since 1964 all major parties now have machinery for electing their leaders. The Queen has no choice but to wait and see who is elected, and then send for him or her.

The latter circumstance, in which no party has a clear majority in the Commons, is still very much on the cards. It nearly happened in the spring of 1974. The Conservatives just lost the February general election, which they had called to resolve the industrial, economic, and particularly coal crisis on the slogan of 'Who governs Britain?' Labour won a majority of four over the Conservatives, but a minority of thirty-two against the combined opposition parties, not counting the Speaker. Edward Heath did

not resign at once, so the Queen did not have to decide whom to
send for, namely Harold Wilson. Mr Heath spent four days vainly
negotiating for a coalition with Jeremy Thorpe, the Liberal leader,
even though, in fact, a Conservative-Liberal coalition would not
have commanded a majority over Labour and the other opposition
parties combined. When it became clear that there were no terms
upon which such a coalition could coalesce, Mr Heath resigned,
and the Queen sent for Mr Wilson. Immediately there were threats
and rumours of the opposition parties combining to bring down
the Government, notably on amendments to the Queen's Speech.
If that had happened, Mr Wilson would presumably have asked
for a dissolution rather than resigned. It therefore became more
than a fantastic academic question whether the Queen could in
those circumstances refuse his request and invite somebody else
(Mr Heath? Mr Thorpe? Mr William Whitelaw? An unelected
outsider?) to try to construct a temporary coalition, on the grounds
that nobody wanted another election so soon after the bitter and
indecisive contest of February; and that another election would
probably produce no more decisive a result.

Whatever the constitutional propriety of such a decision, there is
no doubt that it would have caused acrimonious uproar that could
have threatened the position of the monarchy. Labour politicians
are more prone than others to suspect the monarch of bias against
them, and to be suspicious of any extrinsic interference in the
House of Commons machinery. If the Queen had refused a request
for a dissolution by Harold Wilson in the spring of 1974, she could,
and would, have been severely criticized for playing partisan
politics. Fortunately, in the event the Opposition managed, while
continuing to utter blood-curdling threats, to avoid bringing
down the Government. One motive may have been to protect the
royal prerogative: to avoid endangering the Queen's role as umpire of last resort by bringing her into the party conflict. Another
motive was indubitably that the opposition parties, like everybody
else, did not want and could not afford another election so soon.

After this breathing-space, when Harold Wilson asked for and
got his inevitable dissolution in the autumn, the second general
election of 1974 produced a result that was hardly more decisive.
Labour came out of it with an overall majority of four, not
counting the Speaker, but counting John Stonehouse, who did not
stay around the lobbies to be counted for long. The same circumstances were again on the cards. If by sickness, incompetence of
their whips, or lost by-elections the Government had been defeated shortly after the October election, the Queen would have
been presented with an agonizing choice.

Would the country have wanted, and could it have afforded, a
third election, probably just as indecisive as the last two, in less than

a year? Answer, as far as anybody can presume to answer for the country: definitely no. Yet could the Queen have refused Mr Wilson's request for a dissolution and tried to find somebody else to form a coalition to tide the country through the raging economic crisis, without being condemned by Labour politicians, however unjustly, for partisanship and exceeding her authority? In an age that decides the will of the people by simple arithmetic, even if this produces a majority of only one, it takes a brave monarch to interfere with the addition. The Queen is a brave woman, and exceedingly conscientious about her duties; and she would have taken her decision according to the best constitutional advice available in what she judged to be the interests of the nation as a whole, irrespective of the inevitable criticism. Fortunately she was spared the decision. But the possibility remains real. We appear to be moving into a period of dissatisfaction with the two big monolithic parties, which have alternated in power for the past half century: a period of consequent proliferation of small parties. This fragmentation of the big battalions would be greatly encouraged by the introduction of a more equitable voting system of proportional representation. That is why there is no probability of either of the big battalions introducing such a system.

We may be moving into a period of numerous small parties and concomitant coalition governments. If so, the Queen will be called on to use her vestigial constitutional power of choice of Prime Minister, when there is a real choice to be made. Constitutional propriety does not insist that she must follow the advice of the outgoing Prime Minister; but, if it is given and practicable, his advice is usually decisive. No doubt both Queen and politicians would try to avoid such a choice being forced upon her. The Queen would be meticulous to be seen to be choosing fairly, not arbitrarily, like her great-great-grandmother, who did not bother to pretend that she did not have favourites among her politicians, and black sheep like Gladstone, whom even the most convincing majority could hardly persuade her to send for.

Presumably the equitable way to do it would be for the Queen first to try to follow the advice of the outgoing Prime Minister, if he chose to offer her any; then to send for the leader of the next largest party in the House of Commons, to see whether he could form an administration that commanded the support of the House; then for the leader of the next largest party, and so on, almost down to the leader of the Flat Earth and Votes for Dogs one-man-band party; though before she sank that low, she would presumably call a conference of all the party leaders, as her grandfather did. In a time of turbulent, transitional, and turbid party politics, when no clear leader emerges from the muddle, there is great advantage to the nation in having a disinterested referee above the smoke and stir of the fray. It is a heavy responsibility for the Queen, but it is difficult to think of a better solution.

The other circumstance in which Bagehot maintained that the Queen might have to exercise her function of choice of Prime Minister was when the majority party in the Commons possessed no recognized leader. The most recent and probably the last occasion on which the Queen had to do this was in 1963. Harold Macmillan, the Conservative Prime Minister, was suddenly struck down by what he described magniloquently in his memoirs as 'the stroke of fate': to be blunt, the urgent need for a prostate operation. This made it impossible for him to soldier on as Prime Minister through the nadir of unpopularity through which his government was passing until after the approaching general election, as he hoped to do; and then hand over to a new man with a clean sheet, whether he won or lost. The Conservative Party in those days did not elect its leader, but allowed him to emerge after obscure customary processes of more or less informal consultation. Neither the efficiency nor the dignity of this undemocratic procedure was enhanced by the fact that fate chose the eve of the Conservative Party Conference to strike down Mr Macmillan. The Conference was thereupon transformed into an election convention as rowdy and inappropriate for discreet Establishment king-making as an American convention. Numerous candidates threw their hats into the ring, accompanied by the clang of falling coronets, as peers renounced their peerages under legislation made possible, ironically, by the persistence of a Socialist, the former Lord Stansgate, now Tony Benn.

The obvious successor to Macmillan and incomparably the best qualified of the contenders was R. A. Butler, the deputy Prime Minister if such a post existed in the constitution, whom Macmillan had defeated to succeed Anthony Eden in 1957. Macmillan took the view that Butler did not have the steel that makes a Prime Minister, nor the inspiration that a leader needs to pull his party through a fierce general election. His first candidate to stop Butler succeeding him was Lord Hailsham, who became Quintin Hogg again and entered the race in scenes of mass enthusiasm that the fastidious found distasteful. Nor was Hailsham/Hogg's campaign helped, though it was certainly enlivened, by the doubtful advantage of the arrival of Randolph Churchill at the Conference with hundreds of badges marked 'Q' for Quintin. Lord Butler recalls, with characteristic dry wit: 'He came up to my room and obligingly handed me some for my wife, myself and friends. These I consigned to the waste-paper basket'.

After Hailsham's star waned, a number of other *papabili* became available as rivals to Butler: principally Reginald Maudling, Edward Heath, Iain Macleod, and, a dark horse, the fourteenth Earl of

Home, who gave enigmatic patrician signs of not being interested in changing his title for the far less ancient appellation of Prime Minister. With assiduity worthy of a better cause Mr Macmillan orchestrated the customary procedures of consultation in the Conservative Party from his hospital bed and in considerable discomfort.

At the last minute the rivals for the leadership realised that the old walrus had ditched them, and that Lord Home was about to emerge as the candidate with the greatest overall support in the party. On the night before Macmillan resigned, seven or eight members of the Cabinet including all the other candidates decided to sink their rivalry and support Butler against Home. But they were too late. Macmillan rallied Lord Home with the curious observation: 'Look, we can't change our view now. All the troops are on the starting line. Everything is arranged'. He ignored what he described as the organized revolt of his colleagues as being 'distasteful and rather eighteenth century', and resigned. And on the same morning that he resigned he tendered advice to the Queen in the form of a memorandum showing that Home had majority support in all sections of the party. In the case of the Cabinet this memorandum may have been misleading. If he had let the Queen know that Butler was now running Home close in support in the Cabinet, she might have felt bound to reopen her inquiries.

As it was, Lord Home became Prime Minister, and then transformed into Sir Alec Douglas-Home. And after the dust had died down and the blood stopped flowing, Iain Macleod wrote a trenchant account of the selection procedures, attributing them to the occult manipulation of, in a memorable phrase, 'a magic circle' of Old Etonian aristocrats, determined to keep the premiership in their hands. Macleod acquitted the Queen of all complicity in or knowledge of the manoeuvres: 'There is no criticism whatever that can be made of the part played by the Crown. Presented with such a document [Macmillan's memorandum purporting to be the collective view of the party] it was unthinkable even to consider asking for a second opinion'.

But he concluded that the customary process of letting a Tory leader emerge had resulted on this occasion in contradiction and misrepresentation; and had damaged the party, and indirectly the Queen. He suggested that the procedure would not be followed again. Sir Alec Douglas-Home himself introduced an elaborate system for electing a Tory leader, which elected Mr Heath as his successor in 1965, and Mrs Margaret Thatcher as Mr Heath's successor, though he did not want one, in 1975.

None of the Queen's other choices of whom to send for have been as doubtful or as slippery as that three-ring circus of 1963. But she was called upon to exercise her prerogative on another occasion, at a less dramatic transition from one Tory Prime Minister to another. In 1957 Anthony Eden's bad nerves and poor health forced him to resign during the Suez crisis. There were two candidates for the succession: 'Rab' Butler, generally accepted as favourite by the public, that is to say by most lobby correspondents; and Harold Macmillan. Considerable efforts were made to sound party opinion, by canvassing leading backbenchers and prominent figures in the party organization. Two of the eldest elder statesmen in the party, Sir Winston Churchill and Lord Salisbury, were employed as emissaries to carry the verdict to the Queen. With Lord Kilmuir Lord Salisbury interviewed each member of the Cabinet singly, and asked them: 'Well, which is it, Wab or Hawold?' He also interviewed the Chief Whip, the Chairman of the Party, and the Chairman of the 1922 Committee by telephone. The preference was for Macmillan.

The Queen slept on the advice, and then sent for Mr Macmillan. There is no truth in the legend that the Queen postponed her decision overnight in order to emphasize the royal prerogative. Sir Winston Churchill, ever a nonsuch, broke the customary reticence of the customary procedures by announcing to his constituency executive what advice he had tendered to the Queen, and saying: 'I was delighted that my advice was acted on'.

There is no embarrassment of choice when a Labour Prime Minister has to be succeeded, since the Party has always elected its leaders; or when there is an obvious heir apparent to a Conservative Prime Minister, as there was when Eden succeeded Churchill in 1955. But in the terrible summer of 1940, in the hour when earth's foundations fled, Neville Chamberlain was forced to relinquish his pacific grasp on the premiership by a revolt of his backbenchers that Bagehot would have recognized as the House of Commons acting once again as an electoral college. Chamberlain preferred Lord Halifax, his foreign Secretary, as his successor. But there were doubts about whether the Labour Party would agree to serve in a national coalition under a member of the House of Lords. Halifax was also the first and personal preference of King George VI.

The King described his consultation with Chamberlain about possible successors in his diary: 'I, of course, suggested Halifax, but he told me that H. was not enthusiastic, as being in the Lords he could only act as a shadow or a ghost in the Commons, where all the real work took place. I was disappointed over this statement, as I thought H. was the obvious man, & that his peerage could be placed in abeyance for the time being. Then I knew that there was only one person whom I could send for to form a Government who had the confidence of the country, & that was Winston. I asked Chamberlain his advice, & he told me Winston was the man to send for'.

Churchill's account of being sent for includes a rare recorded example of royal banter: 'His Majesty received me most graciously and bade me sit down. He looked at me searchingly and quizzically for some moments, and then said: "I suppose you don't know why I have sent for you?" Adopting his mood, I replied: "Sir, I simply couldn't imagine why." He laughed and said: "I want to ask you to form a Government." I said I would certainly do so'.

Now that the parties have all adopted machinery for electing their leaders, the prerogative of choice of Prime Minister is in abeyance, but not perhaps quite stone dead. It could be needed again if a Prime Minister were to resign before his successor was chosen, or were to die in office. In such a case the Queen would have to send for a caretaker Prime Minister to carry on the government of the country, while his party went through its procedures for electing a new leader. The overriding constitutional duty of the Queen is to ensure that her country is governed. The Labour Party has stated that only its elected leader could accept the premiership; so presumably, if Labour were in power, there would be an interregnum. The Conservatives have complicated machinery for electing a leader, which can result in several polls extending over several weeks. In that not inconceivable situation the Queen would have to choose a caretaker. If the caretaker himself was a candidate for the leadership, the Queen's choice could have an influence on the election, since possession is nine points of the law. There have been instructive examples of this happening both in 1939 and in 1967 in Australia, where the constitutional position in this respect is similar to that in the United Kingdom.

The dignified pretence that the monarch chooses whom to send for also applies to the holders of posts subsidiary to that of Prime Minister. They are known as Her Majesty's Ministers, and are sent for to kiss hands on appointment. But it is one of Bagehot's stately fictions; since now they are appointed only on the nomination of the Prime Minister.

Another dormant prerogative that may not yet be dead is the right to dissolve Parliament without the advice of the Prime Minister. The last time that a monarch dismissed an entire ministry was in 1834, when William IV, who feared the radical reputation of Lord John Russell, dismissed the Whigs from office. The subsequent general election returned the Whigs, and implicitly voted against the King. No succeeding monarch has been so foolish as to repeat the experiment. And it is unlikely that any ever will be so foolish as to try.

Bagehot denied that the sovereign any longer had the right to dismiss a ministry or dissolve Parliament on his own initiative.

Albert V. Dicey, the great constitutional jurist, disagreed with him: 'I entirely agree that the King can do nothing except on the advice of his ministers; I totally disagree with the doctrine drawn from this principle that he can never dismiss ministers in order that he may ascertain the will of the nation'.

This disagreement between constitutional giants was dramatically resolved, for Australia at any rate, in the autumn of 1975. Gough Whitlam, the Labour Prime Minister, was deadlocked by the Senate's refusal to pass his budget. The Australian Senate, unlike the House of Lords, is constitutionally empowered to refuse or defer supply of funds to the Government. Unlike the House of Lords, the Senate is not inhibited by the feeling that it is not democratically elected from opposing the will of the people, as supposed to be expressed by the Lower House. The Senate is elected also. And the Australian system works on a more adversarial relationship between the two Houses than at Westminster.

Mr Whitlam might have been expected to resign or dissolve Parliament, in order to give the voters a chance of resolving the deadlock. Instead he hung on and would not budge. Malcolm Fraser, the leader of the Liberal Opposition, was equally uncompromising in his refusal to let the budget through the Senate. The country was drifting close to the brink of breakdown, with the Government having no money to pay its servants or its bills. The overriding constitutional duty of the Governor-General, as of the monarch, is to sustain constitutional governance in the Commonwealth or United Kingdom, and to prevent it slipping into anarchy. So the Governor-General, Sir John Kerr, reactivated the dormant constitutional power assigned to him by the Queen, and dismissed the Prime Minister. He invited Malcolm Fraser to form a caretaker administration until an election could be held; and the Senate immediately let the budget through to pay the bills.

The effect of the Governor-General's action was as startling to his neighbours in Canberra as a volcanic eruption on adjacent Mugga Mugga or Mount Ainslie. The Labour Party stigmatized the dismissal of their Prime Minister as a reactionary upper-class conspiracy; although, in fact, the Governor-General, appointed by Whitlam, is a boilermaker's son from a working-class district of Sydney, a pre-war Marxist, and an old though now former personal friend of Whitlam. Some Labour constitutional lawyers argued that the Governor-General was 'a merely titular, non-elected head of state', and did not possess the power to dissolve Parliament. But the weight of opinion was that the Governor-General had acted entirely constitutionally in reanimating his reserve power to dismiss a Prime Minister and dissolve Parliament.

Whether he had also acted wisely was another, more doubtful question. It is always a grave risk to force a general election on a

Controversial Governor-General. H. E. Sir John Kerr, KCMG, Governor-General of Australia, stands before one of the ubiquitous formal portraits of the Queen. The Queen is also 'Queen of Australia'.

single issue, since elections are inappropriate machinery for giving simple answers to single questions. Voters who supported the Governor-General's reserve powers, and at the same time supported the Labour Party were torn in half almost as painfully as disjuncture by sprung pine saplings. In a reply to the Speaker of the House of Representatives the Queen put it on record that she had taken no part in the decision of the Governor-General, which had to be taken in accordance with the Australian constitution: 'The prerogatives of the Crown have been placed securely in the hands of the Governor-General, and only he can exercise them'.

There was a similarly instructive crisis in Canada in 1925. The Governor-General was severely criticized for the independent exercise of his prerogative, as he was in Australia in 1975. The Imperial Conference of 1926 passed a resolution that the functions of a Governor-General were 'similar in all essentials' to those of the sovereign. The light that this throws on the question is less than

limpid. It is fortunate that so difficult an issue has not presented
itself in the United Kingdom so far this century.

The last monarch to dissolve Parliament in person and to dismiss
a ministry was William IV in the 1830s. On neither occasion did
the electorate support the monarch's advice, and they are not
happy precedents. However, the reserve prerogative of dismissal is
not quite dead. It would have to be a very extreme case for the
Queen to revive this power: for example, a Prime Minister who
had gone off his head and yet was still supported by his Cabinet;
or a Government which, without the excuse of an emergency,
attempted, against the will of the Opposition, to prolong itself in
power by repealing the Quinquennial Act. These would be dire
circumstances indeed; but in such extremities the power is there
to be used by a monarch brave enough to take it. If she chose the
wrong occasion, or lost the subsequent election, she would
probably never get a second chance, since the powers, and probably the monarchy, would not survive.

The converse of the prerogative of dissolution is the prerogative
to refuse a dissolution. Queen Victoria maintained that these
related personal prerogatives were alive and capable of being
activated, though she never in practice activated them. In a letter of
1846 she wrote: 'She considers the power of dissolving Parliament
a most valuable and powerful instrument in the hands of the
Crown, but which ought not to be used except in the extreme cases
and with certainty of success. To use the instrument and be defeated is a thing most lowering to the Crown and hurtful to the
country'.

Victoria held the old-fashioned view of the government as her
personal ministers; and consequently of a defeat of the government
at a general election as a personal affront to the Crown. Her
descendants have followed her caution about the exercise of the
prerogative of dissolution. The Queen was spared a difficult choice
about whether to grant or refuse a dissolution in the spring of 1974
and again in the winter of 1974–5. In 1972 opponents of British
entry into the European Economic Community argued that she
should insist on a dissolution, in order to get the wholehearted
approval or disapproval of the British people for such a profound
constitutional change. The result of a general election on the issue
at that period, if one imagines it possible to extract a single answer
from a general election, would probably have been 'no' to entry. In
comparable circumstances in 1910 the Queen's grandfather insisted
on a dissolution before agreeing to facilitate the Parliament Bill to
limit the veto of the House of Lords on legislation. Some opponents of British membership of the European Economic Community and also opponents of royal prerogatives (the same people)
argued that on that occasion the Queen gave up the last of her

powers to act independently as the guardian of the constitution. Their argument is not persuasive. The fact that emergency powers are not actuated in one instance does not entail the conclusion that there is no instance in which they could be actuated.

No monarchs have refused a dissolution for well over a century, though they have sometimes used their prerogative to warn their Prime Ministers against it. For example, George V tried to dissuade Lloyd George from dissolving Parliament in November 1918; and similarly tried to dissuade Baldwin in 1923. In each case he eventually granted the request. There would have to be exceptional circumstances for the Queen to refuse a dissolution. But the point about the exceptional is that it can sometimes happen.

It nearly happened in 1950. Clement Attlee had won an election with a majority of only six. It was quite possible that he might be defeated in the House and ask for another dissolution immediately after a general election. A long correspondence was conducted in *The Times*, that tribal wrestling-ground for constitutional experts, on the question of whether in the circumstances the King would be justified in refusing a request for a dissolution. Sir Alan Lascelles, George VI's Private Secretary, brought the correspondence to its quietus with a magisterial letter under the pseudonym of 'Senex'.

In it he argued that it was indisputable that the King had a personal choice of whether to grant or refuse a request for a dissolution. He went on that no wise sovereign would refuse such a request unless he were satisfied that: '(1) the existing Parliament was still vital, viable, and capable of doing its job; (2) a general election would be detrimental to the national economy; (3) he could rely on finding another Prime Minister who could carry on his government for a reasonable period, with a working majority in the House of Commons'. This statement of the constitutional position, although full of slippery value judgments about what is detrimental, viable, and reasonable, still has a ring of reason and authority for modern times. If Attlee had asked for a dissolution in 1950, Sir Alan Lascelles would have advised the King to agree.

Another long dormant prerogative concerns the Royal Assent, the final theatrical procedure that transforms a Bill into an Act of Parliament. The Queen still signifies her assent in ancient Norman French formulae. For a money Bill she says, or in her absence the Lords Commissioner say for her: '*La Reyne remercie ses bons sujets, accepte leur benevolence, et ainsi le veult*'. For all other public and private Acts the formula is: '*La Reyne le veult*'. And for personal Acts it is: '*Soit fait comme il est désiré*'.

The prerogative to refuse the Royal Assent has not been exercised since 1707, when Queen Anne refused her assent to a Bill for settling the militia in Scotland. The form of words used to express this refusal was: '*La Reyne s'avisera*'. It may therefore be safely

The Queen and the Duke of Edinburgh during their state visit to Brussels in 1966 with Princess Paola, King Baudouin, and Queen Fabiola.

assumed that this prerogative is as dead as Queen Anne herself.
That master of misleading cases, the ingenious and magnificent
A. P. Herbert, once constructed a fantasy in which the Queen refused assent to a Bill as a protest against the increasingly unintelligible
gobbledygook of modern legislation. He had her refuse with the
ancient formula: '*La Reyne s'avisera*', with the modern rider: '*La
Reyne ne comprend pas ceste bille*'. That, unfortunately, is such stuff as
dreams are made on. The world would be a better place if some of
A. P. Herbert's fantasies could be realised.

But it is not entirely out of this world to imagine circumstances
in which the royal veto could be revived. Bagehot asserted that
the Queen must sign her own death-warrant if the two Houses
unanimously send it up to her. In such a far-fetched situation the
Queen might be better advised to withhold her assent; and so
either take her chances at a general election, or force her politicians
at least to act unconstitutionally, if they insisted on acting so
unkindly.

In time of extreme national crisis, for example with an administration trying to prolong its life by repealing the Quinquennial Act
without the agreement of the Opposition, the Queen could veto
the Bill rather than revive her prerogative of dismissing a ministry.
This would confine her disagreement with her ministers to the
single issue, instead of staging a general confrontation. It would
put the ball neatly back in the Government's court. Either the
Government could drop its Bill; in which case a dissolution would
follow automatically at the end of five years under the existing
law. Or it could advise an immediate dissolution. Or it could
resign; in which case its successors, being *ex hypothesi* without a
majority in the Commons, would advise an early dissolution. Or
there would be the rumble of tanks down Whitehall, and a ring of
automatic guns encircling Broadcasting House and New Printing
House Square. In every case except the last the Queen, acting as the
long-stop of the constitution, would have preserved the electoral
rights of the people to have the last word about their destiny. Such
a situation is so improbable as to be almost fantastic. But stranger
things have happened in English history. A monarch who chose to
withhold the Royal Assent in any less extreme circumstances
would immediately make himself, in the words of Asquith's
famous memorandum to George V, 'the football of the contend-
ing factions'. He would also, probably, live to see the end of all his
prerogatives, and of the monarchy itself.

The examples of exercise of the royal prerogative just discussed
are in their nature so seldom likely to be needed as to be fanciful.
The royal influence is much more usually exercised by the Queen's
right to be consulted, to encourage, and to warn. Copies of all
important government papers are sent round daily to Buckingham

*The Queen working at state
papers at her desk at
Buckingham Palace.*

Palace, or wherever the Queen is staying, in red boxes. These include reports from ambassadors and ministers abroad and instructions or replies from the Foreign Office, copies of parliamentary papers, copies of memoranda and minutes of Cabinet meetings, and minutes of all important conferences such as meetings of Commonwealth ministers. Lord Adeane, the Queen's former Private Secretary, stated in his evidence to the Select Committee on the Civil List in 1971 that the Queen spends up to three hours a day in reading these state papers in order that, as head of state, she can have a general knowledge of all current problems. The Queen is the best informed person, with the most relentlessly boring reading list, in Britain.

In addition the Queen has private interviews with a daily stream of important people. Every Tuesday evening when she is in London the Prime Minister of the day calls at Buckingham Palace for a talk. The relationship at such meetings has become much less formal over the past century. According to one witness, when Chatham was Prime Minister, he bowed so low at his meetings with the King that you could see his great nose between his knees. When Gladstone went to see Queen Victoria, he remained standing up even when he was well into his eighties. Victoria nursed a passionate hostility to her great Prime Minister, perhaps because of his sternly limited view of her prerogative. He wrote: 'It would be an evil and perilous day for the monarchy were any prospective possessor of the Crown to assume or claim for himself a preponderating, or even independent, power in any one department of state'. On his visits to the Queen today the Prime Minister is allowed to sit down and smoke a pipe, if he is a smoker.

How influential these consultations are is, of course, one of the arcana of monarchy. No Prime Minister could afford to have it known in detail how much he had been influenced by his monarch. It was, for instance, rumoured in the winter of 1975 that the Queen's apprehension of the break-up of the United Kingdom persuaded the Prime Minister to drop from that session's programme legislation to introduce separate assemblies for Scotland and Wales. Certitude is not possible in such instances until the diaries of Queen and Prime Minister are published many years later; and often not then. In this instance it would be as likely a priori that the Downing Street press office, from which such mysterious rumours tend to transpire, was spreading the story to divert criticism from the Prime Minister.

Harold Wilson has recorded in his memoirs about his meetings with the Queen: 'She is astonishingly well informed on every detail'. He recorded that the Queen is a voracious reader of all state documents, 'and if she quoted one I hadn't yet read, I felt like a schoolboy who hadn't done his homework'. In a farewell dinner at

*Harold Wilson greeting the
Queen for his farewell dinner
at Number Ten on the eve of
his resignation in March 1976.
The occasion, which
intentionally echoed the dinner
given by Sir Winston in 1955,
demanded a Churchillian bow.*

Number Ten Downing Street that he gave for the Queen just
before his retirement in March 1976, imitating the precedent of his
improbable model, Sir Winston Churchill, Sir Harold warned
whoever might emerge as his successor not to be taken in too easily
by Bagehot's distinction between the dignified and efficient parts
of the constitution: 'While the executive hopes it is efficient,
though making small claim to dignity, the dignified component
can lay strong claim to efficiency'. He advised his successor: 'to do
his homework before his audience, and to read all his telegrams and
Cabinet committee papers in time, and not leave them to the
week-end'.

Until quite recently the British assumed without question and without humility that their constitution was the best in the world; and that they were the best governed people in the world, in happy contrast with lesser breeds without the law, who are continually troubled by revolution, upheaval, and political crisis. Few would be so complacent today. But the dawning recognition over the past twenty years that the constitution is no longer working well, and that we are less well governed than many other democracies, does not attach any blame to the Queen. What has unbalanced the constitutional machinery is the growth of enclaves of power without much responsibility, as disturbing to the state as the private empires of the medieval magnates. Such irresponsible power can be seen in the growing presidential powers of the Prime Minister; in the vast, independent fiefs of the bureaucracy; in corporate and multinational gigantism; in the autonomous estates of the trade unions; in the disciplined feudal armies of the two great party machines; and in the consequent withholding of consent for parliamentary government; but not in Buckingham Palace. The case can be argued that the constitution would run more smoothly if the Queen had a little more rather than less power.

It is significant that few of those who want to change the constitution want to change it in such a way as to abolish the monarchy or reduce the Queen's prerogative. The Communist Party is the only political party of any consequence to have it on its programme. The manifesto of the Scottish Nationalists states: 'The function of the Crown in Scotland shall be exercised during the residence of the sovereign in and through a Scottish Privy Council, and in the absence of the sovereign by a Council of State appointed from the Scottish Privy Council. It may not be exercised from outside Scotland'. Donald Stewart MP, the leader of the parliamentary Scottish National Party, says: 'Our policy is for an independent country within the Commonwealth, recognizing the monarchy; that is, the same as the constitutional position of Canada or New Zealand'.

Plaid Cymru, the Welsh National Party, adopted a policy of dominion status towards the monarchy in the early 1930s. At that time this involved recognizing the monarchy, and looking forward to the day when the King of England would also be the King of Wales. There has been no change in this policy since the dominions have become free and equal members of the Commonwealth. Gwynfor Evans MP, President of Plaid Cymru, says: 'We still accept the Crown as one of the links between members of the Commonwealth; and there has been no move in the party at all, as far as I know, to change the situation. This does not mean, of course, that there are no republicans in the party; only that the party policy does remain unchanged'.

The constitutional future of the monarchy in the last quarter of the twentieth century and on into the twenty-first is wrapped in turbid and increasingly turbulent mist, like the future of all of us. Now that Britain is a member of the European Economic Community, shall we see the Queen gaining a European role, like her Norman and Plantagenet ancestors? It is no great leap into fantasy to imagine the president of another member of the Community inviting the Queen to some grand state occasion, to lend it more majesty. It is possible to imagine the Queen opening the European Parliament, so perhaps, in a small way, encouraging the rest of us to take it more seriously. Might she perhaps become the first head of state for Europe, acting in rotation with Europe's other heads of state?

In 1854 Baron Christian Frederick Stockmar, Prince Albert's earnest Belgian political adviser, whose misconceptions of the British constitution were as unfortunate for his royal employers as his pedagogic notions were disastrous for the education of the Prince of Wales, wrote to Albert about what he took, erroneously as usual, to be the unconscious crypto-republicanism of the Whigs: 'If the English Crown permit a Whig ministry to follow this rule in practice without exception, you must not wonder if in a little time you find the majority of the people impressed with a belief that the King in the view of the law is nothing but a mandarin figure which has to nod its head in assent, or shake it in denial, as his minister pleases'.

Quite properly in an age of democratic party politics the constitutional powers of the monarch have indeed become emergency powers since Baron Stockmar wrote. In general the Queen nods and shakes her head as the Prime Minister pulls the strings, even if she finds herself assenting to such improbably anti-monarchical views as an attack on hereditary privilege. As Clement Attlee described it: 'A monarch is a kind of referee, although the occasions when he or she has to blow the whistle are nowadays very few'. But if you take the whistle completely away, you might as well not have a referee at all. And games without a referee have a tendency towards chaos and bad temper. If every last discretionary power were to atrophy, you might as well not have a Queen. A waxwork in regalia could ride in the gilded coach, entertain distinguished foreign visitors, and mouth the Queen's Speech stereophonically. Without her constitutional prerogatives of last resort, the Queen's influence and prestige would be greatly diminished. It is doubtful if there would be any point in maintaining a monarchy on such terms. As it is, the machine works, and provides a safeguard for unforseen emergencies. We may be grateful for it sooner than we think in the hazy but troubled political seas that lie ahead.

3 Foreign and Commonwealth

Foreign affairs once held an important place in the royal prerogative. They are still an important part of the Queen's function.
One of the chief roles of any head of state is as representative and
host on behalf of her country to foreigners. Millions of ordinary
people, from tribesmen just emerging from the Stone Age in
Papua to the shanty-dwellers of Rio de Janeiro, have only one
image of Britain: that of the Queen.

In the Middle Ages the kings, dressed in suits made by black-
smiths not tailors, led their armies out to capture each other's
adjacent territory, like wanton boys playing at internecine French-
and-English. Even in the nineteenth century monarchs still strode
the diplomatic stage beside their ministers, making treaties and
fixing alliances, like babies in crowns and silk hats playing with
dynamite. War was the trade of kings. And the English kings
retained their prerogative to make treaties, to cede or accept
territory, to declare war, and to make peace, long after they had
surrendered their right to tax to Parliament, and their right to try
judicially to the law courts.

Queen Victoria, who was related to all the monarchs of Europe,
and Prince Albert, who was a continental European, demanded the
right not just to be consulted, but also to vet and initiate British
foreign policy in the diplomatic and monarchical upheavals of
their time. They seldom got their way. Lord Palmerston, their
Foreign Secretary so greatly unappreciated at court, was a master
at circumventing royal interference in foreign policy. Either
he sent off his gun-boats or his dispatches without consulting
the Palace. Or he delayed sending the drafts to the Queen until
the dispatches themselves had been mailed. Or he blandly ignored
alterations that the Queen thought he had agreed to. Prince Albert
and his adviser, that egregious ass Baron Stockmar, wrote wordy
memoranda about Palmerston's *bocks*, or blunders, in every crisis
from the chronic Schleswig-Holstein question to the Don Pacifico
affair. Most contemporaries saw, and the retrospective eye of
history sees, that 'Pam's' policies were not so much *bocks* as usually
successful, and, better still, right.

It is easy to overestimate the influence exerted by modern

royalty in foreign affairs. The Germans certainly did so in the case of Edward VII, mistaking the royal symbol of British foreign policy for its substance. So the Imperial Chancellor, Herr von Bethmann-Hollweg, could declare in the Reichstag: 'King Edward VII believed that his principal task was to isolate Germany. The encirclement by the *Entente* with openly hostile tendencies was drawn closer year by year'. And no less an authority than the Italian Foreign Minister, who should have known better, could describe Edward as 'the arbiter of Europe's destiny'.

The wits of Paris bestowed on him the title of *l'oncle de l'Europe*, which was itself the title of a book about Edward published as early as 1906. Queen Victoria had been, literally, the grandmother of most of the monarchs of Europe.

Edward was in no way the arbiter of Europe's destiny. By the beginning of this century European politics had outgrown the tutelage of monarchical dynasties, great and small; though contemporaries were slow to recognize the process. The King had neither the imagination nor the power to conceive and carry through a policy for the realignment of European alliances. What he could do with his contacts in high places, love of foreign travel, and exquisite manners, was to create the atmosphere in which such a realignment could function smoothly. At practical diplomacy the King was an amateur and at times a bungler. He once handed over to the Kaiser a confidential British memorandum not meant for those suspicious eyes, simply, it has been suggested, to get rid of the wretched thing. Atmosphere and panache were the King's forte, not detailed diplomacy. Although widely credited for it, particularly by the Germans, Edward VII did not plan or carry out the *entente cordiale* between Britain and France. The expansion and aggressive imperialism of Germany made such an *entente* inevitable. Edward made it *cordiale*. In foreign policy he was the last British king to play a personal part, which, though less important than his contemporaries supposed, was not without significance.

The world earthquake of 1914–18 finally persuaded people that foreign affairs and wars were matters too serious to be left to kings and even kaisers. Since then the constitutional position of the monarch has been that defined, with characteristically lapidary clarity, by Sir William Anson, the constitutional jurist: 'The Sovereign does not, constitutionally, take independent action in foreign affairs. Everything which passes between him and foreign princes or ministers should be known to his own ministers, who are responsible to the people for policy, and to the law for acts done'.

One department of monarchical diplomacy has waxed this century, while the rest of the monarch's autocratic old diplomatic role has waned to an ornamental vestige. That department is the Commonwealth. The Queen's grandfather presided over the generally peaceful transformation of the British Empire into a Commonwealth of self-governing nations. The Delhi Durbar of 1911–12 was the apotheosis of the Victorian concept of Empire; and at the same time held the seeds of the new idea of the Crown as symbolic link between free and independent peoples. The Queen's father was the last king to bear the title of Emperor of India. He used to say that the outsider, looking at the bewildering anomalies of the British Commonwealth of Nations, must have the same reaction as the man who, on first seeing a giraffe, exclaimed: 'There ain't no such animal'.

The Commonwealth is a giraffe that has grown bigger, and more anomalous, and more spotted since then. The Queen has inherited an extraordinarily diverse and ramshackle legacy and role in the Commonwealth, which somehow still works and is considered of value by its members. It consists at present of thirty-six sovereign independent states, of which the latest to join were Papua New Guinea in September 1975, and the ninety-two Seychelles Islands in the Indian Ocean, which became an independent republic within the Commonwealth in June 1976. It is an extraordinarily diverse congeries of states, with little in common apart from the Commonwealth connexion and the ancient accidents of British imperialism. That useful and intelligent Martian would be hard put to discover the common denominator that qualified members for the Commonwealth club.

They range in size from Nauru, the Pacific island just over eight square miles in size and with a population at the last count of 6,768, to the vast sub-continent of India with its teeming population of 550,000,000. They include a broad cross-section of the diverse races, cultures, colours, and creeds under the sun. Some of the old dominions were originally colonized by British settlers, speak English, use British forms of government, appeal to the Judicial Committee of the Privy Council as their supreme judicial authority, and appear more British than the British. Others, like Cyprus, Fiji, and Tanzania, seem engagingly alien.

The systems of government range from parliamentary democracy on the Westminster model, through various forms of one-party oligarchy and dictatorship, to racist tyranny in Uganda. By an unhappy irony 'Field Marshal' Idi Amin seized power in Uganda while his predecessor, President Milton Obote, was in Singapore for the 1971 Commonwealth Prime Ministers' meeting. The only common denominator of membership is that members accept the Queen as the symbol of their free association, and, accordingly, as head of the Commonwealth.

Some members, including the old, white dominions, recognize

The Queen riding on an elephant with the Maharaja of Jaipur during her state visit to India in 1961.

the Queen as their Queen and head of state. In each of these the Queen is personally represented by a Governor-General, who in many respects holds the same position in relation to the administration of public affairs as is held by the sovereign in Britain. The exception is that certain constitutional functions, such as the appointment of the Governor-General himself, and the award of honours in those countries that accept such baubles, are performed by the Queen herself on the recommendation of the Prime Minister of the nation concerned. The Governor-General is wholly independent of the British government, and is now usually a national of the country in which he holds office.

The Queen as Queen of Australia is a wholly independent entity from herself as Queen of the United Kingdom, and wholly separate again from herself as Queen of Jamaica. This position, which Gilbert and Sullivan could have made something of, is a kind of new Athanasianism of many Crowns in one monarchy. It is fraught with the embarrassing possibility of the Queen being pulled asunder by being given conflicting or contradictory advice by some or all of the twelve Commonwealth countries that recognize her as their Queen and head of state. So far that embarrassment has been avoided; but at times it has been a near thing, notably when South Africa left the Commonwealth and became a republic in 1961.

The twentieth Governor-General of Canada, Roland Michener, defined his function in 1975 with a precision that, *mutatis mutandis*, defines the function of the Queen in the United Kingdom: 'As I see my official role, I am the one person in our political system who is above party affiliations and in a position to represent and speak for Canada in its collective whole. This has become more evident in recent years when Canadians have been appointed to the office. In effect, the Governor-General has become the unique symbol of the unity and of the continuity of our institutions and political life, and of our collective identity as a sovereign nation. He should contribute both to unity amongst our diverse regions and people, and to stability in our society'.

But it is not necessary to recognize the Queen *qua* Queen to be a member of the Commonwealth. This was the position until the Second World War, which was a turning-point for the monarchy and the Commonwealth, as for much else. The status of members of the Commonwealth was defined by the Imperial Conference of 1926 and given legal substance by the Statute of Westminster, 1931. This defined members of the club as: 'Autonomous communities within the British Empire, equal in status, in no way subordinate one to another, but united by a common allegiance to the Crown and freely associated as members of the British Commonwealth of Nations'.

King George VI with his Prime Ministers at Buckingham Palace during the Commonwealth Prime Ministers' Conference of 1949.

The constitutional position of the Commonwealth in 1939 at the beginning of the war was that of a small group of nations, all white, in which the United Kingdom was *primus inter pares*. Westminster could not legislate for another member of the Commonwealth except at the request of the Parliament of that country. Each had a Parliament on the Westminster pattern, possessing full powers to legislate on all matters affecting its own country. Each recognized George VI as King, and took all formal action in the King's name.

After the war the idea of one country ruling another as its colony was discredited in Western Europe; although it was enforced with an iron hand in an iron glove over Eastern Europe. The colonies claimed their independence in rapid succession, starting with that jewel of the Imperial Crown, India. Some, like Burma and Palestine in 1948, left the Commonwealth upon becoming independent. A conference of Commonwealth Prime Ministers met in London in 1949 to devise a formula to keep the Commonwealth together in a post-imperial world that had little respect for the monarchical principle. With the flexible empiricism that is the glory of British government as well as of British philosophy, the Conference came up with the definition of the King as 'the symbol of the free association of the independent member nations of the Commonwealth, and as such the head of the Commonwealth'. This Conference is a conspicuous landmark in the evolution of the Commonwealth and the monarchy, as important as the Balfour Formula of 1926, and the Statute of Westminster itself. It enabled countries like India, which understandably wished to be republics with their own native presidents instead of maintaining the symbol of their colonial subjection, to stay in the Commonwealth. George VI recognized the importance of the new club rules when he congratulated his seven Prime Ministers and the Canadian Minister for External Affairs, representing his Prime Minister, at the close of the Conference: 'The problem of which you have just offered me your solution is one that has given us all very grave concern. That solution is a striking example of the elasticity of our system. So far, it has stood tests such as no other association of nations in history has ever survived. Believing as I do that it has in it immense powers of good for humanity generally, I sincerely trust that it may not in the future be subjected to any greater strain'.

Today nineteen members of the Commonwealth, including India, are republics with presidents as heads of state. Western Samoa has a head of state, His Highness Malietoa Tanumafili the Second, whose functions are analogous to those of a constitutional monarch. Lesotho, Tonga, and Swaziland are monarchies with their own kings. And, just to complete the gamut of constitutional music, Malaysia has a system of electing one of its state rulers for a term of five years as *Yang di-Pertuan Agung*, or monarch and head of the federation. The temporary holder of the title in 1976 was His Majesty Tuanku Yahya Putra Ibni-Marhum Sultan Ibrahim, the Sultan of Kelantan. These states, so various that they seem to be not one but all mankind's epitome, have only two things in common: a connexion at some date with British history, and the recognition of the Queen as symbol and head of the Commonwealth.

As if this were not convoluted enough, complication is further complicated by the dependent territories and associated states, being regarded as forming part of the Commonwealth by virtue of their relationship with member states of the Commonwealth. These dependencies include such nice distinctions of nomenclature and constitution as colonies or settlements, protectorates, protected states, condominiums, and one leased territory. This last consists of the New Territories, a peninsula in the southern part of the Kwangtung Province of mainland China, with its adjacent islands. They were leased to Great Britain for ninety-nine years in

The Queen visiting Hong Kong, the one leased territory, during her Far East tour in 1975. Here emulating her husband's talent as a painter, she dots the eyes of a traditional Chinese dragon at Tsuen Wan Sports Ground.

1898, and are administered by the Government of Hong Kong.

Some do consider the modern Commonwealth a chimera, or purely mythical creature kept alive by the fabulists of public relations. And it is true that the Commonwealth link is sometimes hard to detect. India and Pakistan contrived to fight wars against each other while both being members of the Commonwealth; Pakistan resigned its membership in 1972. Uganda brutally expelled its Asian citizens, in spite of the protests and pleas of the rest of the Commonwealth. Members of the Commonwealth have no compunction about putting their own interests first; ignoring the interests of other members; and, on occasions, roundly abusing the policies and behaviour of another member, usually the United Kingdom. The Commonwealth has no common policy. Its meetings of heads of government, which have replaced the more formal

pre-war Imperial conferences, consult frequently on major issues of international affairs and other matters that affect them all. But they tend not to pass resolutions or formulate policies, for the sensible though unstated reason that nobody would feel obliged to follow them if they did. On occasions members of the Commonwealth have subscribed to general and conveniently vague statements of principle: such as the Commonwealth Declaration agreed at Singapore in 1971, and a statement on nuclear weapon tests issued by the meeting at Ottawa in 1973.

Carpers say that these practices mean that the Commonwealth is no more than a grand talking-shop under royal patronage, of no more weight than the hot air it regularly generates. Such a view is short-sighted. As Churchill said, jaw-jaw is better than war-war. In this world of frightening disunity and irrationality, any talking-shop that aims at unity, cooperation, and rational discourse between different nations and races has the angels on its side. The Commonwealth has not yet realised its full potential as a multi-racial partnership. But without such a partnership, the future of the human race looks nasty, brutish, and short. The Commonwealth ideal put into practice could be the fugleman for a saner and safer world.

It is clear that the Queen at least takes the Commonwealth and her responsibilities as its head as seriously as any of her constitutional functions. She came of age in Cape Town during the 1947 South African tour with her father and family. She used the occasion, on the threshold of her tremendous destiny, to make a

The Queen, wearing the Order of Canada, seated with the Duke of Edinburgh and Prime Ministers and delegates at the Ottawa Commonwealth Prime Ministers' Conference in 1973. The group includes Pierre Trudeau, Edward Heath, General Gowon, Dom Mintoff, and Gough Whitlam. Despite conflicting interests, they still managed to subscribe to conveniently vague statements of principle.

dedicatory and hierophantic broadcast by radio to the five hundred millions of the British Commonwealth. Her theme was the Commonwealth ideal. She said: 'I should like to make that dedication now. It is very simple. I declare before you all that my whole life, whether it be long or short, shall be devoted to your service and the service of our great Imperial Commonwealth to which we all belong. But I shall not have strength to carry out this resolution unless you join in it with me, as I now invite you to do; I know that your support will be unfailingly given. God bless all of you who are willing to share it'.

A lot of water has passed under the Commonwealth bridge since that broadcast. South Africa has left the Commonwealth, because her policy of apartheid is incompatible with a multiracial association. And dedicatory declarations have gone out of fashion. The words of Princess Elizabeth today sound charmingly dated, like Peter Pan appealing to the audience to shout that they believe in fairies in order to save the life of Tinkerbell. But the sincerity of the Queen's belief in the Commonwealth is no fairy story. It persists. In 1959 she gave Marlborough House in Pall Mall, which Wren built for the great Duke of Marlborough, and which was the London home of her great-grandfather when he was Prince of Wales, as a Commonwealth centre for government conferences. So far as so loose an association can have a centre, Marlborough House is the headquarters of the Commonwealth.

It is sometimes suggested by Commonwealth enthusiasts that the Queen should take up periodic residence in the other countries besides the United Kingdom that recognize her as Queen. The old dominions of European settlement, Canada, Australia, New Zealand, and South Africa, fought beside Britain in two world wars largely because they felt they were kith and kin of the old mother country; this feeling being symbolized in patriotic loyalty to the monarch. How long can such a loyalty subsist for an absentee monarch, away in Never-Never Land on the other side of the world? It is not very logical for the Queen to be called Queen of Australia, and Canada, and New Zealand, when she visits each of them on average once only every five years, for a formal sightseeing tour of a few weeks. But then people who want logic are not likely to go in for a Queen or a Commonwealth in the first place.

Selwyn Lloyd, when he was Foreign Secretary between 1955 and 1960, supported the idea of sharing the Queen more equitably around the countries that recognize her: 'I think it should be arranged for the Queen to spend a month in Australia each year; perhaps a fortnight in Canberra, and a week in two of the states by rotation. I should like her also to have a week in New Zealand, and to commute to Canada perhaps three or four times a year. Of course, her engagements in the United Kingdom would have to be substantially curtailed to enable her to do this'.

Such suggestions have always been received with the emphatic silence that indicates disapproval from Buckingham Palace. For one thing there is a great deal of routine business for the Queen to transact in the United Kingdom. Her routine would indeed have to be substantially curtailed. For another, it was felt that the head of the Commonwealth should normally be resident at its centre, and available to meet its visitors, public and private. And for another, the Queen is already one of the most peripatetic travellers in the world. When she is abroad in a country that is not accustomed to her presence, she is always on parade. At home, particularly at Balmoral and Sandringham, she can occasionally get away from the theatrical aspects of her profession. It is not easy to imagine her being allowed any private life if she started, like medieval monarchs, to go on permanent progress around her Commonwealth kingdoms.

She likes her present routine, and does not want to spend more time away from home than she already has to in the ordinary run of business.

Prince Philip put this last point bluntly during the royal tour of Canada in 1969, when there was a tide of hostility to the monarchy, particularly from French Canadians. It is a traditional and useful function of the consort of a British queen to express controversial truths that she is inhibited from expressing herself, because of her constitutional duty to be above controversy, a hieratic figure who is all things to all men. The Duke fulfils this function and appears to enjoy it, delivering pep talks like a hearty and testy naval captain of the old school about pulling our socks up, and, on one famous occasion, getting our fingers out. He lectured the mutinous Canadians: 'The answer to this question of the monarchy is very simple – if the people don't want it, they should change it. But let us part on amicable terms and not have a row. The monarchy exists not for its own benefit, but for that of the country. We don't come here for our health. We can think of better ways of enjoying ourselves'.

That may not go down in the record books as the Duke's most diplomatic pronouncement; but it contains more truth than tact. It appears to rule out any question of the Queen ever going international, as occasional monarch in residence in Ottawa, Canberra, or Wellington. But as one of the Queen's wisest and most experienced press secretaries warns: 'Never say that the Queen never does something or never will do something, because as soon as you say that, she will find some reason for doing it'.

Now that the Prince of Wales is adult, he would be competent to discharge all the royal functions as first Counsellor of State, while his mother and father were abroad resident in one of their other kingdoms. On precedent, which counts for more in monarchical affairs than in most things, it is more likely that the Queen's children will be used to domicile the Queen's image in her other kingdoms than that she will do it herself. One of the traditional problems of royalty is to find useful work to keep the heir apparent and other royal children busy and happy. It is not fantastic to imagine the Prince of Wales, particularly when he is married, or his sister or brothers in a few years' time, being sent as Governors-General to Commonwealth countries. The suggestion would have to come from the Prime Minister of the country concerned; and the British Government and Buckingham Palace would need to be convinced that the appointment would be generally popular in that country. There are several precedents for such an appointment of a member of the royal family.

The British Commonwealth is an illogical and extraordinary institution. As such it is quite suitable that it should have a queen as its symbol and its head. It seems to work so far. And it has incalculable potential for good. No doubt other symbols and other heads could be devised. But it seems more likely that so nebulous an association would dissolve and evaporate if you started to reorganize its constitution. The Queen defined her function as head of the Commonwealth precisely and without exaggeration on her visit to Australia in 1954. She said: 'The Crown is a human link between all peoples who owe allegiance to me – an allegiance of mutual love and respect and never of compulsion'. She did not make the mistake of some enthusiasts in describing the Crown as the only possible link for the Commonwealth nations, but correctly saw herself as 'a human link'.

One of the most striking differences that distinguishes the Queen's performance of her office from that of her predecessors is the new mobility of the second half of the twentieth century. Blériot first fluttered across the Channel during the reign of her great-grandfather. Today Concorde can take her to New York in shorter time than it took Queen Victoria to drive from London to Windsor. During her reign television has turned the Commonwealth into a multinational global village, whose members all round the world can hear the Queen and see her in colour as, for example, she speaks her Christmas message from Buckingham Palace.

Lord Adeane made this point about mobility and communication succinctly: 'In what respect has the life of the sovereign altered from that lived by Her Majesty's predecessors? Briefly, in two main respects. First, the Queen has come to stand much nearer to her people in all her realms than her predecessors. Secondly, and this follows to some extent from the first answer, the mobility of the monarchy has enormously increased since 1952'.

In addition to travelling farther, the Queen has met immeasurably more people of all sorts and conditions than her predecessors. The term 'walkabout' was first popularized in 1973 on her visit to Australia to open the Sydney opera house, to describe an informal stroll to meet the people, as an Australian aborigine goes walkabout in the Outback. This style of meeting and chatting to the ordinary people whom chance, sometimes helped by an equerry or local official, throws in her way is now part of all her tours, domestic and foreign; far more useful than the shaking of hands of worthy dignitaries formed up in a stiff line.

Television and still photography have made the image of the Queen one of the best known icons in the world. If you were, in a fit of magnificent absurdity, to conduct a universal public opinion poll of the best known faces of living contemporaries, there is little doubt that the Queen would come in the top ten, along with, Muhammad Ali, Fidel Castro, and a selection of currently fashionable but ephemeral pop and television stars. If she was portrayed wearing the regalia, she would come top.

In the twentieth century it is not peripatetic kings on chevachee, but peripatetic Kissingers shuttling between capitals who make foreign policy. Nevertheless, the Queen's travels make even Henry Kissinger's look like the desultory journeys of a stay-at-home. Since her accession in 1952 she has averaged two major foreign visits a year, each visit usually taking in several adjacent countries. In 1954, in a demonstration of the new mobility that characterizes her reign, she became the first monarch to circumnavigate the globe; scarcely setting foot during the entire voyage on any territory that was not part of the Commonwealth. She has probably visited more countries than any other living person, and travelled more miles than any but the longest serving of long distance airline pilots.

The Queen's travels fall roughly into two groups. First, visits to Commonwealth countries, which are made at the invitation of the country concerned, after preliminary consultation with the Foreign and Commonwealth Office and Buckingham Palace.

The second group consists of state visits to foreign countries outside the Commonwealth. These are usually made on the advice of the United Kingdom government to serve what it sees as its diplomatic interest, and at the invitation of foreign heads of state. A Foreign Office minister accompanies the Queen on such visits to deal with the practical implications on politics and trade.

A sceptic might question what practical purpose is served by such vast and meticulous labours and incessant journeyings. The conventional answer is that royal visits are Britain's grandest form of international public relations. They show the flag, beat the drum, cement international friendships, and, anyway, they are

Although the term 'walkabout' was first popularized in 1970, President Truman had encouraged Princess Elizabeth to get out among the people in Washington as early as 1951.

The Queen became on honorary citizen of New York during her state visit to the United States of America to coincide with the Bicentennial celebrations in the summer of 1976.

good for trade. Unfortunately for this image of the Queen as apotheosis of travelling export salesman, Andrew Duncan demonstrated in *The Reality of Monarchy* (1970) that state visits do not necessarily boost British trade. British exports to Brazil fell and imports thence increased in the year following the state visit to that country in 1968. In the year following the Duke of Edinburgh's very hard-sell campaign in the United States in 1966, which he disliked and said he would not repeat, British exports to the United States fell by £28 million. A more sensible answer is that the primary function of state visits, as of the monarchy itself, is not a practical one. The Queen on tour spreads an image of Britain and mutual *entente* that cannot be measured in dollars, but is nevertheless real and valued by both British diplomats and the host country. There is always a long waiting-list of requests for a royal tour.

Foreign travel, with the complications of foreign punctiliousness involved with convoluted native British etiquette, is a labyrinth in which even the most careful Ariadne can slip into solecism. An eagle-eyed enthusiast for such niceties spotted the

The giving and receiving of gifts is an important part of every state visit. Here the Queen opens a present given by the King of Thailand. The Queen of Thailand and the Duke of Edinburgh watch.

Queen wearing the riband of the Order of the Royal House of Chakri from the wrong shoulder on her state visit to Thailand in 1972. That was just about venial, the Order not being one that she wears regularly in the evening. It is less easy to forgive Sir Christopher Soames, then the British Ambassador in Paris, for wearing his Grand Cross of the Order of St Michael and St George from the wrong shoulder during the state visit to France in 1972. The French all managed to drape theirs around themselves correctly.

As well as ribands, sashes, garters, equally nice protocol envelops royal visits. The Queen makes a state visit as head of state to head of state. She has never yet made one twice to the same foreign sovereign or head of state, and is extremely unlikely to do so. When the head of state changes, she can then make a second state visit. For example, she visited King Frederik of Denmark in 1957, and will return to visit his daughter, Queen Margrethe II, within the next few years.

The Queen would not visit a country privately until she had visited it publicly. For instance, she normally goes to the weddings of her godchildren. But she did not go to Spain in 1972 for the wedding of her godson, Crown Prince Alexander of Yugoslavia. Apart from offending the protocol of royal travel, this would have been taken to confer unwanted warmth on Britain's cool relations with Franco's Spain, and unwanted chill on Britain's relations with Yugoslavia, which shows no signs of wanting Crown Princes any more. The national symbol cannot stir without symbolic interpretations being inferred from her movement. Princess Anne went instead of her to Alexander's wedding. Thus the Queen is normally represented by a senior male member of the family business – the Duke of Edinburgh, the Prince of Wales, Lord Mountbatten – at all *recognized* funerals: for example, those of King Gustaf, and Presidents de Gaulle, Pompidou, Eisenhower, and Kennedy. But for General Franco's funeral the British Ambassador represented the Queen. The Duke of Edinburgh represented her at Juan Carlos's accession ceremonies, making a significant distinction, for those with eyes sharp enough to read the small print, between Britain's attitude to Spain under Franco and after Franco.

After a state visit, the rules allow the Queen to return to the country for a private visit. For example, she spent a private weekend with King Frederik of Denmark some time after her state visit to him. And, after her Italian state visit, she spent some time travelling round Italy from the royal yacht. Any such private visit is cleared with the president or monarch of the country concerned. Monarchs, in their ancient trade union, are the very pineapples of politeness about not trespassing on each other's territory without permission. If the Queen goes to France privately, to a horse race or to look at horses, the President is always formally informed. The only real exception to the Queen's regular pattern of overseas visits seems to have been her visit to the Netherlands in 1962 for the silver wedding celebrations of Queen Juliana and Prince Bernhard.

Her official visits abroad are, of course, arranged by the government, and often have some explicit or implicit diplomatic purpose. A good example of this was her state visit to France in 1972, which was clearly intended as the ceremonial crowning of Britain's accession to the European Economic Community. Whether the Queen herself was in favour of British entry was irrelevant. Some opponents of entry counted her as one of themselves, on the grounds that entry curtailed the royal prerogative in some respects. Such evidence as there is, including her family's inveterate inclination towards internationalism in general, and *entente cordiale* with France in particular, suggests, on the contrary, that as a private person the Queen was an enthusiastic supporter of British entry.

But she was sent to France not because she was personally pleased about British entry (though she was), but to celebrate the achievement of a dream of greater European unity desultorily aimed at by successive governments and the Foreign Office for twenty-five years, and finally fulfilled by Edward Heath's government. The French had stopped blocking British entry, so we sent the Queen to thank them ceremonially.

The converse of this is that denial of a state visit can be used as a penalty, in the opposite way to a visit from the Queen being used as a symbolic reward. When this happens, Buckingham Palace makes the announcement that the tour has been cancelled, stating that it is 'on government advice'. A recent example was when the arrangements for the Prince of Wales to pay a ten-day visit to India in 1975 were cancelled. This had no implication one way or another about the Prince's own attitude to India. It was a signal that the British Government disapproved of the abrogation of the constitution and imposition of Congress Party oligarchy by Mrs Indira Gandhi. Princess Margaret was scheduled to go to Cairo in November 1973 in order to open the British Council office. Sir Alec Douglas-Home, the Foreign Secretary, cancelled the visit 'for diplomatic and safety reasons': in blunter words, the fighting in the Middle East. The Queen's visit to Nigeria planned for October 1975 was postponed, for the diplomatic reason phrased with diplomatic euphemism by the Foreign and Commonwealth Office, that it would be 'more tactful to wait'.

The converse of a state visit by the Queen is a state visit to the United Kingdom by a foreign head of state: a home match as opposed to an away match. The Queen is as much visited against as visiting. Such visits are ceremonial government business, arranged through Foreign Offices and embassies, and often having some diplomatic purpose or point to make. One of the Queen's most important duties is to act as hostess of the United Kingdom on such state visits. When the head of a foreign or Commonwealth state visits Britain, he or she stays at Buckingham Palace, Windsor Castle, or the palace of Holyroodhouse. His entertainment, organized by the Queen, includes banquets, receptions, often a special performance of ballet or opera, and visits to places throughout the United Kingdom that are considered likely to be of particular interest to the visitor. Guests are nearly always treated to a banquet in Guildhall. They always lay a wreath on the tomb of the Unknown Soldier in Westminster Abbey. And they often take tea with the Queen Mother, who does not go to Victoria Station with the rest of the family to meet them. The same rules apply to home as to away fixtures: one state visit is the ration for one head of state. When the head of state has changed, the new man can have a return match and come to Buckingham Palace on a state visit.

The heads of state who have been paraded in a state coach beside the Queen through streets decorated with their national flags, wined, dined, danced at at Covent Garden, escorted around steel-

Entente Cordiale 1976. President Giscard d'Estaing entertains the Queen at the French Embassy on the last evening of his state visit to Great Britain in June. It is traditional for a visiting head of state to entertain the sovereign before he goes home.

works and schools, and made speeches at by the Queen, are a team as extraordinarily varied as foreign affairs themselves are varied. They range from General de Gaulle to President Tubman of Liberia, and from the Shah of Iran to Grand Duke Jean of Luxemburg. The public business on such state visits is necessarily imposing and formal. No doubt useful diplomatic discussions take place privately during them between officials and even heads of state behind the gold plate, bunting, and ballerinas. Occasionally you can see and hear that something more is being transacted than the normal anodyne compliments of such grand package tours. For example, on President Giscard d'Estaing's state visit in the summer of 1976 he and the Queen both called publicly for an end to the old rivalries and suspicions between their countries and the establishment of a new and more confident *entente cordiale*. This aspiration was made practical by an agreement that the President and the British Prime Minister should visit each other for discussions regularly once a year.

The mutual visits between the Queen and Emperor Hirohito of Japan were used formally to bury one hatchet of the Second World War. There was considerable hostility to Hirohito's state visit in 1971. Earl Mountbatten of Burma, who was Supreme Allied Commander in the Far East at the end of the last war, boycotted the state banquet in an uncharacteristic fit of being a shrinking violet and a wallflower at a royal occasion. There was uproar about the Queen returning to the Emperor the Order of the Garter, from which Order he had been expelled when his banner was removed from St George's, Windsor, in 1940. A symbolic tree planted by the Emperor in Kew Gardens was promptly and predictably chopped down by an ex-prisoner of the Japanese. And *Private Eye* welcomed the visitor with a front cover under the headline 'There's a Nasty Nip in the Air'. In her speech at the state banquet the Queen allowed herself to step beyond the polite platitudes expected on such occasions: 'We cannot pretend that the past did not exist. We cannot pretend that the relations between our two peoples have always been peaceful and friendly. However, it is precisely this experience which should make us all the more determined never to let it happen again'.

When the Queen made her state visit to Japan in 1975, Hirohito responded with Delphic discretion: 'Friendship between our two countries had to undergo a severe trial with the vicissitudes of time'.

The Queen is no longer allowed even as little personal initiative in foreign affairs as her great-grandfather, the uncle of Europe, exercised on his continental jaunts. A king on the chess-board of modern diplomacy has been deprived of all power to threaten or capture pieces. He moves and speaks as directed by his ministers.

In 1975 the Queen paid the first state visit of a reigning British monarch to Japan. The Emperor Hirohito confessed: 'Friendship between our two countries had to undergo a severe trial with the vicissitudes of time.'

No doubt the Queen exercises her constitutional right to be consulted, to encourage, and to warn, in foreign as in domestic affairs. No doubt her advice is often sounder than the opinions of her ministers: she has had more experience than any of them; she takes a particular interest in foreign, and especially Commonwealth affairs; and she has sources of information, such as her Governors-General, independent of the Foreign and Commonwealth Office. But only on rare occasions can the Queen's personal opinion on an issue be seen behind the official vizard of the government line that she has to wear.

An instructive example of the Queen following a personal line in foreign affairs can be seen in her resolution to go ahead with her state visit to Ghana in 1961. Kwame Nkrumah, the President, was in the process of imposing a police state. Opposition leaders, including Dr Joseph Appiah, Sir Stafford Cripps's son-in-law, were locked up and bombs were exploding in Accra. The United Kingdom Government and Parliament had grave doubts about the wisdom of risking the Queen's safety in such circumstances. The Queen was determined to go ahead, on the grounds that cancellation of her visit would be such a rebuff that it might drive Ghana out of the Commonwealth. She said: 'How silly I should look if I was scared to visit Ghana, and then Khrushchev went a few weeks later and had a good reception'. Duncan Sandys, the Commonwealth Secretary, volunteered to go to Ghana in advance and 'try it out on the dog'. He flew to Accra, and bravely assuming the role of the dog, drove with stately deliberation, accompanied by President Nkrumah, along the royal route, in accordance with the projected royal timetable. He survived to tell the tale.

Another personal initiative by the Queen in Commonwealth policy came to light in 1965. Ian Smith, the Prime Minister of Rhodesia, was locked in inextricable dispute with the British government over his refusal to allow his African population, which outnumbers the European by a ratio of twenty-one to one, to make any substantial progress towards getting the same voting rights as whites.

Mr Smith and other white supremacists and intransigents were making propaganda that their quarrel was not with the Crown or their kith and kin, the British people; but with the British Labour Government and its ludicrous ideas of equality between races. The Queen dispelled any such notion in the minds of Rhodesians, who were claiming to be more British than the British and more loyal than the Union Jack, by writing a personal letter to Mr Smith in her own hand.

It ran: 'Dear Mr Smith, I have followed the recent discussions between the British Government and your Government with the closest concern, and I am very glad to know that Mr Wilson will be paying you a visit. I earnestly hope that your discussions will succeed in finding a solution to the current difficulties. I cherish happy memories of my own visit to Rhodesia. I should be glad if you would accept my good wishes, and convey them to all my peoples in your country, whose welfare and happiness I have very closely at heart. Yours sincerely, Elizabeth R.'

This letter, with its significant use of 'peoples' in the plural, did not succeed in its appeal; but at least it made it clear beyond fudging that it was not possible both to practise white supremacy and to protest loyalty to the Crown and Commonwealth. A fortnight later Mr Smith made a unilateral declaration of independence, and Rhodesia retreated into the hopeless constitutional impasse where it lingered until 1976, without benefit of Union Jack.

The Queen's personal initiative in that letter may seem modest and couched in discreet and indirect hints. But it is a great deal stronger than the modern monarch is usually allowed to be in foreign affairs. In the twilight of peace before the last war the Queen's father was eager to take some personal initiative to stop the slide to war. He prepared a draft of a personal letter to Hitler on the basis of 'one ex-serviceman to another'. But although he pressed several times to be allowed to send it, Neville Chamberlain and his Foreign Secretary, Lord Halifax, refused to let him. Their reasons were, first that they thought they were the only ones capable of handling Hitler. And second and more correct, that such a letter would have no effect. A letter from the King would have forced the matter to a direct decision, leaving no more room for manoeuvre. Kings are too important as national symbols to be allowed to involve themselves in the rough and tumble and potential humiliation of day-to-day diplomacy.

Chamberlain was right not to let the King become involved in negotiations with Hitler. When his policy of appeasement failed, he and his political colleagues carried the blame and the odium. The monarch, the national symbol, cannot be allowed so close to a particular piece of foreign policy that its failure scars him.

A more effective personal intervention into foreign affairs was made by George VI over Indian independence. Winston Churchill and other diehard Tories of the old Imperial tie attacked the postwar Attlee Government bitterly for 'throwing away the Empire'. In his Christmas broadcast of 1948 the King rebutted this argument and asserted that the extension of independence to the new states of Asia had strengthened the Commonwealth: 'Our Commonwealth – the British Commonwealth – has been subject to the laws of evolution. But it is stronger, not weaker, as it fulfils its ancient mission of widening the bounds of freedom wherever our people live; and for myself, I am proud to fulfil my own appointed share in that mission'.

The Queen is a figurehead in foreign policy; she has to travel which way her ministers steer her. But she is a person as well as a figurehead. She has a memory, and experience. She has travelled farther and has a wider acquaintance of foreign heads of state, diplomats, and politicians than her ministers. She has a devout personal faith in the ideals of the Commonwealth. The influence of the advice of such a figurehead on the direction of British foreign policy is invisible now; it will only become partly visible in fifty years time, when the relevant letters and diaries are published. And British foreign policy is no longer a major factor in the power politics of the world. But it is likely that the Queen's influence will prove to have been considerable for a figurehead, particularly in Commonwealth affairs.

4 Social Influence

It is possible to define with some precision the Queen's role in political and foreign affairs. Her social influence is far more pervasive, but it eludes precise definition. It is easy to assert that her example and tastes, broadcast daily by a powerful but discreet publicity machine, have enormous influence on society. It is less easy to measure actual cases. What effect do the Queen's attitudes to contemporary social or moral questions, so far as they can be known or guessed, have on general attitudes? What connexion is there between her patronage of some good cause, or some breed of dog, namely corgis, or some fashion of dress, and their popularity with the public? Clearly there is a connexion, otherwise good causes and charities would not solicit her patronage with twenty times as many invitations as she can accept.

One obvious advantage of getting the Queen or a member of her family to open the fête, or cut the tape, or lend her name to an appeal, is the intense publicity concentrated on everything she does. Bernard Shaw asserted as a paradox that kings were not born, but made by universal hallucination. The British public generally, led by television, women's magazines, and the rest of the mass media, hallucinates happily over the most trivial activity of the Queen.

Critics complain that the Queen's social influence is excessively neutral, unadventurous, and conservative. Who better than a queen, they ask, to champion women's liberation and other advanced social causes, and be the leading woman of International Women's Year? Instead they compare her to Mrs Dale of the long-running radio serial, or Mrs Miniver of the wartime film: the perfect upper-middle-class lady of the 1930s leading a cosy, leisurely, and gracious country existence, opening hospitals instead of fêtes, having royal garden parties in Buckingham Palace instead of village garden parties on the vicarage lawn, and entertaining visiting heads of state instead of the neighbouring gentry.

Such criticism, though witty, is misconceived. The Queen is head of state for the whole nation, and its symbol of unity. Particularly in this increasingly disunited age her duty where possible is to avoid taking sides among her people, causing offence,

The Queen photographed in her coronation robes in 1953. She wears the Imperial State Crown and holds the sceptre and the orb. The coronation was the first royal television spectacular.

or exacerbating controversy. As she must never be suspected of favouritism in party politics, so she must be all things to all her subjects in her social influence. To take a trivial example, the Queen and her family are suspected of blasphemy against Saints Jacklin and Oosterhuis by finding golf boring. Her father, by contrast, was a keen golfer, and played a notable challenge match in 1924 against Frank Hodges, leader of the miners' union, on a miners' course in the Rhondda Valley. Her uncle, Edward VIII, also swung a brassy with more enthusiasm than proficiency, and was captain of the Royal and Ancient golf club of St Andrews. But never by nod, wink, speech, or conspicuous refusal to attend golfing occasions must the Queen offend the large group of her subjects who find amusement and even a curious beauty in hitting small white balls into holes with sticks.

The Queen with her trainer, Ian Balding, on the Berkshire Downs early one morning in 1969.

To take the converse effect in an equally trivial sporting field, there can be little doubt that lawn tennis acquired great social prestige from royal patronage. Queen Mary, the Queen's grandmother, and Princess Marina attended Wimbledon with a devotion above and beyond the call of duty; and the Duke of Kent and Princess Alexandra still do so. George VI was a good enough left-handed player to appear in the men's doubles of the champion-

An informal view of the Queen beside her Land Rover in Windsor Great Park during the Royal Windsor Horse Show in May 1976.

ships in 1926, being knocked out without disgrace in the first round. Such royal interest made Wimbledon gradually usurp the position in the fashionable social events of the London season formerly held by Henley Regatta and the University and Eton and Harrow cricket matches. In a more complicated relationship of cause and effect, the Queen's coronation in 1953 gave as great a stimulus to television-watching as the General Strike, with its lack of newspapers, gave to radio-listening.

As head of state, the Queen has a duty to be, as far as possible, above factional controversy. As a woman, she has as much right to a private life and likes and dislikes as any of her subjects. It is not easy to distinguish the monarch and the individual in separate compartments. The Queen's uncle, the Duke of Windsor, never managed to conceptualize this distinction, which was why he had to stop being King. But it is irrelevant and unfair to criticize the Queen for her likes and proclivities as a private individual; they are the product of her upbringing and heredity, and too inveterate to change now, anyway. It may be that as a private individual she prefers the company of horses and country people to that of intellectuals and artists. It is a preference probably shared by the majority of her subjects. But so long as she shows no bias in her public life, and takes an official interest in all the main streams of national activity, she must be allowed to do what she likes in her necessarily limited private life. Harold Macmillan wrote of the Queen in 1961: 'She does *not* enjoy "society". She likes her horses. But she loves her duty and means to be a Queen and not a puppet'.

In Walter Bagehot's analysis the social influence of the monarchy was its most important function, and the secret of the benevolent confidence trick of the British system of disguised republic. The attention of the nation was concentrated, he said, on one person doing interesting actions, instead of on the politicians with the effective power doing uninteresting actions like issuing white papers, legislating, amending, and generally running the country. He recognized that this influence was hard to analyse or define: 'The mystic reverence, the religious allegiance, which are essential to a true monarchy, are imaginative sentiments that no legislature can manufacture in any people'.

We have travelled on a century since Bagehot, and in some ways grown wiser. But the social influence of the Queen is still potent, and still hard to define. In one minor aspect the influence of the Queen has faded to invisibility in the past century, and that is in the role assigned to the monarch by Bagehot of being head of society. Under Victoria 'society' had a specialized meaning as the leisured, cultured, and fashionable class conceived as a pyramid with the monarch at its top. Bagehot considered it an important function of his ideal monarch to preside over the levees and drawing-rooms, presentations and balls, and the whole silly season of high Victorian society. His argument was that the British upper and middle classes were so snobbish and envious that without a hereditary head of society to look up to, they would trample each other to death in a Gadarene stampede for social pre-eminence: 'If the highest post in conspicuous life were thrown open to public competition, this low sort of ambition and envy would be fearfully increased. Politics would offer a prize too dazzling for mankind; clever base people would strive for it, and stupid base people would envy it'.

This was not an accurate picture of society under Victoria, particularly after the death of the Prince Consort, when she retired into mourning purdah from high and indeed all society. It was more accurate under her son, who was the last monarch to preside over a court that Bagehot's sharp and cynical eyes would have recognized.

'Society' and rank were killed by two world wars, and today the Queen presides not over a pyramid of the upper classes graded into tidy ranks; she sits in lonely isolation above an egalitarian but divided society, which still retains some of the low sorts of

The last year's giggle of debutantes queue for the last presentation party outside Buckingham Palace in March 1958.

ambition and envy identified with such relish by Bagehot. Presentation parties for debutantes were ended in 1958. At these curious occasions, the peaks of the London season, young upper-class girls were said to come out, or make their debuts, by parading in evening dress, three-quarter length gloves, and assumed demureness in front of the Queen, and curtsying. They wore three curled ostrich feathers in their hair, and ushers stood by with long rods to sweep up each debutante's train and throw it deftly over her arm as she finished her curtsy. There was elaborate protocol about who could be presented, by whom, and how. Item, from the regulations for the last presentation party: 'No applications can be accepted from ladies wishing to be presented; their names must be forwarded by the ladies who wish to present them. Unmarried ladies are ineligible to make presentations even though they themselves have been presented'. It was a self-perpetuating privilege, since only those who had been presented themselves were eligible to present to the Queen their daughters, or friends' daughters, or girls whose parents paid them a sufficient fee. To have been presented at court conferred social standing and the right of entry to courts abroad.

When the presentation parties were abandoned as being ludicrous and socially divisive, the number of garden parties was increased to enable the Queen to meet a wider cross-section of her subjects. These garden parties were started by Queen Victoria in order that she could meet more of society. Since 1958 the Queen has given three garden parties a year in June and July in the grounds of Buckingham Palace, and one at Holyroodhouse on the outskirts of Edinburgh. About eight thousand are invited to each, some directly by the Palace, others on the recommendation of Lords Lieutenant, High Commissioners, politicians, chairmen of national organizations, and so on, all of whom get a quota of invitations. Great efforts are made to invite guests from all walks of life, but inevitably they tend to come mostly from the established, prosperous, deferential, and garden party classes.

Male guests tend to look supercilious or sheepish in morning dress, with their hired tails hanging down behind them and smelling of moth-balls. Lounge suits are permitted, but considered vulgar. The guests are let loose to wander through thirty-nine acres of close-cropped lawn of Buckingham Palace, while Guards' bands alternate in playing selections from *The Merry Widow* and other suitable garden party music. One-legged on the lake the flamingos, as pink and rare as a politician's apology, start in horror at the annual horde of humans, and poke their heads in the mud again. The most luxurious collapsible men's lavatory in the world is discreetly hidden behind the rhododendrons: a twelve-seater, all flush, carpeted, with running water and running attendants with clothes brushes in a pavilion of which a Roman emperor would have been proud.

Social prestige still attaches to an invitation to a garden party. Whips of the last Macmillan government threatened rebellious backbenchers with the ultimate deterrent of being deprived of their tickets for the Queen's garden party. It is one way for the Queen to meet her people.

A garden party at Buckingham Palace in July 1964.

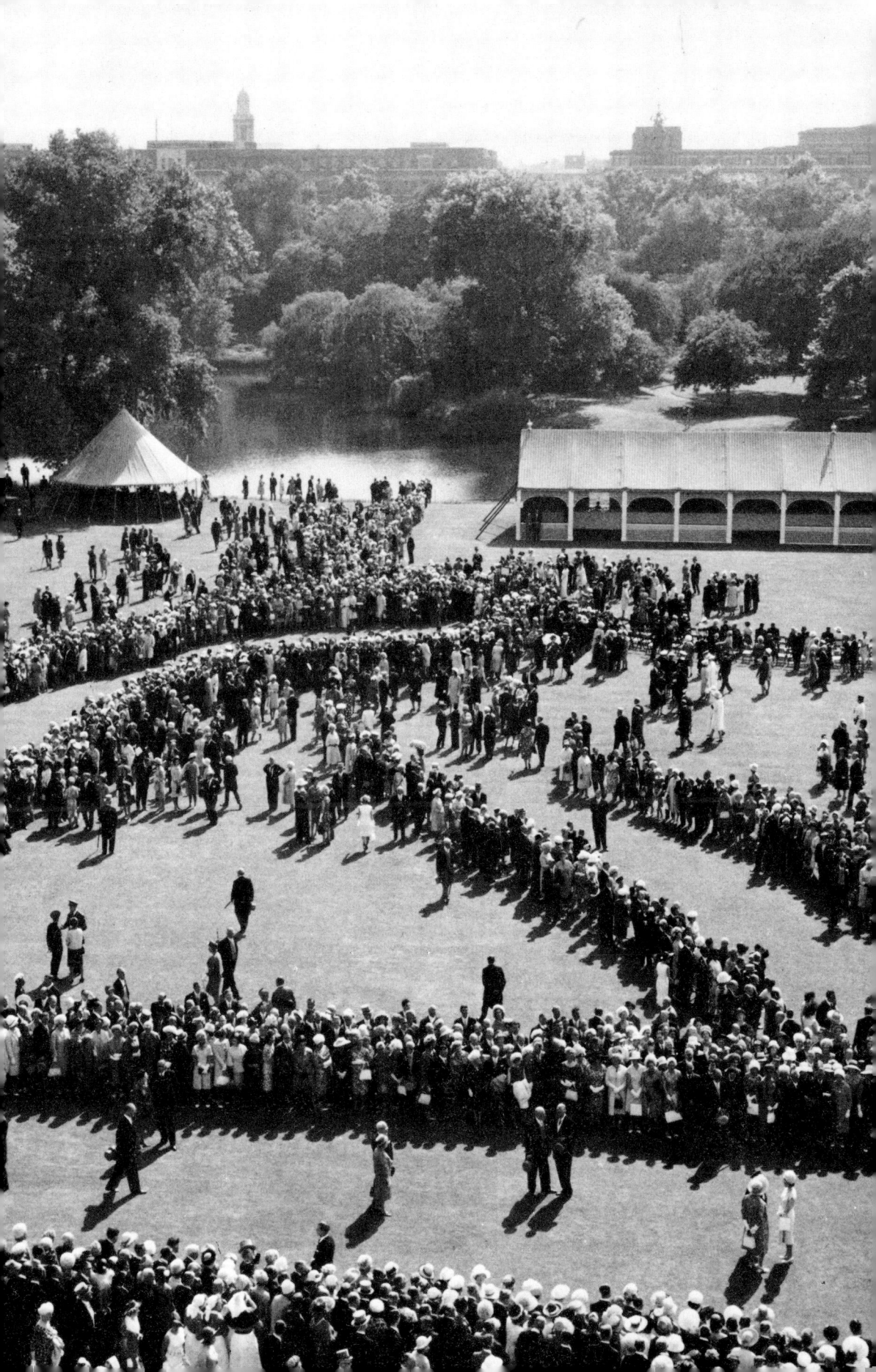

A better though necessarily smaller way is the informal lunch, an innovation introduced by the Queen in 1956. These lunches are intended to enable the royal family to meet a wider range of their subjects in depth and at length than is possible at official functions. An average of six a year have been given since 1956, fitted in whenever there is room in the royal programme. The original plan was to have informal dinners also, but these lapsed in 1960 after sixteen had been held: it proved to be too difficult to find evenings when both the Queen and the Duke of Edinburgh were free simultaneously.

There are always eight guests at the lunches, the Queen and Prince Philip, and either two members of the household, or the Prince of Wales, Princess Anne, or Princess Margaret, if they are available: twelve lunchers in all. The sort of people who get invited come from such diverse places that it is hard to generalize about them. But the intention is to introduce people to the Queen and the Duke whom they do not generally come across in their official lives. On formal occasions inevitably they tend to meet only top people. The lunches are to let them meet people from all walks of life below the top: junior ministers and backbench Members of Parliament instead of Prime Ministers and Cabinet Ministers; junior doctors instead of eminent consultants and hospital adminis-trators; working journalists instead of editors and newspaper pro-prietors. Nevertheless, in the nature of things, they are usually safe, established people of some standing, who can be counted on to accept an invitation to lunch with the Queen and behave them-selves when they get there. You meet what Auberon Waugh described as 'the Arthur Askey sort of person' at the lunches.

Levees, the male equivalent of the evening presentation courts for debutantes, were abandoned during the Second World War without regret by George VI. He disliked social ostentation anyway, and understandably found this all-male afternoon assembly of social climbers in fancy dress silly and offensive during a desperate war. This curious vestige of the custom of gentlemen with the entrée to court gathering to greet their sovereign when he got out of bed in the morning was fortunately not revived after the war.

Such social functions of the monarch, which Bagehot found dignified and important, have either atrophied or been changed so as to be no longer restricted to a small, exclusive class. But there is strong evidence from scientifically conducted public opinion polls that people still look up to the Queen as head of society in the unexclusive, national sense. An interesting regular series of polls shows that large and steady majority of the people look to the Queen and her family for a set of values that they admire, even if they no longer practise them personally. Bagehot noticed that

The Queen between the Archbishops of Canterbury and York at the inauguration of the General Synod of the Church of England at Westminster Abbey in November 1970. She wears the same dress and hat that she wore at the investiture of the Prince of Wales in 1969.

under George III and more particularly Victoria we have come to believe that it is natural to have a virtuous sovereign, and that the Queen should be an exemplar of domestic virtue. The rest of society may be increasingly permissive, but it still expects its Queen to be a model of old-fashioned virtues, moral standards, and religion.

Part of the Queen's official title is 'Head of the Church and Defender of the Faith'. The faith is Anglican, and the church is, of course, the Church of England, which derives its status as the established church of the land from the Reformation. The Supremacy Act of 1534, which formalized Henry VIII's break with Rome, declared him to be 'the only supreme head in earth of the Church of England'. The Act of Settlement of 1701, designed to prevent by law the reunion of the Church of England with the Church of Rome, lays down that the monarch must be a communicant of the Church of England, and excludes from the Crown and Government anybody who 'should be reconciled to the Church of Rome, or should profess the Popish religion, or marry a Papist'.

The Regency Acts of 1937, 1943, and 1953 specify that the Counsellors of State, empowered to act on behalf of the Queen during her illness or absence abroad, shall not be Roman Catholics. And the Queen was required to make the following declaration of faith, when she opened the first Parliament of her reign in November 1952: 'I, Elizabeth the Second, do solemnly and sincerely, in the presence of God, testify and declare that I am a faithful Protestant, and that I will, according to the true intent of the enactments which secure the Protestant succession to the throne of my realm, uphold and maintain the said enactments to the best of my powers according to the law'. Her grandfather, George V, had this milder, more liberal form of declaration substituted for the zealously anti-Papist statement previously extracted from a new monarch by the Declaration of Rights.

Erastianism, the ascendancy of the state over the church in ecclesiastical matters, was imposed on the Church of England by the Reformation. Gradual religious toleration and its progression towards indifference have greatly diminished this ecclesiastical ascendancy of the Crown, and there have been some changes in the law to conform to the change of social attitudes. But Erastian features persist in three forms in particular: an ultimate jurisdiction of ecclesiastical causes by Crown courts; parliamentary veto over changes in the liturgy and formularies of the Church of England; and the nomination by the Crown of bishops, deans, and some other dignitaries. The Crown refused to surrender this last right in the summer of 1976.

The consequences of the Church's establishment in England are mutual obligations: privileges accorded to the Church balanced by duties that it must fulfil. The national church is built into the fabric of the state. Archbishops, bishops, and deans of the Church of England are appointed by the Queen on the advice of the Prime Minister; so are some canons and the incumbents of a number of livings. For his part the Prime Minister consults the Archbishop of Canterbury before making ecclesiastical appointments; and, for appointments in the northern province of the Church, he consults the Archbishops of Canterbury and York. All clergy take an oath of allegiance to the Crown. The Church has to obtain Parliament's consent to change its forms of worship, which are contained in *The Book of Common Prayer* of 1662; although it has temporary powers to use alternative forms without the need for parliamentary approval. And the two archbishops, the bishops of London, Durham, and Winchester, and twenty-one other bishops chosen according to their seniority as diocesan bishops, have seats in the House of Lords. Clergy of the Church of England, together with those of the Church of Scotland, the Church of Ireland, and the Roman Catholic Church, are legally disqualified from sitting in the House of Commons.

A Church commission recommended in 1970 in its report *Church and State* that this ancient relationship between Queen, Church, and State should be modified: the Church should remain established, but should now be given final authority over its forms of worship and doctrine; alterations should be made in the present procedure for the appointment of bishops; ministers of all churches should be permitted to stand for election to the House of Commons and, if elected, to take their seats; and leading members of other churches should be invited *ex officio* to sit alongside Church of England bishops in the House of Lords.

Up to 1976 Parliament has not found the time or the inclination to enact these modifications. If it ever does get round to them it would do well though uncharacteristically to reconsider the constitutional prohibition on a monarch or heir to the throne marrying a Roman Catholic. At present if the Prince of Wales decided to marry a Roman Catholic he would have to give up his claim to the throne. There would be no constitutional impediment, though there might be some conventional embarrassment, if he wanted to marry a Muslim, an Animist, a cannibal, or a girl of any other religion.

So far as the Queen is concerned, her links with the Church are fundamental. The coronation service is built around the act of communion. This service, which confirms the official contract of employment of the monarch, falls into four successive phases, each of which possesses historical symbolism going back more than eleven centuries: the recognition, which derives from the ancient procedure of recognition of the first kings of all England by the Witenagemot, the Anglo-Saxon national council that elected its kings; the oath, which symbolizes a contract between the Queen and her peoples; the anointing, which represents consecration by the Church; and the homage of the Lords Spiritual and Temporal, but not, it will be noted, of the House of Commons. The homage is a feudal survival. The Commons, who have had supreme power in the state for the past three centuries, do not pay homage, because originally they were not consulted about who should rule them, and had no part in his coronation.

It may be asked what practical effect all this has on the social influence of the Queen. No doubt these ancient traditions are ecclesiastically and historically interesting; as well as deplorably illustrative of the religious intolerance in which England emerged as a modern state. But formal religion has declined so far that there

are those who describe this as a post-Christian era. Only a small fraction of the population goes regularly to church, whereas a century ago it was morally obligatory for anyone who wanted to be considered respectable to turn out at least once on Sunday. The Queen is probably head of more Hindus and Muslims in the Commonwealth than even nominal Anglicans; taking no account of Roman Catholics, Jews, agnostics, and other faiths and doubts. George Orwell argued that the common people of England are without definite belief, and have been for centuries. The Anglican Church, he said, never had a real hold on them, and the Nonconformist sects influenced only minorities. 'And yet,' he wrote, 'they have retained a deep tinge of Christian feeling, while almost forgetting the name of Christ.'

Nevertheless, the Queen's position as head of the Church still has enormous though unmeasurable influence. The Anglican communion in Britain and overseas has a membership of more than sixty-five million. Although fewer Britons go to church regularly than when it was socially advisable to do so, a great many still go on special days like Easter Sunday. The majority still choose to be married in church, to have their children baptized, and to be buried with some religious ceremony. Most confess in public opinion polls, the modern confessionals, to some sort of qualified religious faith.

The Queen takes her Christianity seriously and without qualification. She goes to church religiously, often with other members of her family, every Sunday, almost as if she is acting as representative for her lukewarm and idle subjects, for whom car-washing and colour supplements have become substitute Sunday rituals. Nobody can doubt the depth or reality of her personal faith.

The royal family leave St George's Chapel after the quincentenary service on St George's Day, 1975. The Queen is escorted by the former Dean of Windsor, the Right Rev. Launcelot Fleming. Following them are the Queen Mother and the Duke of Edinburgh; Prince Edward with Prince Andrew; Princess Margaret with Lady Sarah Armstrong-Jones; Princess Alice, Duchess of Gloucester, the Duke of Gloucester, and Canon Bentley; Canon Fisher with Princess Alexandra, the Hon. Angus Ogilvy, Prince Michael of Kent, and Canon Dyson. In the background stand the Military Knights of Windsor.

She has an ecclesiastical household, which comprises a college of no less than thirty-six chaplains headed by the Clerk of the Closet, who is always a bishop. At present he is the Right Reverend Roger Wilson, a great sportsman in his youth, like so many Church of England clergymen, and Bishop of Chichester until 1974. The office of Clerk of the Closet goes back at least to the twelfth century, though its pristine function is obscure. The duties of the ecclesiastical household are not onerous, being mainly honorary; members of the college are often invited to preach in the Chapels Royal. Their influence, however, is considerable. The Dean of Windsor always buries royals, helps to christen, confirm, and marry them, and in between generally advises them. The Bishop of Worcester, the Right Reverend Robin Woods, was an influential adviser to the Queen and Prince Philip when he was Dean of Windsor. It was no surprise to the *cognoscenti* when Trinity College, Cambridge, the Bishop's old college, was chosen for

Prince Charles. The Bishop had always had a hand in the discussions about the education of the Prince of Wales. Robin Woods has an engaging expression that he uses: 'The Sovereign and I . . .'

The Chapels Royal are private chapels attached to the Queen, whose members and furniture used to travel around with the monarch in the Middle Ages, when the court was a travelling circus always on the road on regular chevachee. Today they consist of: St Peter ad Vincula in the Tower of London, where notable victims of state executions were buried, than which there is no sadder spot on earth, according to Macaulay; the Chapel of St John in the White Tower, with its tunnel-vaulting the most impressive piece of Early Norman architecture in England; and the Chapels Royal at St James's, Buckingham Palace, Hampton Court, Windsor Castle, and the Royal Chapel in Windsor Great Park, where the royal family worships on most Sunday mornings. The Queen's Chapel of the Savoy, beside the Strand in the shadow of the great hotel, is a private chapel of the Queen in her right as Duke of Lancaster. Accordingly when the National Anthem is sung there, it runs, with an engaging disregard for feminine designations that would gratify extreme women's liberators: 'God save our gracious Queen, Long live our noble *Duke*, God save the Queen.' The Savoy Chapel is the chapel of the Royal Victorian Order.

In addition the Queen has two Royal Peculiars to which she is directly linked. A Royal Peculiar is the peculiar name for a church directly linked to the sovereign and independent of all provinces of archbishops and dioceses of bishops. The Archbishop comes to a Royal Peculiar by invitation only, whereas he comes to any other church in his province by right. The Royal Peculiars are Westminster Abbey, the precinct of coronations, and St George's Chapel, Windsor, home of the Order of the Garter and necropolis of modern royalty, in some respects the symbolic home of English nationalism.

These many and strong connexions between the Queen and the established Church of England are an example of the Queen's position as embodiment of the Establishment: the imprecise vogue phrase introduced in the 1950s to describe the consensus by which the ruling classes contrived to keep power in safe hands. It has been over-popularized. Henry Fairlie, one of its begetters, has recorded sadly: 'Intended to assist inquiry and thought, this virtuous, almost demure, phrase has been debauched by the whole tribe of professional publicists and vulgarizers who today imagine that a little ill-will entitles them to comment on public affairs. Corrupted by them, the Establishment is now a harlot of a phrase'. The Duke of Windsor was much addicted to the phrase, and saw his matrimonial intentions as a collision with the Establishment. His doubtful interpretation of the doubtful word was that neither he nor the Duke of Edinburgh were members of the Establishment; and that his clash with it had been beneficial, because it had revived the thinking of the Establishment, and broken its ancient prejudices.

Nevertheless, the Establishment still well expresses the way in which the Queen is expected to represent continuity rather than change, stability rather than social experiment, old-fashioned virtue rather than modern permissiveness. A conspicuous example is the royal attitude to divorce. In the past generation the general public has become far more tolerant of divorce, which today carries no social stigma; and the law has been changed so that the grounds for divorce are the irretrievable breakdown of a marriage rather than some matrimonial offence, a phrase that has connotations of crime and punishment. At present about nine decrees of divorce are made absolute every year for every thousand married people in England and Wales. But the Church of England continues to regard matrimony as a unique sacrament 'until death us do part'. And the Queen, both as head of the Church and from personal belief, has difficulty in accepting officially what used to be called the guilty party of a divorce. Her uncle, Edward VIII, chose to give up the throne to marry the woman he loved on this issue, thus becoming the first English monarch in more than eleven centuries to give up the throne voluntarily. Mrs Wallis Simpson was ultimately unacceptable as Queen of England not because she was a commoner and an American; but because she was divorced, with two former husbands living. The Duke of Windsor made it clear in his memoirs that, even after his abdication, he still had not grasped the strong, atavistic, and hypocritical attitude of the British public to its monarch. He still thought that his abdication had been forced on him by a conspiracy of the Establishment organized by his Prime Minister, Stanley Baldwin, and embracing the established Church, the Conservative Party, the Opposition leaders, and *The Times*.

He was right in thinking that public opinion was moving in the same direction as his own in favour of the remarriage of divorced persons. But he completely failed to distinguish between what people will approve of in themselves and among their acquaintances, and what they will approve of in their king. Nor did he seem to understand the full implication of his marrying a divorced woman on his position as head of the Church of England.

There never was the slightest chance, as such supporters of Edward VIII as Lord Beaverbrook and Winston Churchill urged, of a groundswell of popular support from a 'King's party' in favour of his marriage. All the evidence of ordinary public opinion at the time, as reported by backbench Members of Parliament from their constituencies and by readers' letters to newspapers, shows that, although the public felt great sympathy for the King, they would not have accepted a twice-divorced woman on the throne of Queen Mary, Queen Alexandra, and Queen Victoria. Although public attitudes to public morality have become far more liberal since 1936, it is doubtful whether today there would be general acceptance of a divorced person on the throne. The British public is contradictory as well as ridiculous in one of its periodical fits of morality.

Thus there was widespread revulsion when Cosmo Lang, the Archbishop of Canterbury, made a broadcast about the abdication intended to be admonitory and sympathetic, but widely received as sanctimonious and merciless. It included, for instance, the implacable sentence: 'Even more strange and sad is it that he should have sought his happiness in a manner inconsistent with the Christian principles of marriage and within a social circle whose standards and ways of life are alien to all the best instincts and traditions of his people'. Gerald Bullett, the writer, produced the most excoriating retort to the broadcast:

My Lord Archbishop, what a scold you are!
And when a man is down, how bold you are!
Of Christian charity how scant you are!
And, Auld Lang Swine, how full of cantuar!

The abdication crisis shook the monarchy. Experienced observers of the House of Commons calculated that, if a vote had been taken in its aftermath, as many as a hundred Members would have voted for a republic. It is not surprising that the royal family has a personal as well as a professional aversion to divorce. They see the Duke of Windsor as having failed in his professional duty; as having forced his brother to succeed him extremely reluctantly but, for the monarchy, therapeutically; and as having thus shortened George VI's life by imposing on him the burden of worry and work of being king through a world war and a period of profound social change. The Queen said, revealingly, in 1949 that divorce caused 'some of the darkest evils in our society today'.

As Tacitus wrote of the transitory Emperor Galba in his famous epigram: *Capax imperii nisi imperasset*. As Prince of Wales he promised golden; nothing became Edward VIII in his reign like the leaving it. But the decision to abdicate shook the monarchy.

Ecclesiastical and royal abhorrence for divorce is still potent. It prevented Princess Margaret in 1956 from marrying Group Captain Peter Townsend, an equerry to George VI and the Queen, and in other respects an eminently suitable husband for her, because he had been the innocent party in a divorce. Princess Margaret, after earnest consultation with her family and the Archbishop of Canterbury, issued a moving statement: 'I would like it to be known that I have decided not to marry Group Captain Townsend. I have been aware that, subject to my renouncing my rights of succession, it might have been possible for me to contract a civil marriage. But

mindful of the Church's teaching that Christian marriage is in-
dissoluble, and conscious of my duty to the Commonwealth, I
have resolved to put these considerations before others'.

Many would feel that in this changed world members of the
royal family, certainly those not in direct line of succession, should
be free to marry whomever they want. But it is significant that
Princess Margaret's renunciatory statement referred to those two
pillars and justifications of the monarchy, the Church and the
Commonwealth.

The only close member of the royal family to have been personally involved in divorce is the Earl of Harewood, elder son of
the Princess Royal and so first cousin of the Queen, and eighteenth
in line of succession; unless the Sex Discrimination Act 1975 is
taken to make women equal with men in the inheritance of thrones
by primogeniture, in which case he jumps to eighth place, his
mother having been older than her brothers, the Dukes of
Gloucester and Kent. The divorce of even so remote a potential
heir to the throne was considered embarrassing. The Royal Marriages Act of George III was invoked; Lord Harewood had to get
the Queen's permission in Privy Council to marry his second wife,
Bambi Tuckwell, an Australian; and by then they already had an
illegitimate son. The second Lady Harewood is not a recognized
member of the royal family, and the Harewoods were accordingly
not invited to Princess Anne's wedding, although they both went
to the funeral of the Duke of Gloucester, Lord Harewood's uncle.

The Queen's attitude to divorce is just one example of her social
influence and attitudes on the side of traditional morality. A more
positive example is her Christmas broadcast. Her grandfather
started the custom in 1932, and achieved great influence by introducing the voice of the formerly remote hierophant speaking
intimately and paternally over the radio into the living-rooms of
his subjects. George VI continued them, spreading a feeling of
concord and security during the dark days of the war, as well as
sympathetic unease that he might not be able to get through his
message without being impeded by his stutter.

The Queen now broadcasts her Christmas talk around the
Commonwealth by television as well as wireless, usually spreading
a simple seasonal message about families, and unity, and the
Christian faith. Satirical critics have sometimes found the message
unduly bland, and the Queen's delivery unduly stilted. But they are
a tiny minority. Vast numbers discover almost the only ritual of
national unity in the entire year when filled with turkey and plum
pudding around their television sets after Christmas lunch. As
Lord Adeane said: 'Television, more than anything else, has made
the Queen, as she follows her various daily duties and interests,
familiar to her people and has brought her into their homes'.

Another pervasive channel of royal influence on the nation is through the honours system. For such a supposedly democratic people the British are absurdly greedy for pretty distinctions to discriminate them from their neighbours. The Queen is still formally known as the fount of honour, from the Middle Ages, when the monarch personally rewarded his deserving or rapacious followers with money, jewels, titles, and, more solid than a title, the land that went with it. Today the machinery is in fact pumped behind the scenes mostly by the Prime Minister and his government machine. Twice a year it gushes: the New Year's honours list and the Queen's birthday honours list in June.

There has been a natural inflation in honours as in sterling. Today there are more than thirty different ribbons, stars, and titles available for distribution; and for the past ten years each half-yearly honours list has averaged more than two thousand awards. It sometimes seems that few manage to escape the distinction of the Order of the British Empire: the Empire no longer exists, but its Order has a hundred thousand members and medallists. There may be a few cases of unrecognized merit left out in the cold without an honour, but they are far less numerous than the cases of recognized demerit. In particular, an honour appropriate to his grade used to be considered a perquisite for a civil servant in recognition of his self-effacing and unselfish service of the public at a salary presumed to be lower than that which he could command in the harsh world outside Whitehall. Few outside the civil service today still adhere to the touching faith that British bureaucracy is the best in the world. The civil service must take its share of responsibility for the national decline and uncertainty of purpose of the past thirty years. But civil service salaries and security now compare very favourably with salaries outside Whitehall; and, in addition, the pensions of civil servants have been proofed against the inflation for which they are partly responsible. However, only a very unworldly man would imagine that this means that civil servants and politicians have stopped taking the giant's share of the honours.

There is an instructive contrast with the treatment given by the honours system to British industry, on whose increased efficiency Britain's prosperity depends. To encourage industry and particularly exporters the Queen's Award to Industry was introduced in 1966. It is always presented on the Queen's birthday in April, and lasts for five years. The letter announcing its award does not exactly ring with the terminology of the white hot technological revolution that its founder, Harold Wilson, hoped for: 'Greeting! We being cognizant of the industrial efficiency of the said body as manifested in the furtherance and increase of Export Trade and being desirous of showing Our Royal Favour do hereby confer

A kiss for the Queen from her cousin, the Duke of Kent. The Duke, as Grand Master of the the Order of St Michael and St George, bids farewell to the Sovereign of the Order outside St Paul's Cathedral. The Duchess of Kent is in the background.

upon it The Queen's Award to Industry . . .' The award has on several embarrassing occasions seemed to be the kiss of death for the recipient firm. The Queen herself was only tenuously involved in the scheme. The hundred or so winners each year received their awards on their premises from the hands of the Lord Lieutenant of their county. In 1976, in order to breathe some new life into the flagging scheme and encourage flagging industry, the Queen and the Duke of Edinburgh started receptions to receive representatives of winning firms at Buckingham Palace.

Lord Melbourne said that he liked the Garter because there was no damned merit in it. The honours system generally is ineffective at rewarding truly original merit, particularly in literary and other intellectual fields. Thus Charlie Chaplin and P. G. Wodehouse, two of Britain's outstanding cultural geniuses in this century, were knighted only in 1975 at the very end of their long lives and brilliant careers. Wodehouse died before he could receive the accolade; and Chaplin had to receive his in a wheel-chair. Evelyn Waugh, the best prose writer of his generation, who would dearly have relished a knighthood, was offered only a CBE, Commander of the Order of the British Empire. He wrote back proudly and with a characteristic chip on his shoulder, saying that he would prefer to wait until he won his spurs.

The honours that nominally flow from the Queen, consist of: peerages; baronetcies; knighthoods and membership of other classes of the orders of knighthood; decorations and medals for gallantry and meritorious service; campaign medals; and commemorative medals.

No hereditary peers, who sit in the House of Lords, or baronets, also hereditary, have been created since 1964. The last hereditary peerage was given to Lord Margadale, formerly John Morrison, a long-serving and dyed-in-the-wool loyalist Tory Member of Parliament, who was Chairman of the 1922 Committee, the committee of Conservative backbench Members in the House of Commons. The last baronet to join the roll was Sir Graeme Bell Finlayson, also a Conservative backbencher getting his reward for long obedience to his party's Whips. It is possible that a future Conservative administration will reintroduce hereditary awards, though it was noticed that Edward Heath pointedly did not take the opportunity to do so when he was Prime Minister from 1970 to 1974. The climate of the age is against hereditary distinctions. If hereditary honours have indeed become obsolete, the Queen will be left in increasingly lonely isolation as the last representative of a hereditary system, apart from the advantages of heredity in joining certain privileged unions in the docking and printing industries.

In descending order of splendour and rank the House of Lords holds dukes, marquesses, earls, viscounts, hereditary barons, and life barons. Today just under nine hundred peerages survive, and there are about two hundred and fifty life peers, thirty-five of them being baronesses, and most of them of both sexes being old and reliable warhorses from the political field put out to pasture safely in the upper house. No political party wants to promote its bright or vigorous young people to the impotence of the House of Lords.

There are nine British orders of knighthood; plus plain knights bachelor, who belong to no order, and just have the title 'Sir'. This is still one of the most valued distinctions in our society.

The insignia of the Order of the Garter: the collar, star, riband, and lesser George.

Knights Bachelors' badge; the Order of Companions of Honour (for a lady); the reverse of the Order of Companions of Honour (for a gentleman); the Distinguished Service Order; and the ladies' and gentlemen's versions of the Imperial Service Order.

The oldest and most esteemed is the Most Noble Order of the Garter, which is considered by the English at any rate to be the premier order of knighthood in the world. It was founded by Edward III in 1348 as a fraternity of sporting young nobles and bloods dedicated to jousting and chivalry. The King had hazy romantic ideas about reviving the legendary idealism of King Arthur and his knights of the Round Table.

The popular account of the origin of his Order's association with the garter has some woman whom Edward loved (the Queen, or more probably Joan, Countess of Kent and Salisbury) dropping a garter at a court ball. The King is said to have picked it up and covered her embarrassment by saying: *Honi soit qui mal y pense*: shame on anybody who thinks ill of this. Edward III is believed to have been the first king after the conquest (with the possible exception of Henry I) to have spoken a little English. But it was not a language that he used in ordinary conversation.

There is nothing improbable about an order of chivalry having as its symbol a piece of underwear. Chivalry was solidly rooted in sex. Court ladies not only gave tokens and prizes at tournaments; they often acted as the prizes themselves.

However, there are elements in the famous story that are not persuasive. The earliest authority for it is Polydore Vergil, who came to England in 1502, became the chief propagandist of the Tudor regime, and was not the most reliable of historians on other matters besides garters. Furthermore it took more than a dropped garter to embarrass a lady of the fourteenth century. Dr Margaret Murray, the Egyptologist and student of folklore, adduced the attractive theory that the garter was a secret signal that Edward III was a devotee of the old religion of witchcraft, of which Joan of Kent was the chief witch. Unfortunately this sensational explanation depends entirely on French fifteenth-century evidence; and to have had sorcerous significance, the garter should really have been red instead of blue.

By the middle of this century the politicians, as politicians have a habit of doing, had canalized the honours system to turn the Garter into a political honour given as a party reward. In 1946 Clement Attlee and George VI decided to restore the Garter and its Scottish equivalent, the Most Ancient and Most Noble Order of the Thistle, to the monarch as his personal gift. Today it is therefore one of the few of her honours that the Queen awards herself, without formal submission by the Prime Minister. She usually chooses retired and very distinguished statesmen, noblemen, military men, and Governors-General, who are past the athletic and amorous activities for which the Order was founded. It is the only method of giving an extra honour to the man who has everything, including a dukedom.

Collar, riband, and star of a Knight Grand Cross of the Order of St Michael and St George.

The Irish Order of St Patrick and the two Indian orders of knighthood are obsolete, although recipients of the Indian knighthoods are still living. The Duke of Gloucester's father, who died in 1974, was the last of the Knights of St Patrick.

The Most Honourable Order of the Bath, refounded in 1725 from the medieval order of knights who took a ritual bath and then kept vigil through the eve of a monarch's coronation, is a large order with both military and civilian knights graded in three classes.

The Most Distinguished Order of St Michael and St George, founded in 1818, also has three classes, and is now used mainly for rewarding diplomats and colonial administrators for having done what they were well paid to do.

The Royal Victorian Order, founded by Queen Victoria, is another order that is in the personal gift of the Queen. It is used to reward people who have directly served the royal family. With a luxuriance of differentials that is characteristic both of the Victorians and of royalty, it is divided into eight different grades, five of the Order itself, and three of the lesser Royal Victorian Medal. Edward VII used to carry insignia of the lesser grades around in his pockets, and hand them out on the spur of the moment to a cook who had made him a particularly satisfactory dish, or anybody else who happened to please him. One recipient of the MVO replied to a friend's congratulations with the nonchalant throw-away line: 'Well, I have done my eight years'.

The Most Excellent Order of the British Empire in five classes, founded in 1917, is the commonest order of knighthood, if any such select body can be politely described as common. When the Beatles got MBEs some unmusical or snobbish members of the Order returned their decorations in protest.

The Royal Family Order is an exclusive and unpublicized Order, given by the Queen personally to her female relations. It consists of a miniature of the Queen set in jewels, and its gift is not publicly recorded. The Queen herself wears the Family Orders of George V and George VI.

Possibly the most distinguished of all orders is the Order of Merit, founded by Edward VII on the occasion of his coronation. It is confined to a membership of twenty-four men and women of great distinction in the armed forces (military division), or in science, art, or literature (civil division). Its award confers no title, no robes, no pseudo-medieval mumbo-jumbo, just a simple badge worn on a ribbon, which devotees of heraldry prefer to spell a riband, around the neck. By paradoxical inverted snobbery it is the most highly valued honour, because of its simplicity, and also because, unlike other honours, it really is restricted to merit. Like the Garter and the Thistle it is awarded by the Queen personally, as

Orders of chivalry:

ABOVE LEFT   *The collar, star, and riband of a Knight Grand Commander of the Order of the Indian Empire. For religious reasons the Indian orders had Knight Grand Commanders rather than Knights Grand Cross.*

ABOVE RIGHT   *The Queen's Royal Family Order. This private order is given to lady members of the royal family. It shows the Queen's portrait surrounded by diamonds on a bow of watered silk of chartreuse yellow.*

BELOW LEFT   *The collar, star, and riband of a Knight Grand Cross of the Order of the Bath (civil division).*

BELOW RIGHT   *The collar, star, and riband of a Knight Grand Cross of the Order of the British Empire (civil division).*

*That walking Christmas tree,
Admiral of the Fleet the Earl
Mountbatten of Burma,
arriving for King Gustaf VI
Adolf's memorial service at
Westminster Abbey, sporting
the Order of the Seraphim of
Sweden along with a large
selection of British decorations.*

a consequence of her father having persuaded Clement Attlee that
the Crown should be responsible for some non-political honours.
The highest double in the honours system is to be both KG and
OM: Lord Mountbatten, that walking Christmas tree decorated
with stars, chains, medals, badges, and ribands, and his less
heavily decorated nephew, the Duke of Edinburgh, in 1976 were
the only living persons to have scaled that honorific peak. Prince
Philip got his OM as a birthday present in 1968, on the grounds,
that it was a specific recognition of his achievements in scientific
and other fields.

The Order of Companions of Honour, founded in 1917, is a sort
of junior Order of Merit, intended to dignify persons of distinction. But it is a division lower than the OM, and less rare, being

restricted to sixty-five companions. Like all honours it nominally emanates from the Queen; but, as is the case with most of them, the selection of its recipients has become a perquisite of her Prime Minister.

These are the principal honours; but they by no means exhaust the catalogue, though they may exhaust the student. The British have whole hierarchies of decorations and medals, ranging from the Victoria Cross, the highest award for military valour, founded by Queen Victoria and physically made from a gun captured in the Crimea, to such exotic distinctions as the Queen's Medal for Champion Shots of the New Zealand Naval Forces, instituted in 1955.

Some members of the Commonwealth join in the honours game, their Prime Minister exercising his power of patronage by recommending recipients. Others, like Canada, have abstained since before the last war, because honours were thought undemocratic. In 1967, however, Canada instituted an Order of Canada with two divisions. The Queen is Sovereign of the Order.

Gough Whitlam, the Labour Prime Minister of Australia from 1972 to 1975, abolished the British honours system in his country, and introduced a new Australian system of honours announced on Australia Day. The main difference is that the Australian awards do not confer the prefix 'Sir', which sounds unduly effete and deferential to Australians. They only allow initials such as AC (Companion of Australia) and OA (Order of Australia) to be placed after the surname. Malcolm Fraser, the Liberal Prime Minister who succeeded Whitlam in 1975, made Australia, of all countries, the most potentially heavily decorated in the world by retaining the Australian system and reviving the British one as well.

Harold Wilson was more abstemious in his use of honours to oil the system and reward his friends than some of his predecessors. He stopped making hereditary peers and baronets; and he announced in 1974 that he was no longer going to recommend honours for

LEFT
The Queen's Medal for Champion Shots of the New Zealand Naval Forces: the medal and the miniature.

CENTRE
The Order of Canada.

RIGHT
The Order of Australia, created in February 1976.

political services: a euphemism for rewarding loyal party hacks. He reduced by two-thirds the honours conferred annually and automatically on members of the public and defence services. His subsequent practice did not always live up to this high and incorrupt principle. The distinction between political and public service is too nice a one for most professional politicians to see. Mr Wilson caused loud scandal when he made his political private secretary, Marcia Williams, a life peeress called Lady Falkender, on what seemed to some to be the insufficient grounds that she had always been politically loyal to him. This was the most unexpected elevation since George IV made a knight of his coachman, who had beaten him in a four-in-hand race, or indeed since Caligula made his horse Incitatus priest and consul. *Private Eye* professes that it finds it hard to identify a friend of Sir Harold who has not got an honour.

It was Edward Gibbon, the historian of the decline and fall of Rome not of Britain, who described corruption as the most infallible symptom of constitutional liberty. If Gibbon was right, the distribution of honours has been a signal for all this century that liberty has been flourishing, contrary to the evidence of some other symptoms. The corruption reached a peak under Lloyd George, who sold honours to benefit Liberal Party funds. A Royal Commission under Lord Dunedin to inquire into the honours system led to the passage of the Honours (Prevention of Abuses) Act 1925. It was under this Act in 1933 that Mr J. Maundy Gregory, purveyor of nobility to the gentry, and to anyone else with the money to match ambition, was convicted of touting for honours.

Since then the corruption has become less overt. The plumbing of the honours system is meticulously supervised by the Lord Chamberlain's Office, the Central Chancery of the Orders of Knighthood, and the College of Arms. And the Political Honours Scrutiny Committee and Sir Stuart Milner-Barry, Ceremonial Officer at the Civil Service Department, inspect the honours system to keep it clean. Sir Stuart, a former British boy chess champion and former chess correspondent of *The Times*, has a mind that appreciates the nice discriminations and subtle gradations of the system.

The Committee was set up in the 1920s as a consequence of the scandal of Lloyd George's sale of honours. It is required to vet all recommendations for political honours, which also have to go to the appropriate departments in Whitehall to see whether they have any objections. The recommendation of an honour must be accompanied by a declaration signed by the Chief Whip or leader of the party that states that 'No payment or expectation of payment to any party or political fund is directly or indirectly associated with the recommendations contained in the attached list'.

Even if the Political Honours Scrutiny Committee objects to a name, the Prime Minister can still insist on its inclusion. But the Queen must be informed of any names that have not been approved by her three scrutinizing Privy Councillors. The sovereign has in practice no right to refuse any candidate put forward by the Prime Minister, but she can express disapproval informally, as George V did to Lloyd George on at least one occasion. It is still the case that almost anybody who wants an honour badly enough, and has plenty of money, can get one by expending money sufficiently lavishly on some worthy public or party cause. Lloyd George was more openly mercenary, selling a knighthood for £10,000 and a peerage for £100,000.

The honours system is one of the more delightfully Ruritanian aspects of the monarchy. Stern Puritans and non-Ruritanians with no sense of the absurd would abolish it. However, most countries have arrangements for honouring public service. The Soviet Union has sixteen orders, ranging from the Order of Lenin at the top to the Order of the Glory of Motherhood at the bottom. Thailand actually has an order called the Order of the White Elephant; and Laos until its revolution had the Order of the Million Elephants and the White Parasol. Rather than abolish such a historical institution as the British honours system, it would be more thrifty to rationalize it by greatly simplifying and reducing the volume of honours; and by restricting them to people who actually have performed some public service above and beyond the call of duty. The award of honours would be more convincing if it was removed from the hands of the Prime Minister of the day, and given to some disinterested and high-minded public body. Naturally no Prime Minister is going to volunteer to relinquish so powerful a weapon of patronage. So it will never happen.

The Queen's position as fount of honour is symptomatic of her social influence across whole ranges of national life. Boroughs are jealous of the right to call themselves royal. No regiment is complete without a royal colonel-in-chief. Societies and institutions feel naked without a royal patron. The Queen is the cynosure and validating symbol of the various interlocking Establishments.

Cumulatively the social influence of the Queen and her family on the life, attitudes, and foibles of the nation is considerable, from details as curious as the love of horses and the taste for petal hats to more serious though less quantifiable matters such as attitudes to morality. It is generally an influence towards continuity, old-fashioned virtues and ways, and steadiness. The British are an exceptionally conservative people, and they expect their monarch to behave in a traditional and not in an upsetting or disturbing way.

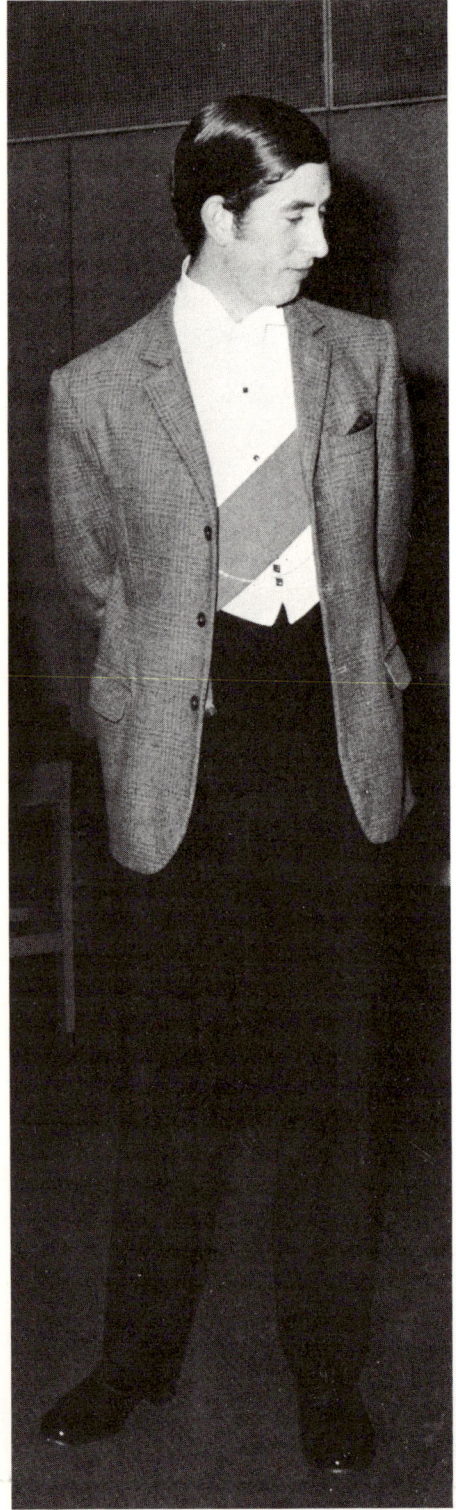

5 Icon and Image

In the case of the monarchy the image is the message. The icon of the Queen is a national symbol as potent and widespread as the Union Jack itself. Official portraits of her hang thick on the walls of British embassies and government buildings. Her head, crowned or wearing a tiara, appears as the legitimating symbol on all seals of state, banknotes, coins, and postage stamps. She must have the best known official features in the world.

Until the present reign the Bank of England and the Post Office considered the plain head of the monarch, on its own or dressed with discreet emblems of royalty, sufficient cachet for our currency and postage stamps. British money and British stamps were majestic in their simplicity and unshakeable in their value; austere, unchanging, and an example to more demonstrative races. However, in the past few years the first Duke of Wellington, Florence Nightingale, and other worthies from history have been obtruded on the banknotes; and the Post Office, in order to exploit the philatelists, issues an incessant stream of garish and vulgar commemorative stamps with the royal image shrunk to minute size tucked away in their corners.

It may be only an unhappy coincidence that since this physical degradation of the currency and postage, money has lost its value quicker than it has ever done, and the cost of posting a letter has risen so sharply that the volume of mail has declined as fast. But there are instructive examples in history of how coinage, which is a pervasive form of state propaganda, tends to become gaudier and more boastful as the state itself declines and loses confidence. In the most high and palmy state of Rome the head of the emperor with the superscription of his name was generally considered a sufficient slogan on its own. But as the Roman Empire declined towards its fall, the inscriptions on the coinage became shriller, as if the masters of the imperial mints were whistling in the encircling gloom. The emperor was regularly designated 'perpetual' with the unconscious irony of black comedy, during a period when emperors were succeeding each other at a rate of almost one a year. The propaganda of the coinage invoked 'concord', when in the harsh world outside there was fatal discord

Royal fashion and influence: the Duke of Edinburgh in knee breeches, with the Garter below the left knee, and wearing the Legion of Honour. The Prince of Wales wears the Garter riband underneath a sports jacket: a joke on the Master Tailors' Benevolent Association in February 1971.

Stamps:
TOP LEFT *Victoria 1d;* TOP
MIDDLE *Edward VIII ½d;*
TOP RIGHT *Elizabeth II 4d*
MIDDLE LEFT *Elizabeth II
1s 6d;* RIGHT *Elizabeth II 5d*

Coins:
*George V, Edward VIII
(model), George VI, and
Elizabeth II displayed on
florins. The new monarch is
customarily represented on the
coinage facing in the opposite
direction to his predecessor; but
Edward VIII was vain.*

between the two halves of the Empire; proclaimed the emperor
'triumphant over the barbarian nations', when the opposite was
the case; and declaimed about the glory of the state, salvation and
security, happiness and peace, when those desirable conditions had
vanished from Italy. The ultimate rhetorical extravagance came in
472, just before the end and the descent of the Dark Ages, when the
transient puppet emperor Olybrius was hailed on his coinage as
'*Salus Mundi*', the salvation of the world. The rhetoric on the
Roman coins shines increasingly brightly in desperation as the
darkness of national danger and humiliation deepens.

By an ancient tradition the British coinage depicts the icon of
each new sovereign looking in the opposite direction to his predecessor. Thus Queen Elizabeth looks to the right, wearing a crown
or what can only be a classical fillet of bay leaves, and displaying
her right profile. Her father looked to the left. Her uncle, the Duke
of Windsor, was designed by iconographic custom to look to the
right, in the opposite direction to his father, George V. However,
he protested vehemently that he preferred his left profile, which

Official royal portraiture is curiously old-fashioned and atrophied.
Timothy Whitbourne's painting of Elizabeth II varies only in quality from Van Dyck's equestrian portrait of Charles I. The Queen wears her uniform as Colonel-in-Chief of the Grenadier Guards.

showed the parting of his hair. With characteristic vanity and iconoclasm of ancient tradition the Duke of Windsor prevailed. But his new coins were not issued before he abdicated; and only comparatively few of his new stamps were printed. The Royal Mint subsequently ignored this aberration, and reverted to the traditional alternating symmetry, with the royal image of George VI looking to the left.

Official royal portraiture is curiously old-fashioned and atrophied. Portrait painting evolved as a new art form during the Renaissance, so coinciding with the evolution of the concept of the absolute and divine right of the Renaissance prince. This coincidence produced the state portrait with its emblems of crowns and other regalia, great swags of velvet curtains, distant palaces, and superhuman props, allusions, and symbols, which has survived little changed down to this day to the bland royal icons painted by James Gunn, Pietro Annigoni, and their peers.

In this century painting of the royal icon has been supplemented by still photography and cinematography, which in their own way are as conventional as the old portraiture. When newspapers publish their annual demotic and indistinguishable portraits of the Queen at the Remembrance Day parade before the Cenotaph, or side-saddle at Trooping the Colour, they are making an iconographic statement that Holbein would have recognized; though he would have been amazed by the mechanical medium of the portraits. Future generations may well find the television film *Royal Family*, produced in 1969 by the BBC and Independent Television, a more effective representation of the royal image than the traditional oil paintings.

Crowns and the other emblems of royal portraiture may be old hat. But one innovation has been made in the presentation of the royal image during the present reign; future generations may come to see it as a most significant development of the monarchy. Buckingham Palace went over from the passive to the active in its image-making and projection of publicity. Since Bagehot it had been orthodox doctrine to believe that the mystery of royalty was its life. He wrote: 'We must not let in daylight upon magic'. During the 1960s the Palace reversed the policy and decided to let in some carefully regulated daylight. The old attitudes of Olympian reticence and exclusiveness were out of place in an increasingly open age, which was suspicious of mysteries and no longer content to be told only as much as was thought good for it. There was a decision by the Palace that the inveterate royal attitude that no news was good news, and no newsmen were even better, was both silly and harmful in an age of mass communication. In a new world in which publicity is king, not even the Queen can afford to neglect her image and leave it to chance. Princess Alexandra expressed the change that has taken place when she said: 'Don't forget that nowadays we have to compete with Elizabeth Taylor and the Beatles'. Queen Victoria would not have been amused by the idea that she had to compete with anyone; most unamused of all that she had to compete with Marie Lloyd. It would have been beyond her comprehension.

It is easier to assert that a change has taken place in the royal image than to give a precise date or occasion for the change. When the Queen came to the throne, her closest advisers were courtiers of the old school, who tended to think all publicity vulgar, and saw the job of a royal press officer as one of shielding his employer from the intrusive attentions of the hacks of Fleet Street. Today the Buckingham Palace press office is as professional about its public relations as any in the harsh, competitive world outside the barrack-like eastern façade superimposed on its offices in 1913 by Sir Aston Webb. Ronald Allison, appointed the Queen's press secretary in 1973, was an eminently proficient BBC football reporter and court correspondent for many years before he got the

Ronald Allison, the Queen's press secretary, arranges a group photograph of representatives from Commonwealth nations aboard Britannia. This group includes Mrs Gandhi, Archbishop Makarios, and Harold Wilson.

job. He gives as his recreations photography, painting, and watching football, and is a man of the press and public as well as of the court. His deputy, Anne Hawkins (Mrs Michael Wall), a niece of Princess Alice, Duchess of Gloucester, also manages to straddle the chasm between Palace and Fleet Street as a bridge not a barricade, and does it very efficiently. The old royal view of publicity, expressed by Oscar Wilde, 'In the old days men had the rack; now they have the press', has been superseded.

The most conspicuous example of the new policy was the royal family film, which bought golden opinions from all sorts of people by taking the cameras behind the scenes, as well as showing the royals on parade. The Queen was cast as a sort of matey, middle-class super-mum. Cut to Prince Philip and Princess Anne grilling sausages and steaks on a family barbecue in the magnificent solitude of the Balmoral estate, with a camera crew lurking in every clump of gorse. Prince Charles, helped by the Queen, mixes a salad dressing. 'The salad is ready', says the Queen. 'Good' says Prince Philip, looking unenthusiastically at a half-cooked steak; 'This, as you see, isn't.' The film was an outstandingly effective and professional piece of public relations. Of course, such intimate exposure worked because the actors in the film were reasonably young, attractive, and glamorous. It would not be such an effective medium at a future date if the incumbent of Buckingham Palace were a dull, degenerate semi-idiot without style. Perhaps the hereditary monarch can survive only if he is also thoroughly educated and a photogenic television performer like the Prince of Wales.

Another instructive example of the new image is afforded by the Queen's Christmas broadcasts. These were started by her grandfather, in a significant step to modernizing and humanizing the monarchy. Those who heard them speak of the extraordinary shock of hearing the rich, deep voice of George V, speaking as a father to his people, issuing from a small box in their sitting-rooms. In recent years these broadcasts have become far more natural and relaxed. In 1975 the Christmas message was filmed out of doors for the first time. The Queen's voice has grown more assured as she has become a more practised public performer; it used to sound alarmingly high-pitched and strained. And on Christmas Day 1975, in a television film called *Pilot Royal*, the Prince of Wales was heard discussing his embarrassment at being filmed flying for millions to goggle at, and referring to 'third degree piles' and 'helicopter haemorrhoids'. Such royal exposure would have given extreme cultural shock to anybody brought up on the old royal image of the Queen as semi-divine. But it obviously makes good sense in an egalitarian and questioning age for the monarchy to take pains to explain its relevance and make itself accessible to ordinary people.

George III was the first monarch to appoint an official publicist, rather than let his image take care of itself. He was so distressed by what he took to be the lies being written about him that he appointed a Court Newsman at a salary of £45 a year. The salary was reduced to £20 in 1909; and a full-time professional press office for the monarchy was started in 1916. Queen Victoria and other monarchs have been sensitive enough about their public image to take a personal interest in drafting the *Court Circular*, the daily and extremely dull record of the doings of the court published in the newspapers.

It is impossible today to take seriously the solemn reverence with which the royal image was presented until the recent revolution in Palace publicity. Even the most boring activity was invested with a quasi-religious reverence. Kingsley Martin said before the last war: 'In the middle of the last century it needed courage to break the religious taboo, to doubt the literal truth of the first chapter of Genesis, or question the scientific basis for belief in the virgin birth. The throne on the other hand was frankly criticized in the newspapers and on the platform. In the twentieth century the situation is exactly reversed'. When George IV died, *The Times* commented on the day of his funeral: 'There never was an individual less regretted by his fellow-creatures than this deceased King'. Such a comment is inconceivable today. Both monarchy and press have become politer.

Upon her accession the Queen was plunged into this unreal atmosphere of sycophancy and hypocrisy that surrounded the throne, and today seems incredible. Her coronation in 1953 was the first spectacular of the television age. Britain, dimly aware that it had lost an Empire without discovering a role, adulated the royal image as a symbol of the old certainties and the end of austerity.

The new image projected by the Queen's Christmas broadcasts. The Queen broadcasts from Government House, Auckland, New Zealand, in 1953 and from in the grounds of Buckingham Palace in 1975.

Politicians and newspapers spoke seriously of a new Elizabethan Age. And the Queen's image-makers presented her with a religious reverence that would have seemed excessive in an age that believed in the divine right of kings.

The high priestess of this cult was Marion Crawford, the governess of the Queen and Princess Margaret, whose unctuous memoirs of her royal charges did marvels for the circulation of women's magazines, but had a maudlin effect on the royal image. 'Crawfie' turned up at any page gives off a mawkish period flavour that could not be intended other than satirically today.

The obverse of this unreal and excessively romantic royal image was that the royals themselves, not unnaturally, believed the rubbish and developed a distaste and contempt for the media of publicity.

The bubble image protecting the monarchy was so unreal that it was bound to be burst by the irreverent post-war age. The bursting was done principally by Malcolm Muggeridge in two articles in 1955 and 1957 entitled 'Royal Soap Opera'; and by John Grigg, the political journalist, who disclaimed the title of Lord Altrincham in 1963, in an article in the *National and English Review*, a political monthly with a tiny circulation, in 1957. It is difficult reading the articles today to comprehend the shock, outrage, and offence caused at the time by these first mild attempts to write objectively about the Queen as if she were a real human being with a real though unusual function. It was as if somebody had shattered an ancient and inviolable tribal taboo of the British.

John Grigg's main criticisms were about the social exclusiveness of the court, and the remoteness from everyday life of the Queen. He complained about the continuance of such grotesque survivals from the past as presentation parties. The Queen's entourage, he observed, was almost without exception people of the tweedy sort. Worse still, courtiers were nearly always citizens of one Commonwealth country, the United Kingdom. The monarchy had become popular and multiracial, but the court remained a tight little enclave of British ladies and gentlemen. He hoped that the Queen would arrange for her children to have a broader and better education than her own; and that, for example, Prince Charles would be able to mix during his formative years not merely with future landowners and stockbrokers.

Much of what John Grigg said was true, sensible, and intended as a constructive criticism of the monarchy. Presentation parties were stopped the year after he wrote. Prince Charles was sent to an off-beat public school and Cambridge, and will be the first monarch to have taken an ordinary university degree, and probably the first since George IV to have been capable of taking one. Court officials these days are selected from classes other than the tweedy,

The scene at Caernarvon Castle when the Queen invested Prince Charles as Prince of Wales in July 1969.

and countries of the Commonwealth other than Britain. The Queen's public speeches have become noticeably less pi, and her voice has become noticeably less priggish.

But in 1957 the scandal and stink stirred up by the article were immense. The Archbishop of Canterbury publicly anathematized John Grigg; a member of the League of Empire Loyalists slapped him; other ancient tribesmen threatened him with horse-whipping, shooting, and hanging, drawing, and quartering; enough dung was put through his letter-box to manure his window-boxes for the season; Commendatore Marmirolli, an Italian monarchist, challenged him to a duel. There was a move to expel him from one of his clubs, and a rumour that he was to be struck off the list of Old Etonians. The uproar seems intemperate, inexplicable, and ludicrous today. But if the monarch is a potent public symbol in the public consciousness and unconsciousness, what is seen by hasty public opinion as an attack on the monarch is taken as a personal attack on the public, and resented accordingly.

The Queen's first reaction to the criticism of her is reported to have been to suppose that Muggeridge and Grigg were mad. This was understandable in somebody who had been brought up as the goddess at the heart of the cult of royal infallibility. Prince Philip is said to have seen at once that the criticism must be taken seriously. The revolution in the Palace's attitude to its image and its publicity can be taken to have started at about this date. Prince Philip and the newspapers have in the past enjoyed a relationship of mutual antipathy: he likes publicity, but dislikes journalists. He once said about the monarchy: 'I entirely agree that we are old-fashioned: it is an old-fashioned institution'. But his approach to his rather nebulous job as consort has been to identify himself with the future rather than the past, particularly with youth, industry, technology, and conservation. And, in spite of his occasionally bad relations with the press, Prince Philip more than anybody is responsible for changing the attitude of royal public relations with the outside world from negative and defensive to positive and outgoing. His Australian private secretary, Michael Parker, an irreverent enemy of pomp and red tape, encouraged him to modernize the Palace's attitude to publicity before he left the Palace for the freer shores of commerce.

A significant date in this process of modernization was the appointment of William Heseltine as the Queen's press secretary in 1968. Since 1972 he has been her Assistant Private Secretary. Heseltine was young, the son of an Australian schoolmaster, and intelligent, with first class honours in history at the University of Western Australia. His previous experience before he came to the Palace had been as a civil servant at Canberra, where he finished as Private Secretary to the Prime Minister: a job in any democracy in

Princess Anne's wedding to Captain Mark Phillips in Westminster Abbey in 1973. To the left of Captain Phillips are ranged what the Court Circular describes as 'the other members of the royal family'.

which a sensitive and constructive feel for publicity is essential. His predecessor, Commander Sir Richard Colville, had been a fine old courtier of the old school, with little instinct or taste for publicity. John Grigg would have found him tweedy. The new style of appointment signalled a new approach to the royal image. At about the same time Prince Charles got his own Private Secretary, Squadron-Leader David Checketts, who had been a professional public relations man in the firm of Neilson McCarthy.

When Heseltine was promoted in 1972, he was replaced by a similar young professional, Robin Ludlow, who was working in sales management and marketing promotion for *The Economist* before he took on the Queen's account. Ludlow unfortunately came to grief over the engagement of Princess Anne and Lieu-tenant, as he then was, Mark Phillips. In the winter of 1972–3 the newspapers kept running stories and pictures with heavy-handed hints of romance between the Princess and Mark Phillips. Ludlow was sent on a tour of Fleet Street to ask the editors to lay off the story, on the grounds that there was no truth in it. Love laughs at press officers, editors, and off-the-record briefings; and a few weeks later the engagement was announced. There had been no conscious deception by anybody. Accurate forecasts are even less possible in affairs of the heart than they are in economic affairs. But Robin Ludlow honourably felt that he should resign after such a classic publicist's catastrophe. His successor, Ronald Allison, is also a young professional, but from the other side of the publicity business, having been formerly a reporter of royalty, and now being a poacher turned gamekeeper.

The results of this sharp change of direction in the presentation of the royal image are apparent. Its first spectacular demonstration was the investiture of the Prince of Wales at Caernarvon Castle in 1969. Some of the ritual of homage whispered the last enchant-ments of the Middle Ages. But television cameras had captured every available turret of Edward I's impregnable and much hated castle. Gross electric cables writhed like serpents over his crenel-lated walls. Investiture mugs and tea towels were on sale in the moat. The town was filled with armadas of mobile lavatories called 'rollalongs'. The Constable of the Castle, Lord Snowdon, wore a dashing Peter Pan costume in hunting green designed by himself; surprisingly it lacked a sword, which is a serious omission for a constable. And with stately echoes of medieval chivalry, with the glare of modern publicity for millions of television viewers, the Queen invested her son as Prince of Wales and presented him ceremonially to his people. The Prince replied partly in Welsh picked up on his crash course of one term at the University College of Wales at Aberystwyth, and made a popular gesture by referring to one of his favourites from the BBC's Goon Show, Harry

Secombe from Swansea. It was a far more professional piece of public relations than the investiture of the Prince of Wales's great-uncle, an unhappy mock-Celtic pageant dreamed up by Lloyd George for political reasons, and remembered by the Duke of Windsor with anger and humiliation.

The investiture has been the biggest set piece of royal variety show since the new image was introduced; but there have been others almost as spectacular, such as Princess Anne's wedding. The cameras and the crowds were allowed closer and more intimately to the ceremony than would have been conceivable a decade before. They got so close in fact that some sharp-eyed observers claimed to detect by the lie of their clothes that Princess Anne and Mark Phillips were wearing bullet-proof waistcoats underneath. The family scenes in the Palace, with the Princess shouting 'Oy, get off my dress' at her younger brothers, have been repeated in the Christmas broadcasts. The Queen has not yet allowed herself to be interviewed, though she allowed herself to be filmed in private and unguarded conversation for the royal film. Most of the rest of her family are regularly interviewed by newspapers, radio, and television, and are remarkably proficient at it. They make speeches that sound as if they are composed by themselves, not a committee of courtiers; they write books and book reviews; they make jokes and off-the-record chats on walkabouts, and generally expose themselves to the public and the media with a freedom undreamed of before the revolution in the royal image. The Queen Mother and Princess Alice, Duchess of Gloucester, were even portrayed by actresses on the stage in 1972 in *Crown Matrimonial*, a play, inevitably, about the abdication crisis. It used to be considered pretty well blasphemy to portray a royalty on the stage until at least fifty years after he or she was safely buried. Until 1968 when Britain abandoned theatre censorship, the Lord Chamberlain, who was for historical reasons the official censor, would certainly have prohibited any attempt to do so. Anna Neagle had difficulties before she was allowed to star in *Victoria the Great* in 1937.

The converse of this new openness of the Palace in its public relations and its image-making is that the royals are exposed to more satire and criticism than was formerly thought dignified. The 'Sixties were a decade of satire, with audiences tasting their own blood and enjoying the taste. And the royals did not escape the attention of *Private Eye*, Gerald Scarfe, that savage descendant of Hieronymus Bosch, and the pack of trendy cartoonists and television scoffers. One of the most notable pieces about royalty was *Love in the Saddle*, a 'true romance' by Sylvie Krin in *Private Eye*, a marvellously funny and soppy cod piece of nonsense about the romance between Princess Anne and Mark Phillips, their difficult families, and their horses with names like Muggeridge and the Arabian Gaddafi. The bogus horsy jargon was almost as inventive as the bogus royal gossip.

To some extent, of course, people at weekend parties have been making jokes about royals and telling unattractive anecdotes about them for years and centuries, their principal motive being to demonstrate their superiority, and to create the impression that they have intimate inside knowledge. But such stuff about royalty in the public prints would have been inconceivable in the 1950s, and would have caused grave public offence. The new climate of freedom is far healthier than the excessive old reverence that treated royals as though they were more than human, and was at the same time slightly patronizing. The British seem to progress in cycles of deferential reverence and rude irreverence towards their royals. There was a a long period of stuffy deference from the second half of Victoria's reign until the current free-for-all.

Satire directed against one's kings and queens and masters is not an English invention. It has a long, honourable, and perilous history stretching back beyond Rabelais to Juvenal and Aristophanes. William Hogarth is generally accredited with having been the founding father of modern caricature. He described his portentous invention: 'I then married, and commenced painter of small conversation pieces, from twelve to fifteen inches high. This having novelty, succeeded for a few years. I therefore turned my thoughts to a still more novel mode, *viz*. painting and engraving modern moral subjects, a field not broken up in any country or any age'. It is certain that George III did not appreciate Hogarth's modern morality, since he figured prominently in it, not on the side of the angels. The Hanoverian kings played party politics, took sides, and were consequently obnoxious to the robust satire and violent scurrility of eighteenth-century politics.

What Hogarth had started, James Gillray, Thomas Rowlandson, Isaac and George Cruikshank, and the lesser lights of that golden age of English caricature took up and carried on with a will. No aspect of royalty, from its morals, politics, and manners to its private parts and George III's madness, escaped their often brilliant malice. The caricaturists had no mercy and no ghastly good taste. They made a mockery out of George III's understandable phobia of being blown up. And the then Prince of Wales's adventurous sex life was a gift to them as well as the satirists.

Princess Charlotte, the Regent's only child, died in childbirth in 1817, leaving the succession in confusion. None of George's three brothers, the royal dukes, had a legitimate heir, though jointly and severally they could muster an impressive team of mistresses and bastards. There was accordingly an undignified and ludicrous scramble by the royal dukes to get themselves legal wives suitable to be queens of the United Kingdom and to produce legal heirs.

The cartoonists and satirists called it 'the great matrimonial stakes', and lampooned it vigorously with racing and other irreverent metaphors.

The race was won, in the event, by the Duke and Duchess of Kent, so giving us Queen Victoria. And the new age associated with the name of Victoria gradually became less violent in its royal politics and blander in its satire, as the monarchy withdrew from partisan politics and became constitutional.

The golden age of British caricature was over. The new cartoonists like John Leech and John Tenniel were not such angry young men as their great predecessors, nor such brilliantly cruel draughtsmen. They had less to be angry about, with the monarch at least, since she interfered less disgracefully in politics than her uncles and grandfather. The temper of society became increasingly prudish. Nevertheless, they managed to satirize Victoria and caricature her with a robust vigour that does not match modern misconceptions about the Victorians. *Punch*, or *The London Chari-vari*, the illustrated weekly comic periodical, was founded in 1841, and was originally a strongly radical and political paper, well to the left of the position that *Private Eye* takes today. *Punch* in its early days devoted much scurrilous and amusing space to the monarchy, which cannot have amused Victoria. Particular targets for *Punch*'s heavy-handed satire were the expense and extravagance of the royal family (an inveterate theme for satire that is still with us), especially the number of children it produced; the Queen's European connexions and her interference in foreign affairs; and the Prince Consort's unfortunate mistake in being born German not

British, and in not showing sufficient humility about this misfortune. A *Punch* cartoon of 1844 called *A Royal Nursery Rhyme* portrays Victoria surrounded by a teeming brood of offspring that threatens to outdo in numbers George III's fifteen unsatisfactory children, who were an advertisement for the desirability of royal birth control.

The satirists were not afraid to animadvert on the domestic purity of the royal household, and on Victoria's supposed sex life, with remarks that seem lese-majesty, if not blasphemy, to our hindsighted perception of the Queen as the chaste national matriarch. The name of John Brown, the Balmoral gillie who became Victoria's personal attendant and closest companion after Albert's death, lent itself to lampoons and the elephantine puns that were as pleasing as *Punch* to Victorians.

After Albert died and Victoria withdrew from public affairs into her private celebration of bereavement, the humour became ruder and harsher. A scurrilous pamphlet entitled 'Mrs John Brown' was circulated. In 1866 *Punch* published a spoof *Court Circular* in the deadpan style of those issued by Victoria:

> *Balmoral, Tuesday.*
> *Mr John Brown walked on the slopes. He subsequently partook of a haggis. In the evening, Mr John Brown was pleased to listen to a bag-pipe.*
> *Mr John Brown retired early.*

The final instalment of the romantic serial, Love in the Saddle, *by Sylvie Krin of Private Eye.*

New Crowns for old; Punch *cartoon, by John Tenniel, caricaturing Disraeli offering Queen Victoria her crown as Empress of India.*

But as the nineteenth century progressed, satire went out, and patriotism and pride in the aged matriarch came in. The satirists certainly had some shrewd fun when Disraeli created the Queen Empress of India in 1876.

But it is remarkable how *Punch*, which had become established and indeed part of the Establishment, now greeted the frequent marriages of the royal children and the birth of more and more royal grandchildren and great-grandchildren with loyal and effusive congratulations, instead of grumbling about the public expense. The royal image entered on a long period of hagiography and reverence in its iconography, partly explained by the long period of war, social change, and loss of Empire that the country was going through. At a time of national crisis, satire and caricature of the monarchy seem dangerously close to attacks on the nation itself, and no longer funny. Max Beerbohm was the best of the Edwardians, but he was gentle compared to his predecessors.

From Beerbohm to *Beyond the Fringe* in 1960 satire was not dead, but generally dormant; and satirical attacks on royalty were generally avoided as being in shocking bad taste, and on the spurious grounds that royalty cannot answer back. From the early 1960s

there has been a recrudescence of satire, from which the royals have not been sheltered. The satire coincided with, and may have interacted with, the new, more open attitude of the royal family to its image. Some people brought up in the sixty bland years of sycophancy for the royal image found the new openness shocking; but in fact the modern satirists are far gentler to royalty than Gillray, Rowlandson, the Cruikshanks, and even the Victorians. Gerald Scarfe, the most original talent of the new wave of caricaturists, is possessed by corruption and death, and shows the skull beneath the skin. But his drawings of the Queen and her family are less grotesque and obscene than his treatment of other public figures. Satire and caricature are concerned with ridiculing the vices and follies of the powerful. The royal family since Victoria has been careful to be virtuous and to give up all political power except its constitutional vestiges. There is therefore less scope for satirizing it. *Private Eye* is comparatively mild and even good-natured in its treatment of royalty.

Princess Margaret and Lord Snowdon were regular targets of *Private Eye*, which concerned itself obsessively with their private lives and matrimonial difficulties. One element in this mockery, and to a lesser extent in the treatment of Princess Anne and Mark Phillips, is a snobbish comment about princesses being married to

Serial

LOVE IN THE SADDLE

by Sylvie Krin

SO FAR: PRINCESS ANNE, ONLY DAUGHTER OF HER GRACIOUS MAJESTY QUEEN ELIZABETH II IS NOW MARRIED TO FIELD MARSHALL SIR MARK PHILLIPS, CHIEF OF THE IMPERIAL GENERAL STAFF . . .

the luxurious Persian carpet, a bowl of heavenly-scented mimosa and Chinese jasmine, a present from the Libyan head of state, Colonel Gaddafi.

And the bed . . .

Yes! Now she heard his familiar footstep on the wooden ballons! Her heart began to beat faster and faster. The boat was rocking like a cradle. The door burst open and Mark rushed towards her, his jaw set strong and firm.

commoners, who work for their livings like other men. This is the exact opposite of the complaints of satirists a century ago that the members of the royal family were always marrying German princelings instead of native spouses, who would not be royal, but would be better than royal, British. You cannot win with satirists; they get you coming and going.

Other contemporary caricaturists such as Giles and Osbert Lancaster have in the past decade found a new freedom to portray royalty and make jokes about it. The portrayal is usually respectful and the jokes are kind, the point usually being that royals are ordinary people just like the rest of us, or at least just like the rest of the stereotypes in the simplified world of caricature.

The new openness about the royal image works both ways. The Queen and the Duke of Edinburgh now feel free to make jokes about their image and the image-makers. In his youth the Duke was involved in a series of extravagantly publicized disputes with the press, which culminated in him appearing to spray photographers with a water sprinkler on purpose, and describing the *Daily Express* as 'a bloody awful newspaper'. Relations have now relaxed in the new approach to public relations at the Palace so that the Duke could say to the anniversary banquet of the Guild of British Newspaper Editors: 'After all, here I am, a figure whom you have been brought up to believe is an implacable enemy of the Press, who goes to any extreme to show his acute displeasure, even using nuts and sprinklers and every other nefarious device. Here am I, not only dining with the great panjandrums of the despicable enemy, but I am actually down to propose their continued good health. But, anyway, it is comforting to know that the members of the Guild also don't believe everything they read in the newspapers'.

The Queen herself, who feels inhibited by the dignity of her office from making public jokes, and finds public speaking harder than her husband, made a delightfully light humorous speech to six hundred guests at the lunch at Guildhall to celebrate her silver wedding. It was the best speech she has made in her life, and demonstrated how much more free and easy the relationship between royalty and the general public has become during her reign.

She started by taking everyone's breath away with a joke against her habit of starting every speech with the phrase 'My husband and I', a trick much mocked by mimics. She said: 'I think that everyone will concede that on this of all days I should begin my speech with the words "My husband and I".' She went on to have a laugh about the royal 'we': 'We, and by that I mean both of us'; and to proclaim that her attitude to family life was as simple as the conviction of the legendary bishop's attitude to sin: 'He was

'Chief PRO of UK Ltd (internal and external relations)': an unkind caricature by Marc.

against it; I am for it'. It may not have been high comedy. But by royal standards it was heady stuff, and symbolized the new royal image. Guildhall resounded to the civilized sound of glasses responding to thumps of applause on the table. Since Sir Martin Charteris became Private Secretary, nice textual critics have detected traces of his whimsical sense of humour in royal speeches.

The Palace's new approach to publicity treads a tight-rope. It is more open and more suited to the spirit of the age than the old sycophancy and hypocrisy. And yet the Queen and her family cannot be marketed exactly as if they are pop stars or breakfast cereals. It is doubtful whether people want the monarchy stripped of all its old dignity and mystery. Scandinavian monarchs bicycle around town and go about their daily business to some extent as if there were no difference between their offices and those of ordinary people. But if there is no difference, there is little point in retaining a monarchy.

Total exposure would make life impossible for the totally exposed; the royal family are on duty all the time anyway, and have a hard enough time securing a private life for themselves. The Palace is therefore still extremely sensitive about intrusion into the private life of its royalties, as in 1964 when photographs of the Queen sitting up in bed in a woollen bed-jacket after the birth of her youngest son, Edward, were smuggled out of Buckingham Palace, and sold to the public prints, no doubt at a great profit.

The royal image depends on more than the Queen, her advisers, and the artists, writers, satirists, and rascally freelance photographers who publicize it. Complex factors change the ways in which a nation looks at itself and sees its symbolic head of state. Everything is in a state of flux, particularly people's attitudes to the society they live in. As Adam said to Eve on their way out of the Garden of Eden: 'We live in an age of transition'. Age and familiarity are potent factors affecting the royal image. This was well exemplified by the changed image of Queen Victoria during her long reign. By its end only her oldest subjects could remember a time when she was not Queen. Victoria had become a national grandmother substitute, appealing to British ancestor-worship and our instinct for continuity and security. Her death was widely felt to be the end of an era.

The present Queen is young enough to see a similar change in the public's attitude to her. Humans need to invent historical landmarks to give a coherent pattern to the flux of events in which they live; and the English have always found the events in their monarchy conveniently personal signposts. An important discovery in this reign has been the recognition by the royal family of the need to present its image professionally and attractively in a world that runs on mass communications, where the image rules.

6 Family

Around the Queen as sun revolve her family as satellites, reflecting and magnifying the royal image, and describing their orbits in the family solar system. Her large family play their supporting parts in the dignified and ceremonial functions of the family business. By their variety in age and temperament they provide royal models of all sorts for those who need a figurehead to look up to and identify with. Bagehot, as usual, did not miss the point: 'A family on the throne is an interesting idea. It brings down the pride of sovereignty to the level of petty life'. Women, he said, care fifty times more for a marriage than a ministry.

The wide public interest still shown for royal marriages, royal babies, and suchlike indicates that Bagehot's cynical and male chauvinist opinion is still valid. Unmarried monarchs with small families to support them, like George IV, tend to be unpopular. The exception to the rule was Elizabeth I. Since Victoria the royal family has generally followed the prescription of Bagehot, the hidden persuader, for stimulating public interest by being philo-progenitive. In the present reign the supporting cast around the protagonist Queen have both been given far more to do in the royal theatre than their predecessors, and also been allowed far greater freedom than their predecessors to follow their chosen paths outside the limelight.

Next to the Queen, but always a literal or metaphorical pace behind her when it matters, stands the Duke of Edinburgh, Prince Philip. The 'Prince' is by way of being a courtesy appellation. George VI, having granted his son-in-law the style of Royal Highness, erroneously supposed that it carried the style of Prince with it, and consistently spoke of him thereafter as Prince Philip. Prince Philip had to be granted the style and titular dignity of Prince of the United Kingdom and Northern Ireland in 1957; and the Queen has also made it clear that he has precedence immediately after her.

The job of Prince Consort is notoriously nebulous, especially in so ill-defined a system as the British monarchy, which depends almost entirely upon custom and precedent, and hardly at all on definitions. The last one, Prince Albert, was a worthy representative of the Victorian age, being earnest, creative, conscientious, and hard-working. His hard work and worry, as well as the frustration of always being kept well away from the driving seat by the unconscious jealousy of Victoria, probably contributed to his premature death at the age of forty-two. Having always to play second fiddle to his wife in public is hard on a Prince Consort's machismo, and demands tolerance and sensitivity.

Prince Philip has defined how he sees his job: 'It is almost like being self-employed in the sense that you decide what to do'. The principal job is to accompany, support, and escort the Queen, stand in for her, speak up for her when discretion gags her, and take some of the weight off her shoulders.

Driving himself in fast cars, piloting his own helicopter, and dashing ceaselessly and busily around the country, the Duke is as representative of the way that his age likes to see itself as Albert was

The Duke of Edinburgh at the controls of a helicopter of the Queen's Flight.

of his age. He projects an image of dynamism, purposiveness, heartiness, and modern impatience with red tape and tradition.

He comes from the formidably clever, ambitious, and arrogant Mountbatten family. With his characteristic pose, with hands clasped behind the back as when standing at ease in the Navy, he still manages to keep his finger in as many pies as possible. His interests range widely, but the causes that he is most closely associated with include conservation and wild life, youth, industry and technology. His interest goes deep as well as wide. His devotion to such causes as his own foundation, the Duke of Edinburgh's Award Scheme, the National Playing Fields Association, and St George's House, Windsor, the residential retreat where clergy can discuss social, moral, and philosophical questions with businessmen and other prominent people, and occasionally the Duke himself, is greater than ducal duty demands.

He was born Prince Philip of Greece, alias Philippos Schleswig-Holstein-Sonderberg-Glücksburg, son of Princess Alice of Battenberg and Prince Andrew of Greece and Denmark, the youngest son of King George I of the Hellenes. So he is a prince of the Greek royal family, which is Danish racially, and a third cousin of the Queen. The name was a mouthful; so when he settled in England with a view to matrimony in 1947 he adopted the surname of Mountbatten, the anglicized version of his mother's maiden name, though she was never called Mountbatten. His mother and father separated, and he shared in the turbulent life of disgrace, exile, and recall that Greeks inflict on their royals. His father had little money to leave him, and he was by royal standards as poor as a royal chapel mouse. He was educated at Cheam School, the oldest preparatory school in England, which removed from its London suburb to Headley in Berkshire while he was a pupil; and at Salem and then Gordonstoun under the German educational innovator, Kurt Hahn, a believer in the virtues of cold baths, leadership, and rugged individual initiative. His surrogate father figure while he was in England as a boy was his maternal uncle, 'Uncle Dickie', Lord Mountbatten who has been a major influence on him all his life and a power behind the throne; though not quite such an influential power as is sometimes imagined. Lord Mountbatten's influence on Prince Philip and on the Prince of Wales naturally decreased as each in turn grew up and came into his own.

From Gordonstoun Prince Philip followed his uncle and his family tradition into the Royal Navy by going to the Royal Naval College, Dartmouth. While a cadet there he first met his cousin, Princess Elizabeth, whom Cupid and Uncle Dickie had already got their eyes on for him. He joined the Navy in 1939, and served with distinction with the Mediterranean Fleet in home waters, and with the British Pacific Fleet in South-East Asia and the Pacific.

By the end of the war it was no surprise to close observers of royalty to discover that Prince Philip and the heir presumptive, Princess Elizabeth, were in love. After the usual procrastination of a fond father, anxious that at twenty-one his daughter was too young to be absolutely certain, George VI gave his consent, granted Prince Philip the title of Royal Highness, and created him Duke of Edinburgh, Earl of Merioneth, and Baron Greenwich. Prince Philip had previously been naturalized as a British subject.

In the generation since then he has become so native a figure in the English scene that it is incredible and absurd to remember the suspicion that once attached to him as a foreigner. A public opinion poll taken in 1947 showed 40 per cent of the sample opposed to his marriage, on the grounds that he was a foreigner. Prince Philip has entirely dispelled this suspicion, and is now reckoned more English than the English. He has thus avoided the problems of nationality that persist with his friend and counterpart, Prince Bernhard of the Netherlands.

His predecessor, Prince Albert, never managed to dispel the mutual suspicion between himself and the ruling classes. He went to his early grave unforgiven for the shameful crime of not being English. Albert was also widely suspected by the silly and the suspicious of being a secret and sinister power behind the throne. Royal marriages are revealing catalysts to crystallize the unpleasant latent chauvinism, envy, and xenophobia in the British character.

Nobody today accuses the Duke of Edinburgh of being foreign or of meddling with power behind the throne. He has established for himself the distinctive job of wide-ranging, free-booting national cheer-leader and critic. He is a first-class speaker, writing his own witty and breezy speeches, and delivering them with the no-nonsense and bluff heartiness of a naval commanding officer addressing his crew of slackers, exhorting them to wake themselves up and pull their socks up. He sometimes sounds like his old headmasters, Kurt Hahn or Harold Taylor of Cheam, ticking off the nation with a magisterial self-confidence in his common sense. For example, 'I'm sick and tired of making excuses for Britain', on the subject of the incompetence of the British at exporting; 'The economists seem to be building up the same sort of structure of dogmas and shibboleths which became the millstones of the old religions'; and, the classic example, on his favourite subject of the shortcomings of British industry and commerce: 'I could use any one of several stock phrases or platitudes about this, but I prefer one I picked up during the war. It is brief and to the point: Gentlemen, I think it is about time we pulled our fingers out'.

His pep-talks occasionally exasperate the sensitive. After his 'sick and tired' speech Clive Jenkins, the general secretary of the Association of Scientific, Technical, and Managerial Staffs, said that the

Duke was the best argument for republicanism since George III. And Prince Philip has become aware of the unfavourable impression that his exasperated gadfly role sometimes creates, and is able to mock himself about it: 'As usual I find myself in the delightful position of telling people who know much more about it what they ought to do, in the certain knowledge that I will not have to attempt to do what I suggest'. Diffidence and humility do not come naturally to a Mountbatten. But Prince Philip has admitted: 'There's an awful lot of things that, if I were to re-read them now, I'd say to myself: "Good God, I wish I hadn't said that".'

'The best thing to do with a degree is to forget it': the Duke's only degrees are honorary. Here he is receiving a Doctorate of Laws at the University of California.

Among the things he wishes unsaid would probably be a number of impatient remarks about education and universities, for which he sometimes shows the intolerant philistinism of a man who worries because he has not had a university education.

There was a good example of his capacity to shock by being outspoken in a television programme in 1968, when he referred to the royal family's finances, a subject considered in bad taste by traditionalists and hypocrites. With characteristic jauntiness the Duke confided to millions of viewers in Britain and America: 'We go into the red next year. We may have to move into smaller premises'.

Such flippant bluntness is for most people a refreshing change from the anodyne platitudes that were expected from royalty in the days when they were worshipped as nodding mandarin figures. The occasional inevitable gaffe can be forgiven a man who speaks his mind without cant, and more often than not comes out with sound common sense.

The Duke's most recent and persistent campaign has been on behalf of the environment and conservation, which he took up before they became a fashionable craze. Monarchs, after all, may also be an endangered species. He wrote a good little book, illustrated with photographs that he took himself, about birds he had seen from the royal yacht *Britannia* on two long voyages in the southern oceans and the Antarctic. The book is an accurate illustration of his style: the practical approach to problems, the insatiable curiosity on every subject from sailors' names for birds to the mechanics of a whale factory ship, the nautical and humorous vulgarity. He is at his best on such subjects as sex and the single gull, and the mating habits of penguins, which have to mate by trial and error because both sexes appear to be identical. Their courtship consists of offering small flat stones to each other for the purpose of making what passes for a nest, and cases have been reported of penguins offering stones to visiting humans. The Duke observed all this, noted that no penguin offered him a stone, and reflected that if penguins cannot tell the difference between humans and themselves, there may be some basis of truth in the theory that they mate by trial and error.

The Duke manages to reconcile his enthusiasm for conservation and love of wild birds with the traditional passion of the British royal family for shooting them. He explains: 'What I am concerned with is the fact that a total species should not be extinguished. If you shoot for sport, you get conservation, because people say: "Well, I want to go on doing this, I am going to make damn sure that the thing continues to exist".'

He is not exactly a true Philip, which means in Greek a lover of horses. But at least he was a furious rider of the beasts, having taken

up polo on the advice and example of Uncle Dickie, and become at
one stage one of the top eight polo players in Britain. He once
described the horse unkindly as 'the biggest animal with the
smallest brain'. Since he had to give up polo, his latest great interest
is driving four-in-hand. He is a keen sportsman, performing
vigorously and formidably at squash, cricket, skin-diving, gliding,
and sailing. He is restless, energetic, practical, impatient, and talented. He is quite a good painter. He does not suffer fools gladly, and
has a tendency to naval irritability, which he is managing to curb
better in middle age. He does not seem like an easy man to have as a
father. He has become a pillar of the Queen and of the Establishment, by far the most successful consort of any English queen; and
he has managed to inspire the public admiration and affection that
eluded Prince Albert. When he described himself as 'one of the
most governed people you could hope to meet' and 'being almost
permanently under arrest', that was an example of ducal irony. He
does the job he has decided to do well, and evidently enjoys it.

The education of their children and particularly of the heir
apparent is a matter to which the royal family in the past has
devoted anxious attention, generally with disappointing results.
Prime Ministers and archbishops were consulted to draw up
the ideal curriculum for a future king. But the boy in question was
seldom an ideal scholar; and tended to grow up isolated from his
contemporaries, with a hatred of learning, and a sense of inferiority
about his intellectual capacity.

The Prince of Wales and his sister and brothers are the first royal
children in history to have had a normal, though not exactly a
comprehensive education. Prince Charles was put through the mill
in his father's footsteps: Hill House, a fashionable Knightsbridge
pre-preparatory school; Cheam; Gordonstoun; half a year at Timbertop, an outpost of Geelong Grammar School, Melbourne, in
the Outback for training in character and Spartan pioneering virtues. The royal family has a curious instinct for balance and
hedging its bets in educating its children. If a Prince of Wales, later
Edward VII, is allowed to Oxford for a year, he had better go to
Cambridge for another year. If Prince Charles goes to Gordonstoun, Timbertop in the Antipodes may be a useful antidote. It was
an exclusive education, and those not persuaded of the virtues of
Kurt Hahn's hearty system of character-training might say a pretty
grim one.

The Prince of Wales survived it, and has no complaints. He says:
'I suppose I could have gone to the local comprehensive or the local
grammar, but I am not sure it would have done me much good. I
think a public school gives you a great deal of self-discipline and
experience and responsibility; and it is this responsibility which is

Father and son in characteristic poses; hands clasped behind their backs, as when standing at ease in the Royal Navy. This time it is an RAF occasion. The Prince of Wales had just received his wings at RAF Cranwell in August 1971.

worth-while. In these times the organization I work for is called into question; it is not taken for granted as it used to be. One has to be far more professional at it than one ever used to be. And I hope that my education and upbringing and all these various schools and establishments will in some way equip me for this role'.

The breakthrough for Prince Charles came with the sensible decision to let him go up to Cambridge to read for the ordinary tripos. Before Cambridge he was sheltered from publicity, shy, and rather dull with the self-conscious dullness of adolescence. At Cambridge he blossomed. He took a respectable honours degree, and led a comparatively normal life as an undergraduate. He

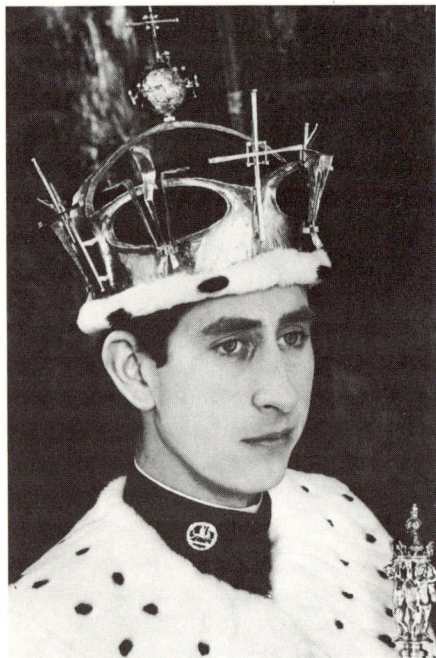

Charles as Prince and pilot.
LEFT, *he wears the crown specially designed for his investiture,*
and RIGHT, *as Red Dragon II, he takes his first dual-control flying lesson at Yeovilton.*

played the cello in the orchestra, and showed an interest in cultural and intellectual matters not characteristic of his predecessors. He emerged as an enthusiastic mimic in the Trinity revues, and showed signs of a dry wit derived from his father's, but more anarchic and less square: the cynical asides; the long words spoken with a straight face to say something rude; the reduction of everything to characters from Monty Python and the Goons.

He naturally followed in his family hoof-prints by being awarded a half blue for polo. Prince Charles commented: 'Half a shirt'. At the end of Cambridge he had come out of his chrysalis as a recognizable person with an agreeable personality, bright, humorous, interested in everybody as the royal family is by training and instinct, intelligent, and showing ominous signs of the Mountbatten self-confidence. When he came of age he was to be invested as Prince of Wales at Caernarvon. He was accordingly packed off for a term to study Welsh at the University College of Wales, Aberystwyth, partly as initiatory ordeal, and partly as a political gimmick and burnt offering to damp down the rising fires of Welsh Nationalism. He says of his time there: 'When I went to study at Aberystwyth, Welsh Nationalism was at its height. Some of it was directed against me; understandably. It was embarrassing, but I could understand the problem. Things are different now. I believe that when I went to spend some time in Wales and showed my interest in and concern about Welsh affairs (and tried to learn the language) a bit of the hot air may have gone out of some of the more negative forms of Welsh Nationalism. I hope that doesn't seem pompous or conceited; I like to think it is true'.

The fires of Plaid Cymru have not noticeably burnt themselves out since then. But it was unquestionably a bold and constructive part of the Prince's education to expose him to the atmosphere of Aberystwyth, beneficial to him at least. He has emerged with some sharp perceptions of the Principality: 'The extraordinary thing about Welshmen is that they have this radical tradition – they are radically traditional and traditionally radical, and this is a curious paradox. They have an old tradition of support for the Labour Party for instance, and yet in the country regions they are also very traditional. And I think there is a certain amount to be said for Wales having been neglected by a central government – it is on the fringes, and this has led to a certain depressed feeling, and perhaps a slight inferiority complex'.

From university the Prince of Wales resumed the family tradition by going into the services, first the Royal Air Force, and then in 1971 the Navy. His careers in them have been far freer and more adventurous than was possible for his predecessors, and more varied than the careers of most of his contemporaries. It is impossible to imagine Prince Albert and Baron Stockmar approving of their Prince of Wales parachuting into the sea from an Andover at 1,200 feet, or piloting a supersonic Phantom jet.

Prince Charles says: 'Some feel that it was the traditional thing to go into the services. But it is also a very sensible thing to do. A period in the services gives you great experience and responsibility: of life, of discipline, and above all of people, and how to deal with people, to discipline them and be disciplined by them'. Discipline is not the most fashionable contemporary virtue, but it is doubtless a useful quality for a Prince of Wales to acquire. And the services have become more sensitive to politics and public relations since Prince Charles's great-grandfather reckoned the Navy inadequate training for a life spent dealing with politicians. He took command of his first ship, the minesweeper HMS *Bronington*, in 1975, and said after a few months of it, with characteristic whimsy: 'I have only been in the Navy five years, and sometimes I feel eighty already. I do not know why my beard has not turned grey'. The Prince's beard is an occasional growth.

In addition to his work in the services, the Prince has been initiated in the mysteries of the family business. For example, he represented his mother at the independence celebrations of Fiji, the 350th anniversary of the Parliament of Bermuda, the memorial service for General de Gaulle, and numerous other state occasions, such as the independence celebration of the Bahamas, the centenary celebration of Fiji, and the coronation of King Birendra Bir Bikram Shah Deva of Nepal.

This again is in marked contrast with the previous practice, by which monarchs have been curiously jealous of their heirs, and reluctant to let them have a foresight of the business they will one day inherit. The most spectacular example of this was Victoria's obstinate refusal to let her eldest son do anything useful or know anything about her constitutional functions. But even as late as 1937, when George VI came to the throne, he told Lord Mount-batten that he had never seen a state paper before. And George VI's plan to educate his elder daughter personally in the business of monarchy was cut short by his premature death. The Prince of Wales has seen plenty of state papers, and has acted as Counsellor of State while his mother and father have been abroad. He shows signs of being politically aware, and of having thought about the monarchy and his future role. When Gough Whitlam's Labour Government in Australia was showing anti-royalist proclivities in 1974, the Prince of Wales made a topical speech to the New South Wales legislative council, justifying the particular brand of Australian and British parliamentary democracy, because of its extraordinary capacity for improvisation: 'This, I do believe, is the system mankind has so far evolved which comes nearest to ensuring stable government. And I also believe that the institution of the monarchy – to which rightly or wrongly I belong and which I represent to the best of my ability – is one of the strongest factors in the continuance of stable government'.

After Britain had joined the European Economic Community the Prince said: 'The drive behind the Commonwealth relationships is one of feeling, of sentiment; the drive behind the European relationship is more practical in character, to do with economics and defence. I'd put it this way: much as I love Europe, and love being a European – after all, I have got plenty of European blood in my veins – what impresses me most about Europeans is the way we differ from one another. Whereas what impresses me about the Commonwealth is how much, in spite of everything, we have in common'.

He is naturally adept at being interviewed, an essential attribute of a modern prince. He made a notably witty maiden speech in the House of Lords on the subject of sport and leisure, and had the peers as near to rolling in the aisles as their dignity and age permit. And he has spoken again, on the subject of voluntary service in the community, and the theme, with intimations of Kurt Hahn, of helping young people to discover themselves through adventure and hardship.

Altogether the Prince of Wales has had a better and more thorough training than any of his predecessors for his inherited job, and shows signs of proving most royal when he is put to it. The job is not a static one, and is likely to change considerably before the end of the century. But however it has by then been modified, Prince Charles will need exquisite discretion and uncommon sense to do it well. The modern monarchy is no longer so essential to the constitution that it can afford an indiscreet or incompetent monarch, or one who is careless of the royal image. He seems to recognize his position and to be in tune with the times. In a recent television interview he said: 'I am one of those people who believe strongly that one should adapt to changing circumstances. The one thing you cannot afford is to get left miles behind. You want to be just a little behind, but ready to adapt gently and slowly'.

The Prince left the Navy at the end of 1976. The question now arises of the next stage in his training. This was the question to which Victoria never found a satisfactory answer for her eldest son. Indeed she never looked for one, but kept him unemployed, resentful, and frustrated until he was nearly the age when ordinary men retire. So much imagination and innovation have already been shown in the education of the Prince of Wales that it is clear that he will not suffer a similar fate of idleness in waiting.

There are precedents for sending a royal son, especially when he is married, as Governor-General to a Commonwealth country that would like to have him. Temporary exile from home and family is a sacrifice demanded of princes, as of men in the armed services and ambitious business executives. Or, like the Duke of Kent, he could take a desk job in some kind of national business enterprise. As Chairman of King George's Jubilee Trust, he launched an appeal for his mother's silver jubilee. An interesting and beneficial way of putting his undoubted drive to use in a non-political way would be for him to go for a time into British industry, which needs all the drive and encouragement it can get. In the new relaxed monarchy of today, with the untraditional affection and easiness between the parents and children in it, it is not inconceivable that the Queen might eventually become the first English monarch to abdicate voluntarily in favour of her heir, rather than soldier on into extreme old age. There is no question of this happening for many years, while the Queen enjoys her work and does not find it a burden. Monarchs, like wine, improve with experience.

Princess Anne has already shown that she has a mind of her own, and a taste for breaking precedents and bones that suits the mood of the times and the modern image of the monarchy. She is the first princess to have been put through a comparatively normal education, having been sent to Benenden, the girls' public boarding school in Kent, from the age of thirteen to eighteen. She quite clearly chose her own husband, Mark Phillips, an officer in the

Dragoon Guards and a notable horseman. This confirmed the trend against arranged dynastic unions, which generally became the thing after the accession of the House of Hanover. Before the Hanoverians it was quite usual for royalty to marry outside the royal circle. After they came in, a superstitious reverence for royal blood made it exceptional, so that eventually it came to seem improper to the Victorians for a royal to marry a non-royal. This reduced the field of possible marriage partners for a royal to a dwindling and unimpressive group that was disappointing for the royal family, and likely by inbreeding to prove genetically disastrous, and to separate royalty dangerously far from ordinary people. Disraeli recognized the danger; and when Princess Louise, Queen Victoria's fourth daughter, broke out of the royal circle by marrying the Marquess of Lorne (not exactly an average commoner, since he was the heir of the Duke of Argyll, but not a royal), he congratulated the Queen on having 'decided with deep discrimination that the time was ripe for terminating an etiquette which has become sterile'.

Princess Anne followed the example of her aunt and the daughters of Edward VII and George V by marrying out of the ludicrously narrow magic circle. Mark Phillips was of neither royal nor noble birth, not selected by any match-making royal computer, but clearly an eminently suitable husband for the Princess.

Another happy precedent set by Princess Anne is that she has risen to the top in her chosen field of excellence. Royalty shines because of its symbolic position. There is great advantage to it if it can be seen to add to the lustre with its own merits and talents. Princess Anne's overriding interest and talent lie, as Stephen Leacock put it about another horseman, in flinging herself upon her horse and riding madly off in all directions. Her great-grandfather rose to the top of the tree in philately, sailing, and shooting. In Princess Anne's field, horses and particularly 'Events', the curious generic name for horse trials, money and leisure to train are not enough by themselves to buy success. She could not have got to the top without endurance, courage, gallantry, good horsemanship, and, in defeat, good sportsmanship: the cardinal virtues of the little country society whose lives revolve around their horses.

Her trainer, Mrs Alan Oliver, analysed her seat, as they say in the horsy world: 'She is a tough horsewoman, completely dedicated to her sport, and capable of competing on equal terms with Olympic champions. Nobody realizes just how hard she has worked to get to the top. She drives over from Windsor every day for between two and three hours' intensive training. Some experts say she is a stylish rider – I think workmanlike is a better description. Besides her tremendous determination to do well, plus a load of guts, she has an ideal temperament. Having grown up as the centre of attraction all her life, she does not seem to suffer from nerves like the normal person'.

Horse trials, whether in one-, two-, or three-day events, consist of three phases: dressage; cross-country speed and endurance; and a showjumping test. The second phase was once considered too tough for women; but in this liberated age horsewomen also have shown that they can be just as tough as men. Princess Anne seems to combine her mother's love for horses and understanding of them with her father's will to win and excel. She has persevered, in spite of breaking her nose in a fall while riding with the Oxford University Draghounds at the age of fifteen, and a number of other spectacular spills and brushes with the press, to become one of the

Princess Anne's boots receive a final polish from Captain Mark Phillips before the dressage competition at the Montreal Olympic Games 1976.

best riders in horse trials in the world. She later had an operation to straighten her nose.

She has fallen or been thrown from horses half a dozen times since she rode to the slippery top of the equestrian world, and she has been unlucky with her horses. Her best horse, Doublet, went lame just before the 1972 Olympic Games, so depriving her of an attempt at her ambition to win an Olympic gold medal. In 1973 she fell during the European three-day championships at Kiev, and was at first thought to have broken her collarbone. In fact she had only, if only is the word, a badly bruised right shoulder and thigh. In April 1976, again an Olympic year, when she and Mark Phillips had been selected as probables for the Olympic three-day event team, she cracked a vertebra and suffered concussion when her horse fell on her during riding trials at Durweston in Dorset. She is courageous and determined, and to ride in the Olympic Games has been her main ambition since she won the European Championships in 1971. Happily she recovered and was selected, the first immediate member of the royal family to take part in the Olympics. Mark Phillips was selected as reserve, and they became the first husband and wife partnership in an Olympic equestrian team.

Those who know her best say that she is the member of the family who most takes after the Duke of Edinburgh. The resemblance shows itself in other ways beside her competitiveness. She is informal, impatient, impetuous, bored with red tape, and imperious, and does not always take trouble to conceal her irritation with intrusions on her private life, particularly by the press. One of the burdens of royalty is that it lives most of its life in public. Losing one's temper with the goggling spectators is counterproductive, as Princess Anne has learned the hard way. Those like Princess Alexandra who go out of their way to cooperate with photographers tend to be the least pestered by them.

There was a spectacular demonstration of this restless temper when Princess Anne, aged twenty, visited the United States in 1970 with her brother as guests of President Nixon's family. She was too young to have learned that a royal must smile and smile in public, and wear the royal mask of interest and pleasure. So at times she did not manage to conceal her exhaustion, boredom, and resentment of what she considered impertinent questions by what she described as 'twenty million reporters on my heels'. This provoked a Washington newspaper to ask: 'Why not limit Anne to opening rhododendron shows in Kent before unleashing her again on foreigners?'

Since then she has become more professional, and accordingly has had a better press. She has started performing her royal duties gradually, only accepting jobs that she thinks she can make some

The Duke of Edinburgh in the full dress uniform of Admiral of the Fleet, photographed at Windsor Castle.

OVERLEAF LEFT   *The Prince of Wales photographed in Canada in 1976.*

OVERLEAF RIGHT   *Queen Elizabeth the Queen Mother on her seventy-fifth birthday in August 1975. Queen Elizabeth wears the collar of the Royal Victorian Order, of which she is Grand Master.*

contribution to. An example is the Save the Children Fund, of which she is president: she is good with her two younger brothers, and children generally, treating them as people, not inferior objects. She made another startling innovation and set another precedent for royalty by going to Kenya to star in a film for the BBC television programme *Blue Peter* on behalf of the fund. In this she was shown more informally than a royal princess had previously, even being seen going underwater swimming with a snorkel. A submarine bodyguard with aqualung and harpoon discreetly escorted her to protect her from sharks. She is natural on television, having been accustomed to being peered at by crowds and photographers at horse trials.

She is developing a self-confident manner of public speaking, with a taste for making jokes characteristic of her father and elder brother. For example, at the mutual admiration festival at which the Society of Film and Television Arts presents its annual awards, the society's president, Princess Anne, can usually be counted upon to be funnier than the professional comedians on self-conscious parade. Her great ambition so far has been to excel at her chosen sport. Mark Phillips has said that he would eventually like to be a farmer; and in 1976 the Queen bought them a country house and farm in Gloucestershire. This caused some people, who noted Princess Anne's early distaste for publicity and the tedium she showed for ceremonial duties to predict that, after their triumphs at horse trials were over, the Princess and her husband would retire from the royal limelight to a country life surrounded by stables and dogs. The prediction does not sound persuasive to those who notice Princess Anne's resemblance to her father: the determined taste for a challenge, the growing proficiency, the sense of royal duty. Princess Anne likes her part in the family business, and is unlikely to retire from it for many years. Few girls would have come undefeated through the hard luck she has had in her early career: the falls and other accidents; the attempt to kidnap her and Mark Phillips in the Mall; and several well-publicized visits to hospital. She must be as tough and determined as her grandmother.

Her younger brothers, Prince Andrew and Prince Edward, have been put through a fairly normal education, and shielded from unauthorized publicity in their childhood even more successfully than their elder brother and sister. They went to Heatherdown, a preparatory school at Ascot, and Prince Andrew followed, Prince Edward presumably will follow the rugged footsteps of their father and elder brother to Gordonstoun. So successfully had they been protected from publicity, that it came as a shock when one day a photograph showed that Prince Andrew had grown much taller than his mother.

Princess Margaret, photographed by Lord Snowdon.

In her salad days the Queen Mother used to be described as a
fairy princess by the gilt-edged prose of the popular press. Today
she has become the matriarch of the royal family. Because of
English reverence for antiquity, she is accordingly widely re-
spected and loved by people and classes not otherwise noted for
their royalist tendencies. Her demotic nickname, the Queen Mum,
is a revealing indication of public affection. Sheer longevity does
wonders for the reputation of royalty, as evidenced by Elizabeth I,
and, most notably, Victoria. Royalties personify the life of a nation
as living almanacs, even though they no longer have much
effective influence on national life. The older they grow, the more
potent symbols of continuity they become.

The Queen Mother has many sterling qualities besides longevity. She was the inconspicuous power behind her husband,
George VI. Without her encouragement, he probably could not
have persevered to overcome the impediment in his speech that
threatened to disqualify him from public life. Without her support
and popularity he might not have managed to make the sudden
and most unwelcome transition to being King; and the institution
of monarchy would not have survived such a failure. Her presence
beside him throughout the Blitz and the rest of the war in London
undoubtedly stiffened national morale. Her steadiness and sense of
the royal duty supported her daughter when she became prema-
turely Queen. Today she is a pillar of the royal family, and its most
polished performer. The reluctant Queen has helped to establish
royalty as a profession. She used to tell her daughters: 'Your work
is the rent you pay for life'. They were never behind with the
rent.

She is not royal by birth, but comes from a family that could not
be described as common. She was born Elizabeth Bowes-Lyon, the
youngest but one, and only survivor, of the ten children of the man
who succeeded to the title as the fourteenth Earl of Strathmore in
1904. She was born in 1900 at St Paul's Walden Bury, her family's
Hertfordshire home, and brought up privately and happily there
and at Glamis, their Scottish castle a thousand years old, and
stretching back through the history of the Young Pretender and
Claverhouse to the black legend of Macbeth. Scottish class distinctions were different from the English variety in those days, less
feudal and in some ways less extreme. Although clearly an upper-
class lady, Elizabeth Bowes-Lyon is more at home with ordinary
people than most high aristocrats. She is at ease with people and has
the common touch, qualities not often found in the royal family
before her marriage into it.

This quality can be seen, for example, when she visits the Black
Watch, her family regiment of which she is Colonel-in-Chief, and
with which her brother Fergus and other relatives were killed in

*Prince Andrew towering over
the Queen at the Badminton
Horse Trials 1976. Prince
Edward stands between them.*

The Queen Mother: an informal pose at the Badminton Horse Trials.

the 1914–18 war. She is quite as much at home with the whisky and broad banter of the corporals' mess as she is with the more respectful atmosphere of the officers' mess. She finds the same down-to-earth escape from protocol at the Castle of Mey (her holiday home, especially in summer), the derelict ruin on the Pentland Firth that she has restored as her country home, that Queen Victoria found among her beloved, democratic High-landers of Balmoral. The earthiness of her language while fishing for salmon or engaged in other country pursuits is spoken of with awe, and no doubt some embroidery, by gillies.

Behind the characteristic boas and toque and fluffy hats, the predilection for baby blue, and the broad smile, which are the public face of the Queen Mother, there is a very tough, competent, and capable person. She never forgave the Duke of Windsor for what she saw as ratting on his royal obligations, so forcing her husband to become king, and possibly shortening his life. After George VI's death the rehabilitation of the Duke and Duchess of Windsor in the English court might have been possible with-out her implacable opposition. Yet when she met the Duke in public she wore her public mask, kissed him, and treated him with royal politeness. She is an excellent actress and a superb pro-fessional in the royal business, the ceremonial side of which is so

The Queen Mother greeting the Duke and Duchess of Windsor in public at the unveiling of the memorial to Queen Mary at Marlborough House in June 1967. The Hon. Mrs Gerald Lascelles stands behind.

closely allied to acting that its performance should qualify royalties for membership of Equity.

She is gregarious, loves talking to people, and enjoys her public engagements; otherwise she could honourably have retired from them long ago. She can always be relied on to prolong her engagements beyond the schedule, as she genuinely loves to chat with everyone. She and the Prince of Wales are devoted to each other.

Racing is her great semi-private passion. After her husband's death she was persuaded by Winston Churchill to carry on racing George VI's horses under his colours, as well as her own steeplechasers under the famous Strathmore colours of her grandfather. She has had more than three hundred winners since 1949; and almost won the Grand National in 1956, when her favourite horse, Devon Loch, collapsed from exhaustion when leading the field only fifty yards from the winning post. She has said that her remaining ambition is to equal the success of her great-grandfather, who won the Grand National once and the Derby three times. The gracious and charming exterior covers a formidable and admirable personality, sensed by the ordinary public, which generally adores her. She has been the chief pillar of the royal family for two generations. Without her it might have lost its job.

It is a shame that public attention for so long concentrated on the matrimonial difficulties, and finally in 1976 on the separation, of Princess Margaret and Lord Snowdon. Few marriages could have survived such a persistent, and hostile campaign by the gutter press. They are in many ways the most adventurous and interesting members of the royal family, and could have built a bridge across the chasm between the monarchy and the artistic and intellectual worlds. He is a talented photographer, sensitive director of television films, and designer of things from the Snowdon Aviary at the London Zoo to wheelchairs, his own spectacles, and, less successfully, his costume for the investiture. She is interested in the theatre, and has a good collection of modern art, especially of Bryan Organ, whose portrait of her is one of the most successful and unconventional pieces of modern royal iconography. Epstein, not a safe royal sculptor, made a bust of her. She is musical, a clever mimic, a good pianist, and, as Sammy Cahn put it, 'sings well for a princess'.

Princess Margaret by Bryan Organ, 1970.

The Snowdons could have been creative trend-setters, expanding the horizons of the Palace. Somehow it never worked. They, and especially Princess Margaret, tried to have their cake and eat it. When it suits her she stands on protocol and insists on being treated royally. Such hierarchical attitudes are irrelevant and objectionable in the world of art and ideas.

It is also true that the Snowdons have had a bad press, not all of it deserved. Almost since the day of their marriage the press, fed by bitchy society gossip, took a prurient and intrusive interest in their private life. The Queen's younger sister is in a vulnerable position anyway, without going out of her way to invite criticism by standing on her dignity. The British notoriously like scandalous gossip and backbiting. The Queen's private life is generally considered inviolable by such malice, as well as being too worthy and dull for it. But Princess Margaret has been reckoned fair, or possibly more acurately unfair, game for our national hypocrisy masquerading as morality. She once complained that she had 'as much privacy as a goldfish in a bowl'. Her elder sister is inevitably the focus for most of the attention and the recipient of most of the perquisites of the family business, as well as the carrier of its main burdens. It was psychologically natural for the lively younger sister to become the royal equivalent of an *enfant terrible*. She is short of the exquisite discretion and majestic humility we demand from our monarchs. When attacked, her instinct is to bite back. Physically and temperamentally she is a Hanoverian.

Her marriage difficulties were an embarrassment to the royal family; partly because of the Queen's public position as supreme governor of the Church of England, which still does not officially recognize divorce; and partly because of the family's private horror of divorce, which brought George VI to the throne, and shook the family business to its foundations. The attitude of the Church in 1976 was more sympathetic to divorce and remarriage than when in 1955 the Archbishop of Canterbury, Lord Fisher, was called in when Princess Margaret wanted to marry Group Captain Peter Townsend, who was in the process of getting divorced. That is why Princess Margaret and Lord Snowdon settled for a legal separation rather than divorce. Although Princess Margaret is only fifth in succession to the throne, if she divorced her example would upset the established principles of Christian family life of the Church of which her sister is head, and attract the disapproval of influential church leaders.

The Queen's cousin, the Earl of Harewood, another musical member of the family, has been isolated as a black sheep from the official business of the royal family because of his divorce. But the closest analogy to the separation of the Princess and Lord Snowdon was the dissolution in 1900 of the marriage of Princess Marie

Louise, a favourite granddaughter of Queen Victoria, who in 1891 made the calamitous mistake of marrying Prince Aribert of Anhalt, who was unable or forbidden or unwilling to consummate the marriage.

In an interview in a French magazine in 1973, Princess Margaret was quoted about her old troubles with the press: 'I had no way to retaliate. I just had to submit and keep quiet. They accused me of everything, and I did not have the chance to give an interview to put the record straight. All that is different now. Apart from taking my clothes off and bathing in the fountains in Trafalgar Square, I can do anything'. Her separation from Lord Snowdon temporarily revived the ancient press curiosity about her private life, and was taken by hard journalists to have justified it. But generally her royal image has now become fixed: talented, artistic, imperious, unhappy, and undervalued and misunderstood. In the past decade the British press have become less keen on blood sports with the private lives of royals as quarry, and have anyway turned to younger prey. It is curious that their hunting instincts are now directed more at Princess Anne, who is luckier than Princess Margaret because she went to school and is tough. In her way Princess Margaret has played a significant part in bringing the monarchy closer to real life. It could have been more significant if it had not been for unfortunate mutual misunderstandings by Princess and public. She is the most culturally aware of the royal family, clearly the most lively companion among them to take to the theatre, and the most interesting to talk to afterwards.

The Snowdon children, Viscount Linley and Lady Sarah Armstrong-Jones, are being educated at Bedales, a boarding public school, and given more privacy and a more normal education than their mother achieved.

Lord Snowdon was Tony Armstrong-Jones before he was elevated to his earldom; and since the separation wishes to revert to his former name for professional and private purposes. In spite of his father's opposition, after Eton and Cambridge, where he coxed the winning university boat in the boat race of 1950, he started work as a photographer with *Picture Post* and *Country Life*, then moved on to *Vogue* and *Harper's Bazaar*. He graduated from fashion photography, and eventually got commissions for taking royal portraits through Lord Rupert Nevill, and then by writing directly to the Duke of Kent. He photographed the Queen's children, and then took the official photographs for Princess Margaret's twenty-ninth birthday. He joined *The Sunday Times* in 1962, and extended his range of work to become one of the brightest and most imaginative professional photographers working in Britain. The royal connexion, of course, helped him to get such sitters as Lady Spencer-Churchill and Agatha Christie. But some of his best work

The Earl of Snowdon prepares
for an exhibition of his
photographs in Los Angeles in
1974.

has been of the obscure, the poor, and the violent in scenes of urban
squalor: for instance, a fine series he published about Detroit in
1974. He takes his art seriously, and has exhibited widely. He
believes in showing photographs in shops and open spaces, not just
in art galleries; and has said: 'A good photograph makes you use
your eyes, has the minimum amount of material, and is quick'. His
maiden speech in the House of Lords was devoted to demanding
more public help in meeting the needs of the disabled. He is an
engaging and unusual member of the royal family, providing a tart
contrast with many conventional royal attitudes. For example, he
goes out of his way to avoid military events. And he said, in
something approaching lese-majesty towards the royal sport of
shooting: 'Any idiot can be a good shot; apart from that, I simply
do not want to kill things any more'.

The Gloucesters are the family of the late Duke, the Field-Marshal and soldier of the family, the third son of George V and Queen Mary, who died in 1974.

His widow, Princess Alice, Duchess of Gloucester, was a devoted wife to the Duke. She is a shy, rather nervous person, very busy and conscientious, a hater of publicity. She has worked extremely hard in the family business, especially when her husband was out of action because of his long last illness from 1966–74. Now she gets a state allowance of £20,000 a year as widow of a younger son of a sovereign; and feels that she has to work even harder to justify it, in spite of the fact that it is well earned, that the Duke's £45,000 a year stopped at his death, and that she was born on Christmas Day 1901. Her main duties are concerned with ceremonial and representative functions in the Army and Air Force, reflecting her husband's background and predilections. She recently became the first lady GCB: Extra Dame Grand Cross of the Most Honourable Order of the Bath. She lives at Kensington Palace and occasionally at Barnwell Manor, the family farm near Peterborough. She is frail, pretty, dignified, a keen gardener and countrywoman, a talented watercolourist, and rich in her own right, being a Montagu-Douglas-Scott, daughter of the seventh Duke of Buccleugh, who was one of the wealthiest men in the country.

Prince William, the elder son of the Gloucesters, was killed when a small aeroplane he was piloting crashed in 1972. The first English Prince William for 153 years had broken new ground for the royal family by becoming the first royal to live in college at Cambridge; the first to attend an American university, Stanford; and the first to become a professional diplomat by working for the Foreign Office. He was a great loss, being a lively, gregarious, and outgoing member of the family.

His younger brother, Prince Richard, accordingly became the new Duke of Gloucester. He is a professional architect, trained at Cambridge, who practised for the old Ministry of Public Building and Works and then as a partner in a firm of London architects, before the dukedom fell upon him in 1974. He still does some work in his architect's firm when he can escape from public and family duties. He has written some attractive books about the architecture and statues of London. The dust jacket of one described its author with charming coyness: 'Richard Gloucester is a 29-year-old architect and photographer who lives and works in London'. He is an artistic member of the royal family, with, by cautious royal standards, Bohemian and trendy left proclivities. He and his wife intended to live on the Isle of Dogs, in the heart of the old East and West India Docks and the Millwall Docks system, in an old warehouse that he was going to convert into a house. But family duty

Funerals are occasions for family reconciliations: Royal mourners at the funeral of the Duke of Gloucester, the Queen's uncle, in St George's Chapel, Windsor in June 1974.
Front row: Prince Richard of Gloucester, the Duke of Edinburgh, the Prince of Wales, the Duke of Kent, Prince Michael of Kent, Earl Mountbatten of Burma, Lord George Scott, and Lord Maclean.
Second row: the Queen, the Duchess of Gloucester, Princess Richard of Gloucester, the Queen Mother, Princess Anne, Princess Margaret, and the Earl of Snowdon.
Back row: the Earl and Countess of Harewood.

overrides personal inclinations. Within a month of his brother's death, Prince Richard and his wife were installed in Kensington Palace, and have remained there.

He has taken on numerous and unconventional official commitments, such as being the patron of Action on Smoking and Health, the anti-smoking campaign. He is the first president of the Society of Architect-Artists; a member of the Anglo-Nepalese Society; president of the Cancer Research Fund; Grand Prior of the Order of St John of Jerusalem, whose unceremonial, very practical functions include the St John Ambulance Brigade. He is patron and an active member of the Victorian Society, and made a lecture tour of the United States on its behalf. In addition to his official and architectural duties, he has had to become a farmer. He decided to keep Barnwell on, and take over the running of the 2,500 acres, which were once considered the most modern farm in the country.

His wife, the Duchess, formerly Birgitte van Deurs, is the daughter of a Danish lawyer. She was a secretary at the Danish embassy in London, and walked out with Prince Richard for years before they decided to get married. She is tough, determined, and better looking than her photographs suggest, and has adapted herself quickly to being royal. She has taken on a number of official commitments, particularly ones connected with nursing: for example, she is president of the Princess Christian Training College for nursery nurses, Manchester, and patron of the Association for Spina Bifida and Hydrocephalus. Their son Alexander is the Earl of Ulster.

The Kents are the family of the fourth and youngest son of George V and Princess Marina, the youngest daughter of Prince Nicholas of Greece and Denmark. The father, known as George to the family, was killed in 1942, when a Sunderland flying boat in which he was en route from Scotland to Iceland crashed into a Scottish mountain. His Duchess, Princess Marina, one of the most cosmopolitan and elegant members of the royal family, died in 1968. The present Duke, known to his friends as Eddie, was educated at Eton and Sandhurst, and commissioned into the Royal Scots Greys, subsequently amalgamated with the Carabiniers to become the Royal Scots Dragoon Guards. In his youth he projected the conventional image of a young royal duke: fast sports cars, which he tended to crash with alarming frequency; winter sports; smart cavalry regiment; and a hint of stiff upper lip and loose lower jaw. But he was also a serious professional soldier, who passed out in the top ten from the Staff College at Camberley. It was a bitter blow for him when he was unceremoniously withdrawn from his regiment after it was posted to Ulster, on the grounds that he made too tempting a target for IRA terrorists; and more particularly as a hostage for kidnap and blackmail. His uncle, the Duke of Windsor, suffered the same frustrations as a young Army officer during the First World War when he was kept away from the front line. When he protested, Lord Kitchener pointed out to the Prince with characteristic bluntness that, although it would not matter very much if he was killed or wounded, it would be extremely embarrassing if he was taken prisoner. The Prince made the point, with equally characteristic insensitivity about his hereditary obligations, that it would not matter if he was killed, since he had four brothers to take his place.

His withdrawal from Ulster cost the Duke of Kent the command of his regiment, and ultimately made him decide to leave the Army and progress to a civilian job. In 1975 he joined the British Overseas Trade Board, the organization that is responsible for marketing Britain's technological skills overseas. He takes a keen and expert interest in technology, particularly electronics, having been encouraged in it by his Army experience and his cousin, Lord

Mountbatten. In 1976 the Board elected him its vice-chairman, and he left the Army to work full time at the important job of promoting British exports. He travels widely in his work, and speaks fluent French. Professionals in the competitive commercial world in which he works say that he is not just a royal figurehead; but also a shrewd and agreeable professional himself, with a good knowledge of the nuts, bolts, and circuits of his chosen career.

His Duchess is Katharine, the only daughter of the late Sir William Worsley, a great Yorkshire landowner, and Lord Lieutenant of the North Riding. She is blonde, beautiful, a lover of country pursuits, and in considerable demand in her own right for charitable and ceremonial functions. There are brains in the family. Their elder son, the Earl of St Andrews, won a foundation scholarship to become a King's Scholar of Eton. Their other children are Lady Helen Windsor and Lord Nicholas Windsor.

The Duke of Kent's younger brother, Prince Michael, was born only six weeks before his father was killed. Franklin Roosevelt was his godfather. He is a professional soldier in the Royal Hussars. His girl friends are considered to be of interest to readers of the William Hickey column in the *Daily Express*. Like his brother, he is good at winter sports, and has won the British bobsleigh championships. Formerly he lived in Kensington Palace; but he has now set up home on his own in the royal borough of Kensington and Chelsea. He spends a lot of time with the Gloucesters at Barnwell. Princess Alexandra, alias Mrs Angus Ogilvy, is the girl in the Kent family. She is strikingly good-looking, and has her mother's gregarious and gracious qualities, and an engaging schoolgirl gaiety. In the bitchy gossip that follows royalty, nobody has a hard word to say about Princess Alexandra. She can charm the persistence out of a Fleet Street photographer: that snapping pack of newshounds considers her the friendliest and most amenable royal to photograph. Like the rest of her family, she has a wide range of musical interests, and plays the piano well.

Angus Ogilvy, her husband, used to be described in the reference books as a company director, but that was an understatement. He once collected directorships as easily as other men collect cold germs. At the time of his marriage in 1963 he had more than fifty, but he reduced the number considerably after marriage. His career crashed in the summer of 1976, when a Department of Trade report severely criticized his conduct while he was a director of Lonrho. It described him as a weak man who, partly because of a financial relationship that developed between him and Roland 'Tiny' Rowland, the chief executive of the company, did not stand up sufficiently to Mr Rowland, and was negligent in his duties. Mr Ogilvy complained bitterly that the report was unfair, but he offered to resign his directorships as the only honourable thing to do. With a good sense of public relations he was at once seen at his wife's side assisting at all her official functions. He is the second son of the twelfth Earl of Airlie, and accordingly a scion of one of the most patrician Scottish families. His line can be derived with high probability from a younger son of Gilbride, who was Earl of Angus in 1138. The history of the Airlie family is woven in the plaid of Scottish history; the ballad, 'The Bonnie House of Airlie', commemorates just one of its romantic and savage exploits. He comes from a Christian Scientist family, though he is not a practising member of the sect. He has had chronic trouble with his back and kneecap. He helps his wife in her official engagements, has accompanied her on most of her foreign visits, and has subsidized the Civil List by paying some of her official expenses. They live at Thatched Lodge House in Richmond Park, one of the Queen's properties. Their children are James and Marina Ogilvy, Angus Ogilvy having considered his old Scottish family name more honorific than any other possible title.

These are the inner circle of the royal family, who help in the family business by regularly undertaking ceremonial and official duties on behalf of the Queen. But it is a prolific family, and the circumferences of its outer circles spread far and wide. The doyenne of the official list is Princess Alice, Countess of Athlone, Queen Victoria's last surviving granddaughter, and a grand old survival from the nineteenth century. She was born at Windsor Castle in 1883, the daughter of Prince Leopold, Victoria's fourth son. She is the Queen's great-aunt; attended Victoria's diamond jubilee celebrations in 1897; was made a Lady of the Order of Victoria and Albert in 1898; and has so far attended four coronations in Westminster Abbey. She married the Earl of Athlone, Queen Mary's brother.

Princess Alice, Countess of Athlone, born in 1883, last surviving granddaughter of Queen Victoria, and great-aunt of the Queen. She wears the Order of Victoria and Albert, given to her by Queen Victoria in 1898.

The Marquess of Cambridge, a nephew of Queen Mary, is another survivor from the reign of Queen Victoria. He was a royal trustee of the British Museum from 1947–73, but apart from that he has not been active at official royal functions for some years. His Marchioness recently edited a cookery book of royal recipes.

The Duchess of Beaufort comes before her Duke in precedence, since she is a niece of Queen Mary, and consequently a member of the old royal family. They are horsy, country, charming people, directly descended from George III, and two of the Queen's closest friends. She and other members of her family regularly stay at Badminton, the stately home of the Beauforts in Gloucestershire, for the Badminton horse trials, the famous three-day event initiated by the present Duke in 1949. The Duke has been Master of the Horse since 1936: an ancient and honorific royal appointment, whose duties today are ceremonial rather than practical. He is also the greatest and most devoted foxhunter in the world, counting all time lost that is not spent in hunting the fox. Queen Mary was made to evacuate London against her will to avoid the bombing of the last war. She took refuge at Badminton, arriving with a convoy of servants and furniture, and staying for five years. She said that she had never seen hay before going to Badminton.

Lady May Abel Smith is the only surviving child of Princess Alice, Countess of Athlone, and therefore a great-granddaughter of Victoria. Her husband, Colonel Sir Henry Abel Smith, is an old Royal Horse Guards officer, and a former Governor of Queensland; during part of 1965 he became temporarily Administrator of the Australian Commonwealth. They live near Windsor, and are always on parade at Ascot, the Windsor Horse Show, the Rose Show, and other local royal events: an agreeable, polite old couple.

Earl Mountbatten of Burma is a royal of the outer circle who is active in the inner circle, and said to have considerable influence there. He is the son of Prince Louis of Battenberg, who was largely responsible for renewing the Royal Navy and preparing it so that it was ready for 1914. Ungrateful anti-German hysteria then forced him out of his office as First Sea Lord, and subsequently caused him to relinquish his title and assume the anglicized surname of Mountbatten. The old Duke of Cambridge, Queen Victoria's first cousin, who died in 1904, made a snobbish and uncharacteristically witty bon mot about the family: 'The origins of the Battenberg dynasty are lost in the mists of the nineteenth century'. Battenberg's son had an equally distinguished and gallant career in the Navy, ending up as Supreme Allied Commander in South-East Asia at the end of the Second World War. It has been said that he would have won the Victoria Cross if he had not been so closely related to the royals. He became the last Viceroy, and negotiated independence for India; and then became the first Governor-General of independent India. He is a busy, restless, ambitious, active man, whose activities, foibles, titles, honours, and vanity occupy more space in *Who's Who* than those of any other individual. In his old age he has more energy than responsibility. It was typical of him that he was the only member of the royal family to turn out in uniform for Princess Margaret's wedding, and full dress uniform at that. And after Princess Anne's wedding, with his usual thrust and initiative, he jumped the queue ordained by protocol in order to arrive back at Buckingham Palace in the main royal procession.

George Lascelles, the seventh Earl of Harewood, is the elder son of Princess Mary, the Princess Royal, the Queen's aunt, who died in 1965. He is a notable and talented musical administrator, managing director of the English National Opera since 1972. He was artistic director of the Edinburgh Festival and the Leeds Music Festival, and has filled a series of important posts in the musical world. Partly because of his musical preoccupations, and partly because of his untidy divorce and remarriage in 1967, he has not taken an active part in royal business.

Gerald Lascelles, Lord Harewood's younger brother, is also musically talented, though he favours jazz rather than classical music. He is interested in motor racing and is chairman of a company concerned with the conservation of green crops.

The Duke of Fife is the son of a granddaughter of Edward VII, Princess Maud: a Scottish landed laird interested in athletics, and a vice-president of the British Olympic Association. He survived a very bad motor accident. He has committed the act embarrassing to royalty by going through the divorce courts.

Captain Alexander Ramsay, Laird of Mar, known as Sandy Ramsay of Mar, is a grandson of Victoria's third son, Prince Arthur, Duke of Connaught. He was a regular soldier and was severely wounded in the Second World War. He is another Highland laird in the royal family, with a predilection for appearing at royal occasions in a kilt.

From him the circles of the royal family spread wider still, like ripples in the genealogical pond, to embrace the Norwegian royal family, a Norwegian family called Lorentzen, another Norwegian family called Ferner, the five Rumanian Princesses, Prince Tomislav of Yugoslavia, and eventually, if you extend the circles far enough, no doubt to Adam and Eve themselves. The Duchess of Windsor, the former Mrs Simpson and aunt by marriage of the Queen, is not a member of the royal family. She is on better terms with the royal family than journalists sometimes suppose. The Prince of Wales calls her Aunt Wallis. And it has long been agreed that when she dies she will have a funeral in St George's Chapel, and be buried beside the Duke at Frogmore.

The royal family is a large, splendidly versatile and varied group of people. Its inner circle of about twenty are powerful reinforcements of the Queen, and, for the most part, ornaments of the throne.

7 Finance

Money is the root of much embarrassment to the monarchy. Money was the weapon with which the Commons broke the autocratic power of the English kings, by periodically insisting that redress of grievances must precede the grant of supplies.

Today the royal finances are still the sharpest weapon in the hands of critics of the monarchy. This has come about partly because of the extreme antiquity and complexity of the royal finances, and partly because of the peculiarity of their terminology. When in 1975 the Civil List, which finances the running of the royal household, was increased, the name household suggested to the uninformed that the Queen was getting a queenly increase in her housekeeping allowance and personal living expenses, inappropriate at a time of general belt-tightening and impoverishment. In fact no element of the modern Civil List is for personal pay, and three-quarters of the Civil List grant is for salaries of staff working in the royal household. Most of these salaries today are directly linked to those of comparable grades in the civil service. It is the inflation of salaries that is the principal cause of the trebling in Civil List expenditure since the beginning of the reign. During the same period the salaries of civil servants and Members of Parliament have more than quadrupled. It would be a harsh doctrine that secretaries and other employees of the royal household, just because they work for the Queen, should be paid progressively less than people doing the same work for employers with less ancient titles.

The royal finances can be seen in perspective in relation to other national expenditure. The Civil List for 1975 consisted of: for the Queen, including royal bounty, £1,400,000; annuities and pensions for retired palace staff, £250,000; supplementary provision, £85,000. This adds up to £1,735,000, half the state subsidy for the Royal Opera, Covent Garden, that year. In addition government departments, such as the Ministry of Defence for the royal yacht and the Queen's flight, had expenditure of £4,643,000 connected with the monarchy. This gives an overall maximum cost of the monarchy of £6,378,000; although abolishing the monarchy would not abolish the cost, or even reduce it by much. Even in a republic the sailors of the formerly royal yacht would remain on the public payroll, constitutional and ceremonial duties would have to be done and paid for, and Hampton Court and Kensington Palace and the rest of the national monuments would have to be maintained. In comparison the state spent more than £15 million in 1975 on overseas information; more than £23 million on the Arts Council; more than £11 million on the British Library. The British public spent thirty-four times as much on football pools (£215 million) as on the monarchy; thirty-three times as much on Bingo (£210 million); and forty-five times as much on one-armed-bandits and other gambling machines (£285 million). The cost of the Civil List was 3p a year for each member of the population: much less than the cheapest fare on a London bus or the Underground; a twenty-fifth of the cost of a gallon of petrol, that is about one mile of motoring in a family car; the same as two cigarettes or half an inferior daily newspaper; a third of the cost of a cup of tea at a London railway station, which is an antidote to thirsting for tea ever again.

In the same way that the royal household is a misleading euphemism for what is in effect a department of state, the name of royal yacht gives intimations of idle luxury in the South Seas, with sails flapping gently in the tropical breeze, while royal bodies in bathing suits lie about the deck sipping cool drinks. In fact HM Yacht *Britannia* is not a yacht, but a medium-sized naval hospital ship of the Royal Navy of 5,769 tons gross weight, built at John Brown's, Clydebank, at a cost of £2,150,000, and launched in 1953. In peace the *Britannia* serves as an official and private residence and as a mobile administrative headquarters for the Queen and other members of the royal family, when they are engaged on visits away from the United Kingdom or are voyaging in home waters. The communications equipment is kept to the highest modern Royal Navy standard, because an essential function of a head of state is never to be out of touch, in case some constitutional duty or crisis demands her. It is very often used on state visits by other members of the royal family as well as the Queen. To take an old example, when the late Duke of Gloucester and his Duchess visited the war cemeteries and battlefields of the Gallipoli peninsula, it was natural for them to use the *Britannia*.

The annual cost of running the *Britannia*, at present between one million and two million pounds, comes out of the Ministry of Defence vote. More than half of the cost consists of the pay and allowances of the crew of 189 on a harbour running basis, and 279 when members of the royal family are on board, or when the ship is required to undertake long ocean voyages. When not needed by the royal family, the royal yacht regularly takes part in naval exercises and demonstrations as a target ship, hospital ship, or

The royal yacht Britannia, *dressed overall.*

convoy Commodore's flagship. It is, therefore, misleading to call it a yacht, an atavistic title derived from the long flotilla of yachts in the service of the royal family. The best known of *Britannia*'s ancestors was the *Victoria and Albert*, which was built in 1901 and was used for royal occasions and junketings until just before the last war. The father of the Prime Minister, James Callaghan, served on it. At the same time, although it serves a more useful purpose than pleasure cruising, it is questionable whether another royal yacht of equivalent size and expense will be built when the *Britannia* becomes unfit for service. Such extravagance belongs to the days when the symbolic Britannia ruled the waves.

The royal finances are a difficult subject, whose complexity is confounded by nomenclature, the politics of envy, and the embarrassment that most people, not just the rich, feel about discussing their money in detail. Self-appointed specialist in the subject, scourge of the monarchy, and keeper of the bees in the royal bonnet is Willie Hamilton, Labour Member of Parliament for Central Fife, and the most conspicuous republican in British politics today. For a generation he has ridden his republican hobbyhorse to tilt at royal windmills, and particularly royal finances. He brings a rude wit and fire to his pet subject that confirm the opinion that his talents would have earned him ministerial office, had he not devoted them so exclusively to such a narrow and embarrassingly sensitive a subject. His principal treatise on the subject, entitled, with characteristic cheek, *My Queen and I*, was published in 1975. It perpetrates some glaring inaccuracies that cast doubt on the rest of his royal arithmetic.

For example, Mr Hamilton misapprehends that the Duke of Gloucester receives £45,000 a year from the revised Civil List of 1971. In fact he received nothing at the time Mr Hamilton's book was published, and today has his official expenses paid by the Queen. It was his father who received the grant, as the son of a sovereign, on the grounds that his birth precluded him from earning his own living. The grant died with the old Duke.

Nevertheless, in spite of its flaws, Willie Hamilton's book has done much to break the taboo on even mentioning the royal finances, a process that was started by the admirably clear and straightforward report from the Select Committee on the Civil List, published in 1971. The Palace cooperated with the Select Committee to make public the most detailed statement of the royal finances published since Domesday Book. The Queen has nothing to lose and much to gain from accurate publicity about her official finances.

The present system of financing the monarchy derives from the eighteenth century. Before then the Crown got most of its money from its private estates, like any other great landowner. The rest came from ad hoc grants of supply from Parliament; from sales of monopolies; in the case of Henry VIII from the seizure of church lands and property; in the case of the Norman and other early medieval kings by treating England as their feudal patrimony; and by other methods that would be tedious to discuss here, and are irrelevant to the present arrangements for paying for the monarchy. Concomitantly with these old revenues, the farther back the finances of the monarchy are taken, the more expenses the monarchy had to bear that are paid today by the central government.

Parliament has made grants for the support of the Crown for many centuries. The first Civil List Act was passed in 1697. But the modern Civil List system of financing the monarchy dates from 1761, when George III agreed to surrender his income from the Crown Estate to Parliament in return for a regular annual grant.

The origins of the Crown lands known today as the Crown Estate go back at least to Edward the Confessor. They consist partly of ancient demesnes of the English and Scottish kings, and partly of recent purchases of land and property over the past hundred and fifty years. They include great tracts of the central administrative and most valuable part of London, including Regent's Park, down Regent Street to Carlton House Terrace, and much of St James's; important properties in Piccadilly, Haymarket, Trafalgar Square, the City, Holborn, Kensington, including Kensington Palace Gardens, the last private road in London, and the address of the Soviet and many other embassies, several theatres, and the government buildings in Whitehall. The Crown Estate includes other urban property, and about 180,000 acres of agricultural land widely spread throughout England. In Scotland they amount to about 105,000 acres of agricultural land, moor, and forest. The oldest known holding is King's Park, Stirling, which is said to have been enclosed and laid out by King Alexander III of Scotland in 1257. In Wales they consist of about a thousand acres of agricultural land, great areas of unenclosed mountain and moor, and extensive mineral rights. Much of the land George III and his successors surrendered in return for the Civil List was stolen from the Church at the Reformation, and could only be said to belong to the Crown in the loosest and most divinely right sense of the word.

The Crown Estate also includes much of the foreshore, which lies between high and low water marks around the coasts, the bed of the sea, which has recently become more valuable than George III ever dreamed possible, mineral, oyster, and salmon rights, and considerable investments in government stocks. At the same time George III surrendered the ancient royal revenues from such things as wrecks, fisheries, and estrays, that is 'any beast not wild, found within any lordship, and not owned by any man'. He gave up his droits, or ancient perquisites, from the Admiralty and Courts of Justice; from fines, recognizances, legal fees, and forfeitures; and from prerogatives connected with the Church, such as the temporalities, or material possessions, of bishoprics during vacancy. Finally, as part of the bargain, the Crown surrendered in return for the Civil List some revenues of the Post Office; the excise on beer, ale, cider, and wine licences; and the four per cent West Indies duties, when in force. It surrendered treasure trove, unwilled money, and the income from the foreshore, except when they occur within the boundaries of the Duchy of Lancaster and the Duchy of Cornwall, when they form part of the revenues of the Duchies. Other curious hereditary revenues include all mute swans, and, by an Act passed in the reign of Edward III, sturgeon caught in the sea or below London Bridge in the Thames. Since then one London Bridge has fallen down, and another has been sold and removed to Arizona, which adds a fishy constitutional problem to the ancient royal finances.

All in all, the Crown Estate constitutes one of the largest, most diverse, and most valuable holdings of property in the capitalist world. In the 1970s urban property produced about three-fifths of their gross revenue; agricultural land about one-fifth; and miscellaneous investments and peculiar ancient revenues the remaining fifth. If the Crown Estate that George III surrendered is taken to have been his patrimony and private property, as it was at the time, the nation has had by far the best of the bargain. Ever since 1760 the annual income from the Crown Estate and small branches of hereditary income has usually been twice and often treble the amount of the Civil List. The contribution of the Crown Estate to the Consolidated Fund was £4 million in 1968–9; it is estimated that it will rise to just over £7 million by 1978–9.

But, however you do the sum, it is hard not to arrive at the conclusion that the nation makes a handsome profit out of the monarchy, given the ancient and whimsical trade of Civil List for Crown Estate. If you add the concealed costs of the monarchy, and subtract the concealed profits, you arrive at the conclusion that such arithmetic is not worth the calculation.

When the Queen succeeded to the throne in 1952, as usual the Civil List for the new reign had to be fixed. Accordingly the Chancellor of the Exchequer, then R. A. Butler, presented an address from the Queen to the House of Commons, unreservedly placing her hereditary revenues at the disposal of the House, and relying on the attachment of her faithful Commons to her person and family 'to adopt such measures as may be suitable to the occasion'.

The measures they adopted in the Civil List Act later that year provided a total annual payment to the Queen as follows:

	£ per annum
Class I: Her Majesty's Privy Purse (the Queen's private expenditure as sovereign, not as private individual)	60,000
Class II: Salaries of Her Majesty's Household	185,000
Class III: Expenses of Her Majesty's Household	121,800
Class IV: Royal bounty, alms, and special services	13,200
Class V: Supplementary provision	95,000
	£475,000

The supplementary provision of Class V was earmarked for three purposes: up to £25,000 was available for the expenses of the official duties of members of the royal family who received no grant from Parliament; the balance was available to meet any excess expenditure under Classes II and III; any surplus in the early years of the reign was to be stockpiled by the royal trustees (the Prime Minister and Chancellor of the Exchequer of the day, and the Keeper of the Privy Purse and the Treasurer of the Queen) to cover inflation in later years. The Privy Purse provision of Class I was not so fine and privy as its name suggests. It was intended to meet the cost of private expenditure arising from the Queen's responsibilities as head of state. For instance, it went to create a pension fund for past and present royal employees; to maintain and run Sandringham and Balmoral; to give additional help to other members of the royal family in their official expenses; to charitable subscriptions and donations; and to welfare and recreation of the staff of the royal household.

In addition the Civil List Act 1952 made separate provision for other members of the royal family as follows:

	£ per annum
The Queen Mother	70,000
The Duke of Edinburgh	40,000
Princess Anne	6,000
increasing in the event of her marriage to	15,000
Princess Margaret	15,000
The Duke of Gloucester	35,000
	£181,000

The 1952 Civil List exceeded expenditure for the first nine years of the Queen's reign. In 1962 the Queen's annual official expenditure began to exceed her income, and the deficit was met from the accumulated surplus of previous years. By 1970 the rising tempo of inflation put the royal finances overall in the red. The Civil List deficits of 1970 and 1971 amounted in total to £600,000; and expenditure for 1972 was estimated at £810,000. The Queen met these deficits from her private resources and from a contingency reserve that had been built up in previous years from unspent Privy Purse revenue. But another year at the prevailing rate of inflation would have made the Queen in her public office bankrupt, which would have been poor publicity for the pound and the national finances.

The 1952 Act had prudently foreseen such a situation, and under its terms the Queen sent a further 'Gracious Message' to Parliament, asking that the original grant should be reconsidered. Accordingly in 1970 a Select Committee on the Civil List was set up under the chairmanship of Anthony Barber, the Chancellor of the Exchequer, and in 1971 it published its report on the royal finances. It made the point that the Civil List is not a form of salary payable in respect of the Queen's public duties, but a reimbursement of the operating expenses of the official part of the royal household: 'The present need for an increase in the Civil List arises very largely from pay increases granted since 1952, not to the Queen or members of the royal family, but to the Palace staff'.

The Committee also went into the sensitive topic of the Queen's private wealth, about which there had been excited and ill-informed public speculation, some of it based on a misunderstanding. The royal palaces, the crown jewels, the royal collections of antique furniture and pictures, and the royal archives (described by one historian as an Aladdin's cave) would be of incalculably vast value in a sale room. However, Lord Cobbold, then Lord Chamberlain, pointed out to the Committee that the royal palaces (with the exception of Sandringham and Balmoral estates, which are the Queen's personal inheritance), the crown jewels, the royal collections of paintings and other works of art, and the prodigious stamp collections amassed by the Queen's grandfather and father were regarded by both the Queen and the Treasury Solicitor as 'passing in right of the Crown from sovereign to sovereign and, therefore, inalienable by the occupant of the throne. In no practical sense does the Queen regard any of these items as being at her free personal disposal'. These precious items bring in no income, cannot be sold, and are costly to maintain.

By any standards the Queen in her own right as a private person is an extremely wealthy woman. The sovereign is exempt from death duties, so that death has not eroded the family fortune. The income from the Duchy of Lancaster (52,000 acres of mainly agricultural land, producing perhaps £200,000 a year) is consider-

Balmoral, where the Queen spends her summer holidays.

able, and tax-free. But her father was a younger son, and had to use much of his inherited wealth to buy Balmoral and Sandringham from his brother, Edward VIII. The Queen when heiress presumptive received no income from the Duchy of Cornwall, which belongs by statute to the eldest son of the sovereign. But she made an unprecedented renunciation of the Duchy revenues on behalf of her son when he was a child. She surrendered eight-ninths of the annual income from the Duchy of Cornwall to the Treasury until the Duke, alias the Prince of Wales, came of age at eighteen, three years before everybody else under the contemporary law. Between the ages of eighteen and twenty-one the Prince of Wales received an additional £30,000 annual income. In 1969 the revenues of the Duchy automatically reverted to him; but he voluntarily surrendered half of them to the Consolidated Fund. The proportion is subject to review on his marriage, or in the event of some other change of circumstances. In 1970 his half share of this revenue was £104,846.

Exactly what the Queen is worth as a private woman is therefore one of those questions, like what song the Sirens sang, that are puzzling if not beyond all conjecture. Lord Cobbold went into the question discreetly in his evidence to the 1971 Select Committee, in view of recent sensational guesswork on the subject. He said: 'Her Majesty has been much concerned by the astronomical figures which have been bandied about in some quarters suggesting that the value of these [private] funds may now run into fifty to a hundred million pounds or more. She feels that these ideas can only arise from confusion about the status of the royal collections, which are in no sense at her private disposal. She wishes me to assure the Committee that these suggestions are wildly exaggerated. Her Majesty also wishes me to state that the income from these private funds has been used in some part to assist in meeting the expenses of other members of the royal family; owing to the progress of inflation, they have, in many cases, heavily outrun the annuities granted by Parliament to cover such expenses at the beginning of the reign'.

The Queen told the 1971 Select Committee that she was prepared to forgo the £60,000 payment a year to the Privy Purse from Class I of the Civil List. The Committee looked at the estimate of £810,000 official royal expenditure for 1972, and recommended that the rest of the Civil List, apart from Class I, should be increased to £980,000 a year. As in 1952 the royal trustees were asked to invest and accumulate unspent surpluses from the grant in the early years to cover later deficits arising from inflation. It was hoped that this arrangement would keep the royal finances out of the red for about five years before a further increase became necessary. This hope proved too sanguine.

The committee increased the annuities to other members of the family as follows:

The Queen Mother	£95,000
The Duke of Edinburgh	£65,000
Princess Anne	£15,000
after marriage	£35,000
Princess Margaret	£35,000
The (late) Duke of Gloucester	£45,000

It increased contingency payments as follows:

Younger sons, Andrew and Edward at age of eighteen and before marriage	£20,000
Younger sons after marriage	£50,000
Daughters at age of eighteen and before marriage	£15,000
Daughters after marriage	£35,000
Putative widow of the Prince of Wales	£60,000
Princess Alice, Duchess of Gloucester, since she was widowed	£20,000
Future widow of a younger son	£20,000

The Committee recommended that £60,000, the sum for the Privy Purse under Class I of the 1952 Civil List now to be given up by the Queen, should be made available to the royal trustees for the official expenses of members of the royal family who receive no grant from Parliament: that is, the present Duke of Gloucester, the Duke of Kent, Princess Alexandra, and Princess Alice, Countess of Athlone.

By 1975 inflation had run away with the royal finances, as with everybody else's. Estimated expenditure had risen to £1,380,000, and the Queen made a personal contribution of £150,000 to the Civil List. The royal trustees (then Harold Wilson, Denis Healey, and Sir Rennie Maudslay) recommended an increase in the Civil List of almost 43 per cent to £1,400,000, and forecast that they would need to come back for more annually so long as inflation continued at its current high rate, and the purchasing power of the Civil List continued to decrease.

The trustees explained why £980,000 had become inadequate so soon. Household wages and salaries had risen from £580,000 in 1972 to £985,000 in 1975; and household expenses from £291,000 to £385,000 in the same period. The trustees outlined the current scale of royal expenses in an interesting appendix to their report: food bills, £73,061; laundry, £12,878; the royal gardens, £23,736; purchase of horses, forage, and farriery, £24,253 (the horses in question are ceremonial beasts, not the Queen's race-horses, which are her personal property, and paid for personally); garden parties, £39,477; flowers, £11,244; and official presents, £9,357.

The details of the wages and salaries of the royal household give an equally illuminating picture of a labour-intensive industry hit by the sharp inflation of the 1970s. The Civil List in 1976 covered 337 full-time household staff (compared to 375 in 1970) and 126 part-time (compared to 100), so there has been a gradual slimming of the royal work-force. The average earnings of all employees in Britain rose by 12.7 per cent in 1973. The figure for the household was 9 per cent. In 1974 the national increase was slightly less than that for the household, but the latter benefited from a Civil Service anomalies award, which was back-dated to November 1973. The increase in the Civil List in 1975 was needed if royal workers were not to be paid less than people doing the same kind of job elsewhere, an event that would have infringed a trade union agreement about the wages of royal employees.

Harold Wilson, moving the second reading of the Civil List Bill in December 1975, told the House: 'Although the Queen has a wider range of activities than any previous sovereign, the number of people employed in her household has been reduced by forty-four during her reign. This is the more remarkable since the Queen is now sovereign of twelve countries, and travels regularly throughout the world, in addition to carrying out an extensive programme in this country'.

The principal purpose of the 1975 Civil List Act was not in fact to increase the money needed to run the monarchy business, but to alter the old machinery for increasing it. The previous system of voting an annual sum that was expected to remain adequate for a whole reign, or at any rate for a decade, was no longer working at a time of such rapid inflation. The Act therefore provided that any further increases in provision for the Civil List, which are going to be needed annually until inflation slows down, should be subject to normal House of Commons supply procedures. Instead of the elaborate machinery of a select committee and a new Civil List Bill to increase the royal money, the Treasury was empowered to make payments out of votes for the purpose of supplementing all or any of the sums to which the Civil List applied. This put the royal finances on the same regular basis as other government expenditure, instead of making them conspicuous and obnoxious to criticism because of the nonsuch system of fixing them. From 1976 estimated increases in the Civil List made necessary by inflation will be presented to the House of Commons like any other vote of money, and Members of Parliament will have the same opportunity to discuss and debate such increases as they have in the case of other government expenditure. The Queen's finances have been removed from the antiquated fixed annuity, and put on an inflationary sliding scale like those of most other government employees.

As part of the 1975 settlement, the Queen offered to take over personal responsibility for the payment of the official expenses of the Duke of Gloucester, the Duke of Kent, Princess Alexandra, and Princess Alice, Countess of Athlone. In 1971 she had surrendered her Privy Purse grant of £60,000 for payments to these four in their public duties. By 1976 their expenses had risen to £120,000, and the Queen agreed to take over responsibility for this payment from the Consolidated Fund. Her contribution inevitably rises year by year with the cost of living. As a consequence, since 1976 the Civil List has provided only for the sovereign, the consort of the sovereign, and for the children of a sovereign, and any widows of those children. In that respect the revised Civil List is simpler. Its new provision for regular annual increases to keep pace with inflation is an honest but terrifying admission by the Treasury and the politicians that they have been unable to control the national finances. It was a sounder and more stable world when a Civil List voted at the beginning of a reign could be expected to remain as adequate and safe as the Bank of England for the rest of that reign, even so long a reign as Victoria's. In those happy days the royal finances could be discussed, fixed, and got out of the way once and for all at the beginning of the reign. The old Civil List procedure took care of the gradual inflation expected by providing for a surplus in the early years of a reign to build up a contingency reserve for later years.

The disadvantage of annual vote provision for the monarchy, which is embarrassing both to the Queen and her government, is that it resurrects the sensitive question of the royal finances once a year, and so provides an annual platform for republican, mischievous, and sensation-loving Members of Parliament to get their names in the papers by having a go at the monarchy. The old system was more discreet, and kept the controversial matter of the royal finances out of sight except for once a generation. Constant recourse by the Crown to Parliament for more money is felt to be undignified. The new system is more democratic and open. If there is nothing to be ashamed of in the royal finances, there is no reason to fear an annual parliamentary debate about them. And such regular discussion might expose by repetition how factious, factitious, and sensational many of the arguments deployed against the monarchy are.

Over the years there have been a number of suggestions for rationalizing the royal finances and making them less complicated. The 1971 Select Committee recognized that the old system of allowing a contingency margin to take care of inflation in later years had broken down because of the acceleration of inflation. At the current rate of inflation it was alarming and impossible to guess a contingency margin big enough to meet future inflation for the whole of the rest of the reign. The Committee considered other ways of avoiding annual involvement of Parliament in the royal finances, while providing a periodical opportunity for Parliament to review the arrangements and to make sure that they are working as intended.

One suggestion considered in 1975 was to adjust the Civil List automatically each year by reference to the movement in some specified index reflecting inflation. The difficulty was to decide what index. Should it be a general index of price movements in the economy as a whole; or more specialized indices, reflecting movements in the main items of costs incurred by the royal household; or different indices for different parts of Civil List expenditure; or an index based on movements in the level of the hereditary revenues surrendered by the Queen in 1952, particularly the Crown Estate revenues?

The flaw in any such scheme of linking the Civil List to an index is that it assumes that the pattern of royal household expenditure will remain in future broadly as it is now, and that the only changes will be due to inflation. But the pattern of royal expenditure has already changed greatly during this reign; and the Committee decided that the assumption that it was not going to change further in future was unrealistic.

The Committee also considered making regular annual increases in the Civil List to keep pace with inflation, to be met from an annual vote, as is done for ordinary departmental expenditure. This expedient was rejected in 1971, because it would entail action by Parliament every year. The Committee felt that it would be quite wrong to allow inflation, for which the Queen has no responsibility, to make changes in the basic principles of the Civil List, on which on all previous occasions Civil List provision has been made. Continuing inflation has eroded such scruples in the politicians, and the present arrangements for the Civil List are for a slight vestige of the old contingency stockpiling for a rainy day, with parliamentary votes to top it up whenever necessary. At the present rate of inflation it will continue to be necessary with melancholy frequency.

Another ingenious suggestion for reorganizing and rationalizing the royal finances is the proposal to set up a Government Department of the Crown, to take over the administration of the Queen's official duties from Buckingham Palace. In many ways it would be a more logical and tidy way of providing the royal finances. Logic and tidiness, however, are not qualities that are valued as being of the first importance in the British way of doing things. Muddling through is an idiom that is dearer to the national idiosyncrasy.

The great disadvantage of such a Department of the Crown

would be that it would finally and completely nationalize the
Queen, and submit her formally as well as in practice to the control
of politicians and civil servants. It may sound only appropriate to
nationalize the head of state. But one of the Queen's functions as
head of state is to stand apart from politics and administration as a
representative of the whole nation.

Another interesting and radical proposal for reorganizing the
royal finances is to link the Civil List directly to the revenues of
the Crown Estate, as a percentage of them. As inflation eroded the
value of the currency, the revenues of the Crown Estate, if it were
managed properly, would rise proportionately to keep pace with
inflation. The Civil List would therefore also keep pace with
inflation, without embarrassingly frequent recourse to Parliament
for a royal 'pay rise'.

The Prince of Wales is already financed on such a sliding-scale.
As Duke of Cornwall he keeps half the revenue of the Duchy of
Cornwall, having agreed to surrender half to the Treasury. Since
the Duchy is well administered, his income keeps pace with
inflation. In the same way the Civil List for the Queen could be
fixed at an amount equal to a predetermined percentage of the net
revenue of the Crown Estate in the preceding year. For example,
the £830,000 Civil List expenditure in 1972 was about 24 per cent
of the revenues of the Crown Estate. That percentage, therefore,
could have been fixed as the annual Civil List of the Queen. Other
members of the royal family could be treated in the same way, by
being allotted much smaller annual shares in the Crown Estate
revenue.

This suggestion is attractive, because it has the automatic capacity to adjust the Civil List to the rate of inflation, unless the
Crown Estate Commissioners are unusually incompetent. This
would avoid the annual appeals to Parliament with what can be
portrayed as a royal begging bowl. Its disadvantage is that it could
remove the royal finances entirely from parliamentary scrutiny;
and it is inflexible, because, like any index-linked scheme, it assumes that the pattern of royal expenditure is bound to remain
unchanged. The pattern of royal expenditure in this reign so far
shows that such an assumption is unreasonable.

Another possible way of adjusting the royal finances to inflation
would be to try gradually to remove from the Civil List the cost of
the Queen's official functions as head of state. It was the established
constitutional practice in the eighteenth and nineteenth centuries
to help the Crown to make ends meet not by increasing the
amount of the Civil List, but by reducing demands on it by
transferring some of the costs of royalty to the departments that
supplied the services. Eventually, if this system could be made to
work, all the official costs of the Queen would be met by the

appropriate department of the government, and would be subject to parliamentary scrutiny with the rest of the departmental estimates. The residual Civil List would be solely for the private expenditure of the Queen and the royal family, and would in effect be their salaries. This Civil List would not be subject to detailed parliamentary scrutiny, in the same way that Parliament has no political or moral right to scrutinize how Cabinet Ministers or Members of Parliament spend the salaries they vote themselves.

The disadvantage of this proposal is that it is impossible to draw a straight line between the Queen's official expenditure as head of state, and her expenditure as private person. In a sense she can never be private. She is potentially on duty for twenty-four hours a day. She never takes a holiday; it is constitutionally impossible for her to do so. Even in her most private moments the national symbol has to maintain high standards of appearance, and dignity, and company. It would be impossible to separate the food eaten, the clothes worn, or the servants employed by the Queen *qua* Queen from the food, clothes, servants, and other expenses of the Queen as private person. When she drives by Rolls-Royce for the week-end to Windsor, where she will receive people officially as Queen, work on government papers, and rest as private person, how much of the cost of the journey should be paid by the government officially, and how much by the Queen personally? What proportion of the salaries of Palace servants should be paid by the Queen, and what by the Civil Service Department? Such a system of making the Civil List a salary purely for private expenses would be repugnant to the Palace, because it would reduce the Queen's residual independence from Parliament. A salaried Queen, with the Civil Service paying her servants and arranging her meals, really would have become a puppet on a purse-string.

A variant of this proposal to reduce the Civil List gradually until it evolves into the royal salary is the proposal to pay the Queen a fixed salary immediately, and pay the expenses of royalty either out of the Consolidated Fund or out of the appropriate departmental vote. This idea is distasteful to the Palace, not least because it would accentuate the present anomaly by which she pays no income tax. This privilege of the royal prerogative makes the Queen immeasurably the richest person in the United Kingdom. The Civil List is not liable to tax. Most of it, as we have seen, would not be liable to tax anyway apart from the royal prerogative, since it is spent on necessary business expenditure. The net revenues of the Duchy of Lancaster accrue to the sovereign by inheritance.

The Prince of Wales is probably the second richest person in the United Kingdom: the revenues of the Duchy of Cornwall are not liable to tax. Annuities paid from the Consolidated Fund or by the Queen to other members of her family are liable to tax in the ordinary way. But the Treasury exempt such proportion of these annuities as in their opinion 'represents a fair equivalent of the average annual amount laid out and expended wholly, exclusively, and necessarily in the performance of the duties in respect of which the annuities are payable'. Most members of the royal family spend all or nearly all their annuities on their official business, and manage to persuade the professional sceptics in the Inland Revenue that they do so.

The Queen is liable to pay rates for Sandringham and Balmoral. Like her subjects, she is liable to stamp duty on her property, and selective employment tax. She is not liable to income tax or surtax, capital gains tax, or capital transfer tax. This total exemption from income tax becomes increasingly anomalous and harder to defend at a time when the majority of Britons are increasingly taxed until their pips squeak. The monarchy has evolved and continues to flourish, like a rose garden, by judicious pruning. It may be that the next thing that needs a little pruning is the royal finances, especially the exemption from tax.

The Queen is in an extraordinary position, and has extraordinary expenses. It makes no sense to have a mean monarchy, or to make the Queen have an average standard of living.

National symbols are meant to be looked up to. It would be silly to make it possible for people to try to keep up with the Windsors, or even look down on them. The Queen and royal family live dutiful and sensible lives. But as the country adjusts to taking a smaller share of the world's wealth, the monarchy may have to adjust to the new standard of living of the country.

Comparisons with the way that other countries manage the finances of their heads of state are not illuminating, because no other country has anything comparable to the British monarchy. The Netherlands radically reorganized their royal finances in 1972, when the Dutch state took over most of the royal palaces and payment and expenses of staff, and the royal family relinquished many tax privileges. In return Queen Juliana of the Netherlands, her consort, Prince Bernhard, Crown Princess Beatrix, and her consort, Prince Claus, were each given a fixed income, which is adjusted annually to keep pace with the rise in the cost of living.

The French presidency cost £436,000 in 1975–6, but this did not include the upkeep of some palaces and the state guest house, or the special allowance for the President's wife. The French President lives in a style somewhere between the Queen's and that of the British Prime Minister.

The President of West Germany is paid and maintained by exactly the same procedure as any other item on the federal budget. In 1975 11.8 million Deutsche Marks (£2.1 million) were allocated to the presidency, compared to 11.6 million Deutsche Marks in the previous year: a modest increase of 1.7 per cent. Out of this total the President receives a personal salary of £36,000 gross, on which he is taxed like everybody else. His official residence, the Villa Hammerschmidt, is paid for by the government, and costs him nothing.

The President of the United States is chief executive and head of government as well as head of state; so his job is not comparable to the Queen's. Some of her symbolic and representative functions are fulfilled in the United States by the Supreme Court and even the national flag, the Stars and Stripes. The President must be the most lavishly maintained and generously paid public official in the world. He has two official residences: the White House and Camp David. He has a yacht, five Boeing 707s, eleven Lockheed Jetstars, and sixteen helicopters. He has a personal bodyguard several hundred strong, and all the status symbols and creature comforts that can be dreamed of in the American way of high life. The bodyguard alone costs 19 million dollars or more than £10 million a year.

The President's salary is 200,000 dollars with a 50,000 dollars expense allowance, which is treated as income. There are considerable perquisites of office. For example, the United States Government spent about 16 million dollars on Richard Nixon's private houses in California and Florida. The President can make a fortune out of writing his memoirs. The Queen cannot.

The Queen is different in constitutional function, symbolic role, and historic tradition from all other heads of state. It is therefore not suprising that the method of financing her is also peculiar and complicated. However, if such items as Windsor Castle and the crown jewels are disregarded, as being historic national treasures rather than personal possessions, she does not appear to be more lavishly maintained or more highly paid than the heads of other developed Western states of the same size. And she has a far more effective and busier constitutional role than other heads of state. The Queen is known and recognised all round the world. But how many people even in Western Europe can instantly name and recognize the faces of, for example, the Presidents of West Germany and Italy?

8 Court

The British genius for adapting old monarchical bottles to hold new constitutional wine means that many powerful and important modern offices retain titles redolent of the flavour of the medieval monarchy. The Lord President of the Council is a senior, freelance member of the government, who takes precedence immediately behind the Prime Minister. They both come behind the Archbishops and the Lord Chancellor in the official league table of national importance, which is, of course, led by the Queen, the Duke of Edinburgh, and the Prince of Wales. The Lord High Chancellor of Great Britain and Keeper of the Great Seal has an office going back more than nine centuries, and is the highest civil subject in the land. To kill him is worse than murder; it is accounted high treason. Behind the majestic title he is just a professional politician and lawyer: the member of the Cabinet of the day who presides over debates in the House of Lords. He is also head of the Judiciary, and appoints all Justices of the Peace, recommends to the Queen the judges for the Court of Appeal, and appoints certain Church livings in the gift of the Crown. The Lord Chancellor is president of the highest Court of Appeal and of the Chancery Division of the High Court of Justice. In charming addition he is also Keeper of the Queen's conscience, which means in practice nothing more than that he must belong to the Church of England.

Many of the other great offices of modern Britain retain their ancient titles. The Treasury, which attempts without much success to control the economy and public finances of the United Kingdom, takes its name from the box in which the Norman kings carried their treasure while on progress around their kingdom, and kept under their beds while they slept. Its political head is a Member of Parliament called the Chancellor of the Exchequer; and he derives his title from the custom, recorded since the fourteenth century, of having a table covered with a chequered cloth at court, on which the accounts of the royal revenue were kept by means of counters on the squares. The old phrase 'to have a friend at court' no longer implies the advantages it used to have, since control of the Treasury, the law, the army, and the other functions of a state have passed from the Palace to Parliament and Whitehall. But it shows where the power used to be, and where the nomenclature of power still lingers because of British reverence for old forms and old names. Whitehall itself, the street and the official sobriquet for the British Civil Service and government apparatus, was the name of the principal Tudor and Stuart palace beside the Thames at Westminster. It was burnt down in 1698, but Whitehall is evidence that there is life after death in the English constitution, at any rate for names and forms.

The Queen, her court, and courtiers no longer run the country, although the terminology of government might suggest the contrary. But the English Crown has been in business for a very long time: according to the *Anglo-Saxon Chronicle* at least since Cerdic, the first King of the West Saxons, who ruled Wessex from 519 to 534 AD. In the fifteen centuries since Cerdic the monarchy has attracted accretions of tradition and offices and pageantry around itself, like coral, so that its presence, though no longer its influence, penetrates every level of national life. You cannot post a letter, or spend a penny, or go shopping down any high street, without being reminded subliminally that you are doing so in a monarchy. Echoes and intimations of the dead royal past permeate the institutions of the modern socially democratic state, giving harmless pleasure to traditionalists and eccentrics (that is to say, most Britons), and frustrating and bewildering radical iconoclasts, who mistake names for facts.

One of the most mysterious of these ancient survivals of friends at court is the Privy Council. This consists of about three hundred and fifty top people: mostly politicians, fortified by a few judges and other eminent persons; mostly citizens of the United Kingdom, fortified by a few Privy Councillors from the rest of the Commonwealth. Privy Councillors are appointed for life, though they have been known to resign; for example John Profumo did in 1963, after his reputation had been destroyed by a combination of sexual scandal and the British public in one of its periodical fits of morality. And John Stonehouse did in 1976. The Duke of Edinburgh heads the list of notable magnates, which includes Nnamdi Azikiwe, the first President of Nigeria, Sir John Kotelawala, a former Prime Minister of Ceylon before it changed its name to Sri Lanka, the Archbishops, Lord George-Brown, the Duke of Beaufort, Tony Benn, Edward Heath, and others of that sort, if a common factor is discernible. Members of the Cabinet must be Privy Councillors. Accordingly most of the Privy Council are members of former Cabinets who have survived. The longest serving Privy Councillor is Sir Henry Slesser, a retired Lord Justice of Appeal and authoritative writer about law, who was appointed in 1929. The most venerable political Privy Councillor is the Earl of Avon, who became a member in 1934.

The active members of the Privy Council are the Cabinet of the day; and any three of them form a quorum, though the usual number summoned to conduct the formalities of British government is four. The main function of the Privy Council today is to give formal effect to proclamations and Orders in Council, which are issued by the Crown under prerogative or statutory powers. Such instruments are enacted 'by and with the advice of Her Majesty's Privy Council', the dignified and formal part of the machinery. The efficient part of the machine that makes the Crown act is the Prime Minister and his inner party committee of the Privy Council, the Cabinet. And where statutory provision exists, the power to act has, of course, been authorized by Parliament through an Act of Parliament.

In addition to the Cabinet, which originated as an informal committee of the Privy Council, there are other committees of the Privy Council, some standing, some ad hoc. The most important is the Judicial Committee, constituted in 1833 'for the better administration of justice in His Majesty's Privy Council'. This is composed of Privy Councillors who are or have been in high judicial office, usually Law Lords and former judges. It has inherited what survives of the ancient judicial powers of the Privy Council, and hears appeals from parts of the British Commonwealth, ecclesiastical appeals from Church courts, and problems referred to it by the Crown, that is the Government.

Like the other institutions of central government apart from the House of Commons, the Privy Council is descended from the *Curia Regis*, the court of the Norman and Angevin kings, itself probably a descendant of the Anglo-Saxon Witenagemot. In those days it was a heterogeneous feudal assembly, including among its members the great officers of state, officials of the royal household, the chief tenants of the king, judges, lawyers, barons of the Exchequer, a varying number of the nobility both lay and ecclesiastical, and others whom the king summoned to advise him. Most of the routine day-to-day work was done by the officials and favourites of the king; but the king with his Privy or Private Council was the supreme government of the country for all important issues. The question of who was supreme within the Council led to a long series of power struggles for dominance within the Privy Council, culminating in the Wars of the Roses, during which the Council disintegrated. The Tudors revived and reformed it as an instrument of government, and began to separate its executive from its judicial functions. The great constitutional struggle between the Crown and Parliament in the seventeenth century swept away the feudal administrative system and all the other accoutre-

The Queen holds a Privy
Council meeting. By ancient
tradition, perhaps to keep the
meetings short, everyone
stands.

The Queen holds a Privy Council meeting. By ancient tradition, perhaps to keep the meetings short, everyone stands.

ments of royalty. The Privy Council fell into abeyance, but it was never legally abolished. At the Restoration it was revived as a functioning body, and its numerical strength was steadily increased, while concomitantly its powers steadily declined. The Cabinet system gradually evolved and eclipsed the Privy Council as an executive organ; until by the time that the Hanoverians inherited the throne, councillors responsible to the king had been almost completely replaced as an instrument of government by ministers responsible to Parliament.

Nevertheless, with the British habit of retaining old forms to do new jobs, the Privy Council survives as the highest formal institution of government in the land, although it is no longer called upon to advise or to govern, merely to approve formally. The responsible departments of government decide. Parliament, when a vote is appropriate, agrees, or, in increasingly exceptional circumstances, disagrees. 'The Queen's Most Excellent Majesty in Council', as the body is still described in the enchanting medieval jargon, adds the dignified rubber stamp to the process of government.

Because it is an autocratic not a democratic instrument of government, it is a quicker and more efficient way of doing things. And the government retains the mask of the Privy Council for performing prerogative powers, that is the residue of once royal powers that do not flow from parliamentary statute. So war is declared and treaties are concluded by 'the Queen in Council'. The Queen in Council mobilizes the armed forces. The Queen in Council prorogues or dissolves Parliament, and summons Parliament; although behind the dignified façade the Prime Minister in the efficient part of the machine takes the decision when to dissolve Parliament himself, without having to consult his colleagues in the Cabinet.

Other prerogative matters for the Queen in Council, acting as a dignified front for the government, are the official appointment of new ministers and the handing over to them of their seals of office. The Queen in Council even fixes the value of money or lets it float, giving dignified endorsement to the efficient decision of the government.

The only occasions on which the entire Privy Council is summoned and has a right to attend are at an accession council, when a new sovereign takes over, and at a council to which the sovereign announces his or her engagement to be married. The last time that the latter romantic formality took place was in 1839, when Queen Victoria announced her intention to marry Prince Albert of Saxe-Coburg-Gotha. She wrote to him after the ordeal: 'The Council was held at two o'clock; more than a hundred persons were present, and there I had to read the Declaration. It was rather an awful moment, to be obliged to announce this to so many people, many of whom were quite strangers'.

A member of her Privy Council who was present at this rare meeting wrote: 'Her eye was bright and calm, neither bold nor downcast, but firm and soft. There was a blush on her cheek.'

Privy Councillors must be British subjects, and are required to take the special, secret Privy Councillor's oath in addition to the oath of allegiance. Its effect is that the new Privy Councillor undertakes to keep secret all matters that the committee has revealed to him, 'or shall be treated secretly in Council'.

Richard Crossman described the formal ceremony of being made a Privy Councillor with customary acerbity in his indiscreet diaries of life as a Cabinet Minister, eventually published in 1975 after much official grief and litigation. He found the business of kneeling, and kissing hands, and walking backwards dull, pretentious, and silly. By ancient custom the Queen sits at a small round table, while all Privy Councillors remain standing in front of her during a Privy Council. On a handful of rare occasions Privy Councils have been held outside Great Britain. George V held the first in Delhi in 1911. The Queen has held a few: in New Zealand, Australia, Canada, and Colombo, the first and last meeting of the Privy Council of the United Kingdom ever held in Ceylon.

Old and obscure custom entitles a Privy Councillor to the august prefix 'The Right Honourable' before his name, and the intials 'PC' after it, just like a police constable. In Parliament it has long been the custom to give priority to Privy Councillors who want to speak in a debate. Although the Speaker has ruled that they have no automatic right to catch his eye before other Members, they somehow usually manage to do so.

The Privy Council of the Norman kings, and the executive departments of government descended from offices of state a

RIGHT   *The Queen receiving a brooch from Captain-General of the Royal Company of Archers in the grounds of Holyroodhouse and* LEFT *Princess Anne and Lord Home of The Hirsel at the tercentary celebrations of October 1976.*

millennium old, are the most notable monarchical survivals and exemplars of the British passion for combining practical change with nominal continuity. Some logical foreigners find this double-think hypocritical. As C. E. M. Joad defined it, hypocrisy combines the smooth appearance of virtue with the solid satisfaction of vice.

But other accretions almost as remarkable have attached themselves to the monarchy over the centuries, and survive, and flourish, to amaze the rest of the world and gratify the sense of heritage of the British. They range from the keeper of the royal racing pigeons, who lives in a semi-detached council house in Norwich, to the Royal Company of Archers, a large number of elderly Scottish noblemen and gentlemen who dress in Border green uniforms and black Kilmarnock bonnets with eagles' feathers stuck in them, carry bows and arrows, and act as the Queen's ceremonial bodyguard when she is in Scotland. Fortunately any practical bodyguarding is done by the Queen's detective and the special branch. The Royal Company of Archers, which is said to have originated in the fifteenth century, is a private archery club as well as the Queen's bodyguard in Scotland. At present it has a membership of just under four hundred. Members buy their own picturesque costumes and bows and arrows, and maintain them.

Another pleasant oddity of the court is the Keeper of the Royal Philatelic Collection. This is a part-time appointment. The Keeper does not trade or swop stamps for the Queen, but is the custodian of the collection accumulated by her grandfather and father.

By far the most influential member of the court that serves the Queen is also one of the least conspicuous, her Private Secretary. By the nature of his work the Queen's chief officer, personal adviser, and official contact with the government, the Commonwealth, and the world at large must be a person of almost superhuman discretion and judgment. He must also be able to get on with all sorts and conditions of men at all levels. Professor Harold Laski, a man above suspicion of courtierly tendencies, once defined the qualities needed by the Private Secretary: 'He is the confidant of all ministers, but he must never leave the impression that he is anybody's man. He must intrude without seeming to intrude. He must be able to carry the burden of the sovereign's mistakes. The royal secretary walks on a tight-rope below which he is never unaware that an abyss is yawning. I do not think it is beyond the mark to say that a bad Private Secretary, one who was rash, or indiscreet, or untrustworthy, might easily make the system of constitutional monarchy unworkable unless the monarch himself was a person of extraordinary wisdom.'

The monarchy and the country have been well served by a remarkable series of Private Secretaries over the past century since the position was formalized. From those eminent Victorians and Edwardians, Colonel Henry Ponsonby, Lord Stamfordham, and Lord Knollys, the succession of personal advisers almost invisible behind the throne have done much to save the monarchy, by helping it to adjust to the realities of the modern world, while preserving as much as was useful and possible of the royal prerogative.

The Private Secretary, like so many other pillars of the constitution, is descended from the medieval Privy Council, in which Lords of the Council assisted by clerks and secretaries advised the monarch. Secretaries of State emerged during the reign of Elizabeth I. By the time that the Hanoverians succeeded to the throne, executive power had passed from the Privy Council to its inner committee, the emergent Cabinet. It had until then been customary for the monarch to attend meetings of his Council. But George I and George II often absented themselves and left the government of England to their First Ministers: they were often in Hanover, spoke little English, and did not understand English politics. It became constitutional doctrine that the Secretary of State for the Home Department was also the King's Private Secretary; and that it was undesirable and dangerous for anybody who was not a Privy Councillor to have access to Cabinet secrets.

George III was the first king to break this tradition by appointing a Private Secretary from outside Parliament and the Privy Council: Lieutenant General Sir Herbert Taylor. The appointment was unprecedented but essential, since the King was rapidly losing

The royal procession at the state opening of Parliament, in which the Duke of Norfolk (Earl Marshal) and the Marquess of Cholmondeley (Lord Great Chamberlain) walk backwards.

not only his sight but his sanity. After the final onset of permanent insanity in 1810, a Regency was established, and the Prince Regent sought to appoint a Colonel McMahon as his Private Secretary. There was uproar in Parliament about the irregularity of the appointment, as there tended to be about many of the activities of the Prince Regent. One Member declared that the office of Private Secretary was 'dangerous and unconstitutional, rendering the person holding it the secret adviser of the sovereign, with a degree of influence over his mind totally at variance with the forms of government in England. The office would be destructive of a fundamental principle of the constitution, which was that no one ought to use the name of the sovereign, give him advice, or be the bearer of his commands, unless he be one of the responsible ministers of the Crown, and answerable to Parliament.' Nevertheless the House voted for the appointment.

William IV recalled Sir Herbert Taylor from retirement to be his Private Secretary. And Victoria shortly after her accession consulted Sir Herbert about the appointment of a Private Secretary. He asked her: 'Is Your Majesty afraid of the work?' She replied: 'No.' 'Then don't have a Private Secretary', said Sir Herbert. She took his advice, with first Lord Melbourne, and then Prince Albert and Baron Stockmar performing many of the duties of the Private Secretary. But when the Prince Consort died, Victoria found that she could not cope with the volume of business on her own, and appointed General Charles Grey as the first of the line of fully developed modern Private Secretaries. The line stretches unbroken from him through a succession of quiet men of great influence and excellence to the present Private Secretary, Sir Martin Charteris. Sir Martin was born in 1913, a grandson of the eleventh Earl of Wemyss, and married the daughter of Lord Margesson, a former Conservative Chief Whip, and Secretary of State for War in Churchill's wartime coalition Government. He was educated at Eton and the Royal Military College, Sandhurst, and served as an infantry officer in the last war, coming out of it as a Lieutenant-Colonel. In 1950 the then Princess Elizabeth appointed him her Private Secretary. And when she succeeded to the throne two years later, he followed her to Buckingham Palace as Assistant Private Secretary.

He writes most of her speeches, a job of great delicacy and ingenuity, since the official words of the monarch are subjected to minute textual analysis worthy of an ancient manuscript. She must never be allowed to deviate from the policy of her ministers, or unnecessarily offend the susceptibilities of her subjects. Sir Martin is an amateur sculptor, a wildfowler, and a man of great charm, cultivation, and unobtrusiveness, exemplifying the essential qualities of the Private Secretary. He has a nice sense of humour,

The throne in the robing room at the Palace of Westminster.

which sometimes can be allowed to show itself briefly in the Queen's speeches. When she made a joke about George Washington in Boston on her visit in the summer of 1976, Sir Martin was observed laughing heartily and clapping with engaging lack of modesty at a joke he had written himself.

His immediate predecessor, created Lord Adeane in 1972, was another model of a modern Private Secretary: grandson of the great Lord Stamfordham, the Private Secretary of Victoria and George V; Eton; a first in history at Cambridge; a professional soldier; shooting, fishing, and other country recreations; courtier of modern courtiers. He composed the masterly memorandum to the 1971 Select Committee on the Civil List, which defines more succinctly and eloquently than any other authority the life and functions of a modern monarch, and, incidentally, demonstrates the intellectual qualities of analysis and expression needed by a modern Private Secretary.

Lord Adeane's predecessor, Sir Alan Lascelles, served three monarchs, Edward VIII, George VI, and the Queen, and is still a flourishing example of the diplomacy, quick-wittedness, and discreet sense of humour that characterize the Private Secretary. Sir Alan once defined the job: 'It is not by any means beer and skittles. The Private Secretary's work, both in volume and responsibility, is continually increasing. In my office at present we compare unfavourably with our relative opposite numbers in the Civil Service, as regards man-hours per day, as regards pay, and as regards leave. We serve, I may remind you, one of the very few men in this world who never gets a holiday at all and who, unlike the rest of us, can look forward to no period of retirement at the end of his service, for his service never ends.' The royal film showed that the Queen summons her Private Secretary, although a fully invested Knight Grand Cross of the Order of the Bath and in spite of his eminence in the hierarchy, by ringing for him on a bell as for any other flunkey.

An Act of Henry VIII of 1539 listed 'the great officers of the realm' in order of precedence. The offices all survive, though their functions have either been subjected to parliamentary control, or have atrophied to dignified skeletons. They are: the Lord Chancellor; the Lord President of the Council; the Lord Privy Seal; the Lord Great Chamberlain; the Lord High Constable; the Earl Marshal; the Lord Steward of the Household; the Lord Chamberlain; and the Master of the Horse.

The Lord Chancellor has become the member of the Cabinet who is head of the judiciary and president of the House of Lords.

The Lord President of the Council is in charge of the Privy Council office. These departmental duties are formal and slight.

The Lord Chancellor, Lord Elwyn-Jones.

Accordingly, like holders of other non-departmental offices, he is a useful freelance and senior member of the Cabinet, whom the Prime Minister can entrust with some special or ad hoc task. The custom has recently grown up that he should also be Leader of the House of Commons.

The Lord Privy Seal once did what his title says, and looked after the private seal of the early kings of England, which was the particular instrument of the royal prerogative. A Keeper of the Privy Seal is recorded in the archives from 1275. In 1311 he became a Minister of State on the same footing as the Chancellor and the Treasurer, though of somewhat lower dignity. The use of the Privy Seal was abolished in 1884. The Lord Privy Seal is another impressive old title for an auxiliary member of the Cabinet, who may be in either House, and can be put in charge of matters of special urgency or political importance.

The Lord Great Chamberlain, who is not to be confused with the Lord Chamberlain, used to have jurisdiction over and management of all the royal palaces. The first known holder of this great office of the realm was Alberic de Vere, appointed by Henry II in 1133. The office is hereditary, and unlike the office of Earl Marshal, which is only transmissible through the male line, it can be passed through the female line in default of male heirs. This has produced genealogical tangles of marvellous intricacy, and frequent disputes about the right to the office. The Committee of Privileges of the House of Lords finally resolved the matter in 1901 with a suitably convoluted compromise. This was that the family of Cholmondeley (pronounced 'rumly' and indeed extraordinarily for foreigners) was entitled to the office in alternate reigns. In every other reign, when a Cholmondeley was not Lord Great Chamberlain, the office was to alternate between the Earl of Ancaster and the Marquess of Lincolnshire. The Marquess of Lincolnshire was also the third Baron Carrington. The Lincolnshire title became extinct in 1928, and the share of duty has devolved on Lord Carrington.

Thus, under George VI, the Earl of Ancaster was Lord Great Chamberlain. Under the present Queen the office has been held by the Marquess of Cholmondeley, who succeeded his father 'Roc' (from his earldom of Rocksavage) in the office in 1966 and the title, on his death, in 1968. When Prince Charles succeeds it will be the turn of whoever is then Lord Carrington.

Although the dignity of the Lord Great Chamberlain is great, the duties today are light. Until 1965 he was the nominal chief authority in the Palace of Westminster, and exercised a complete authority there when the Houses were not sitting. In that year the Queen agreed that, although the Palace of Westminster should remain royal, control and occupation should be vested in the Lord Chancellor for the House of Lords, and the Speaker for the House of Commons. The Lord Great Chamberlain retains responsibility for the robing room, staircase, anteroom, and royal gallery. When the Queen opens Parliament, he adds a touch of suspense to the occasion by walking precariously backwards in front of her in the procession, and selects the peer who carries the Sword of State. He has ceremonial duties at the introduction of new peers into the House of Lords, at the homage of bishops after their consecration, at coronations, and at the funeral of a sovereign. The present Lord Great Chamberlain is George Hugh Cholmondeley, sixth Marquess of Cholmondeley, Eton, Cambridge, an officer in the Royal Dragoons in the last war, during which he was awarded the Military Cross. He lives in Cholmondeley Castle, the family seat in Cheshire.

The Lord High Constable used to be the commander-in-chief of the Army in the absence of his monarch, and the supreme judge of questions of chivalry. The office was forfeited in 1521, and is virtually extinct. The title though not its functions is periodically revived for particular occasions, especially coronations. The powers are now so potentially dictatorial that the appointment lasts for just one day. At the last coronation Field Marshal Viscount Alanbrooke was appointed Lord High Constable. The position is quite onerous in that its holder has to ride on a horse close to the royal carriage.

The Earl Marshal used to be the deputy of the Constable in the medieval army of England. The first Earl Marshal was appointed in 1385; before that the officer was simply known as the Marshal. His office has survived the erosion of the centuries better than that of his commander-in-chief. The Earl Marshal has become the ring-master of state ceremonial, who organizes and carries out some of the most ancient and splendid ceremonies in the world: the coronation, the state opening of Parliament, and other state ceremonials. His duties include responsibility for the Ascot office in St James's Palace, which decides who can be allowed into the royal enclosure at Ascot racecourse, and what they shall be permitted to wear. In recent years he has become more liberal about the dress he allows inside but not much more liberal.

He is also head of the College of Arms, the ancient college of English heralds, whose titles and functions date from the Middle Ages. The days of chivalry may be dead, but the interest in arms and pedigrees is alive and well. Garter King of Arms and his subordinate heralds, with their ancient titles ringing with echoes of the Wars of the Roses (Bluemantle, Portcullis, Rouge Croix, Rouge Dragon Pursuivant) research arms and genealogies. The Queen delegates to the Kings of Arms – Garter, Clarenceux, and Norroy – the right of granting arms, subject to the approval of the Earl Marshal. There is a continual search for arms, both by those who wish to discover whether they have a hereditary right to armorial bearings, and by new knights and life peers and corporate bodies who apply for arms. Under the Earl Marshal the heralds, in their medieval tabards looking like a royal flush in a game of poker, organize the state ceremonials, which are the glory of the tourist industry.

The office of Earl Marshal is hereditary in the Howard family who are the Dukes of Norfolk, the premier dukes and the leading Roman Catholic laymen of England. There is a nice tolerance and irony in the tradition that puts a Roman Catholic in charge of organizing one of the most solemn rituals of the Church of England, the coronation of a sovereign.

The late Duke of Norfolk, Earl Marshal of England, leads the procession at the state funeral of Sir Winston Churchill.

The present Duke of Norfolk and Earl Marshal was born Miles Fitzalan-Howard, and after Ampleforth and Christ Church, Oxford, became a professional soldier, and rose to the rank of Major-General. He was at one time Director of Service Intelligence at the Ministry of Defence, and head of the British military mission to Russian forces in Germany. He retired after thirty years in the Army in 1967, and went into the City, as a director of a merchant bank. Then in 1975 his cousin, the old Duke of Norfolk, Bernard Marmaduke Fitzalan-Howard died without leaving a son; and the mantle of Earl Marshal of England fell on the present Duke. His predecessor, a martinet and perfectionist of ceremonial, organized among much else: the funeral of George V; the proclamation of Edward VIII; the proclamations and the coronations of George VI and the present Queen; the funerals of George VI, Queen Mary, and Sir Winston Churchill; and the investiture of the Prince of Wales. At the first of his state ceremonies he was only twenty-seven. With his red, reptilian face, heavy pouches under his eyes, and massive competence and belief in ceremony, he became a reassuring national totem at state occasions. His successor inherits the title of Earl Marshal; his fee of £20 a year, fixed at that sum in perpetuity by Richard III in 1483; and the obligation of carrying a staff with the royal arms in gold at one end, and the arms of the Duke of Norfolk at the other.

The office of Lord Steward of the Household dates from at least the twelfth century. It is of great dignity and antiquity, but of little practical business these days. Technically and traditionally the Lord Steward is in charge of the staff who run Buckingham Palace and the other royal palaces. In practice this job is now done by the Master of the Household. The Lord Steward takes over the formal arrangements for state banquets and other ceremonial occasions. The office is not hereditary. The holder of the office since 1973 has been the tenth Duke of Northumberland, a great landowner at Alnwick Castle and Syon House, agricultural expert, and lover of horses and country matters.

Nominally under the Lord Steward, but in practice the man who runs the domestic arrangements of the palaces is the Master of the Household. Since 1973 he has been Vice-Admiral Sir Peter Ashmore, a retired naval officer who served with distinction in destroyers in the last war, and subsequently rose through staff jobs to become the Chief of Allied Staff at Nato naval headquarters. His department has the medieval title of the Board of the Green Cloth, and he employs staff with titles almost as antique, such as yeomen of the wine cellars, pages of the back stairs, pages of the presence, the royal pastry chef, and the palace steward.

His responsibilities include the interior and domestic arrangements at Buckingham Palace, Windsor Castle, and the Palace of Holyroodhouse; domestic arrangements for Sandringham House and Balmoral Castle; royal and staff kitchens; catering and entertainments on the royal yacht; state banquets; the garden of Buckingham Palace; the court post office; the Palace police; royal standards; security passes; wines, plate, china, and glass. The Master of the Household is also responsible for liaison with the local depots of the Department of the Environment in the royal palaces; the purchase of food and most other supplies for the royal household; and travel arrangements for the court and individual members of the household, officials, and staff on official journeys by rail and air.

The Lord Chamberlain, who is not to be confused, if possible, with the Lord Great Chamberlain, is the senior officer of the royal household, and has overall responsibility. In practice such different departments as those of the Private Secretary, the Keeper of the Privy Purse, the Master of the Household, and the Crown Equerry, are largely autonomous. But the Lord Chamberlain is the official head of the household, and handles an extraordinary multitude of duties that do not fall into anybody else's department. Before censorship of the theatre was abandoned in 1968, the Lord Chamberlain was the official responsible for censoring, cutting, and if necessary banning stage plays. These ancient powers were first given to the Lord Chamberlain by Charles II of all monarchs, under whom the theatre was the bawdiest in history. They were invidious and controversial, and frequently got their holders into stormy water before they were abrogated. The last play to be banned by the Lord Chamberlain was *Hair*.

Ceremonial is one of the main responsibilities of the Lord Chamberlain, who arranges such matters as state visits, royal weddings, christenings, and funerals, garden parties, the flying of flags, and the multitude of other ceremonial activities of royalty. He and the Private Secretary are in charge of the rich royal library and archive at Windsor, but they delegate professional responsibility to eminent historians. The Lord Chamberlain has overall responsibility for the Queen's medical household of fourteen surgeons, physicians, and apothecaries, and her ecclesiastical household of thirty-six chaplains.

Under the Lord Chamberlain also parade the Gentlemen-at-Arms and the Yeomen of the Guard, the ceremonial royal bodyguards, the Gentlemen Ushers, and the Gentleman Usher to the Sword of State and the Gentleman Usher of the Black Rod.

The Gentleman Usher of the Black Rod, Admiral Sir Frank Twiss.

The latter is the chief parliamentary officer of the House of Lords, custodian of the House, and officer in charge of its administration. The appointment dates from the reign of Henry VIII, and was constituted to be the chief of all the ushers of the kingdom, and to have care and custody of all the doors of the High Court called Parliament. The ancient decree establishing the office lays down that it must be held by 'a gentleman famous in arms and in blood'. Today this condition is met by appointing distinguished retired naval, military, and air force officers to the post in succession. The present incumbent since 1970 is Admiral Sir Frank Twiss, who was Second Sea Lord and Chief of Naval Personnel when he retired. His title is derived from the ebony rod of office surmounted by a golden lion rampant that he carries in his right hand. He is the official who goes from the Lords to summon the House of Commons to such occasions as the opening and proroguing of Parliament, and the giving of the Royal Assent to Bills. By custom dating from the constitutional storms of English history, the Commons, in order to demonstrate their autonomy, bar their doors against the royal messenger until he has rapped three times with his black rod, in which a sovereign is embedded. Black Rod degrades Knights of the Garter on the Queen's orders by tapping them with his eponymous rod of office. It is several centuries, unfortunately, since he was called on to perform this interesting act.

The Lord Chamberlain is responsible for all appointments to the Queen's household, including those of the Lords and Grooms in waiting. The only exceptions are three members of the Government party in the House of Lords, and three in the House of Commons, who have ancient titles of courtiers, but have become political appointments with political functions, usually as Whips. The Treasurer of the Household is the dignified old title for the Deputy Chief Government Whip. The Comptroller of the Household is another Government Whip; and so is the Vice-Chamberlain. The jobs were created to give the politicians access to the court. The Vice-Chamberlain has the residual courtierly duty of writing in longhand a daily personal report for the Queen about what has been taking place in Parliament. His report is delivered to the Queen before dinner wherever she is in Britain, a punctuality that rather loses its point because the main votes in Parliament are usually taken after dinner. If she is at Buckingham Palace, it is taken to her by dispatch rider. If she is at Windsor, Balmoral, Sandringham, or elsewhere, it is telegraphed direct from the post office in the House of Commons. This personal account of the day's proceedings in the House of Commons used to be the job of the Leader of the House; but Stanley Baldwin delegated it to the Vice-Chamberlain.

The Lord Chamberlain's office also includes the Central Chancery of the Orders of Knighthood, the headquarters and registry of the honours system. This office prepares the formal announcement of the honours lists, and arranges for recipients of honours and awards to attend investitures at Buckingham Palace, and for the dispatch of insignia and medals.

With the Department of the Environment, the Lord Chamberlain is responsible for the royal palaces, and maintains the state apartments and the state collections of paintings, furniture, and other works of art. He is also the official custodian of the regalia and crown jewels, an onerous responsibility that he delegates to the Keeper of the Jewel House at the Tower of London, who is at present Major-General William Raeburn, another old soldier.

Under the Lord Chamberlain come such famous and delightful royal appointments as: the Poet Laureate, who is at present Sir John Betjeman, the whimsical singer of suburban bliss and the vanishing delights of Victorian architecture; and the Master of the Queen's Music, who since 1975 has been Malcolm Williamson, born in Australia, pianist, organist, and composer of operas and film scores. The Poet Laureate gets a small salary from the Civil List, which has remained unchanged since Ben Jonson was Poet Laureate from 1619–37, and received such a stipend from James I. Charles I later awarded him in addition an annual terce (42 gallons) of Canary wine. These modest but poetic emoluments continued unchanged until in 1800, when Henry James Pye was Poet Laureate and a constant butt of contemporary ridicule, the terce of wine was commuted to a sum of £27 a year, which remains the going rate.

The Lord Chamberlain is also responsible for the Queen's Bargemaster, Mr H. A. Barry, in case she wants to go boating on the Thames, which was the favourite form of transport of her predecessors four centuries ago; and for the Keeper of the Swans, who is Mr F. J. Turk. Sadly the Queen seldom travels by royal barge. But her Bargemaster and four Watermen accompany her coach when she drives from Buckingham Palace to Westminster to open Parliament, and attend her at functions connected with the London river. Swans are still considered royal birds, on the doubtful grounds that Richard I introduced them to England from Cyprus. Mr Turk's appointment is not a full-time one: he is in business on the river as a boat builder and boat hirer. His duty as Keeper of the Swans is to look after the welfare of the swans on the Thames, and he finds more to do than he should in these days of increasing vandalism. Every July Mr Turk performs the ceremony of swan-upping. This strange custom consists of rounding up all the new season's cygnets on the Thames between London Bridge and Henley, marking those that belong to the Dyers and the Vintners, two of the City livery companies, and counting the

Swan-upping at Kingston-upon-Thames.

several hundred that still belong to the Queen, but leaving their beaks unmarked. The first man to sight a brood of swans shouts 'All-up'. The Keeper of the Swans receives a small honorarium and expenses, and royal prestige. The object was originally to prevent poaching; now it is useful for conservation and recording swans.

The Lord Chamberlain, that man of many and curious parts, is responsible for everything from the state invitation office to the curator of the royal print room. He issues the royal warrants to shops and commercial firms, as a prized royal cachet that royalty shops there, or has shopped there in the past. The criterion for getting the useful advertisement of being able to display the royal coat of arms and boast that royalty are among the customers is at least three consecutive years of 'substantial service to the Sovereign'. There are well over a thousand such warrants extant today, going back as far as George V, and ranging from purveyors of rifles and Highland dress to manufacturers of cornflakes, shoe polish, dog food, and lavatory paper. The warrant of royal appointment to the Queen or one of her immediate family is a jealously guarded advertisement; and anyone who uses it too ostentatiously or vulgarly as an advertisement does not keep the warrant for long. About twenty new warrants are issued each year. There are occasional criticisms that the custom is individious or snobbish. But it is usually justified as being of great commercial value to the export and tourist trades.

The *Court Circular*, the stiff daily record of the official activities of the Queen and the royal family published in the newspapers, is another ultimate responsibility of the Lord Chamberlain's department. It is a marvellous exercise of nice courtierly discrimination over titles and tittles, discernible only by the expert. Thus official members of the royal family are dignified with a capital T to their precedent definite articles, as: Queen Elizabeth The Queen Mother. Others get no capital, as: the Duchess of Windsor. The *Court Circular* style for married couples is: The Princess Margaret, Countess of Snowdon, and the Earl of Snowdon. However, since the last two separated, the punctilious *Court Circular* has deleted the 'and'. It is The Prince Andrew, because he is the son of a sovereign; but plain Prince Michael of Kent, because he is only a grandson of George V. Similar subtle punctiliousness is shown in the degree of grief that the *Court Circular* attributes to the Queen when there is a death in the family. If the deceased is the child or has married the child of A (with a capital A, as no doubt the *Court Circular* would have it) Sovereign, the Queen is said to have 'received' or 'learned' the news with 'great' regret. If the deceased is only a grandchild or other more distant relation of A Sovereign, the Queen receives the news with plain regret. When her mother-in-law, Her Royal Highness Princess Andrew of Greece, died in December 1969, the Queen was reported to have 'heard' the news with great regret, indicating to the *cognoscenti* that Princess Andrew had died upstairs at Buckingham Palace, enabling the Queen to hear rather than learn or receive the news.

According to the College of Arms the *Court Circular* is in error in putting the definite article before courtesy titles, as in the Lady Susan Hussey and the Hon. Angus Ogilvy. As they are courtesy titles, the correct style is Hon. Angus Ogilvy. A full grammar of the *Court Circular* would take more space than it would be worth. But when it states that 'The Queen has arrived at Windsor Castle', it means that the Queen and court have moved into official residence there for a time. It no longer breathlessly records her visits to polo matches and other minor social and recreational events, as it did of Queen Victoria.

The Lord Chamberlain has his multifarious offices in St James's Palace. The post is not hereditary. It has been held since 1971 by

Lord Maclean, a life peer, and a Scottish baronet and landowner, whose home is on the Isle of Mull. He was Chief Scout of the United Kingdom and the Commonwealth for many years, and, when he can escape from his office, he has outdoor interests in such appropriate things as Highland cattle and the Argyll and Sutherland Highlanders.

His chief executive and assistant is called the Comptroller of the Lord Chamberlain's Office. Since 1964 the Comptroller has been Lieutenant-Colonel Sir Eric Penn, a retired Grenadier Guardsman.

The Master of the Queen's Horse since 1936 has been the Duke of Beaufort, the grandest horseman and most ardent foxhunter in the kingdom. Everybody calls him Master, not as Master of the Horse, but as Master of his own famous pack of foxhounds, the Beaufort. He is a close personal friend of the Queen's, and she often stays at his stately home of Badminton. The ancient duties of the Master of the Horse include being responsible for the Queen's safety whenever she is mounted on a horse or in a carriage. This means that he rides as close to her as protocol allows. At the Queen's birthday parade, he rides in the group immediately behind her. When the Queen opens Parliament, the Master of the Horse must ride in the next carriage. Queen Victoria was not married when she was crowned; so her Master of the Horse rode with her and the Mistress of the Robes in the state coach.

The Master of the Horse as titular head has overall responsibility for the royal stables in the royal mews at the back of Buckingham Palace. He inspects them periodically, and is consulted about the purchase of new horses. It is a part-time and unpaid position.

But the day-to-day running of the royal mews department is done by an official called the Crown Equerry, assisted by equerries, a royal veterinary surgeon, a comptroller of stores, and other horsy officials. The Crown Equerry is the Queen's transport officer, and responsible for all the Queen's travelling arrangements, except when she flies. He is in charge of the royal coaches, horses, and cars, buys new ones when they are needed, and sees that the right transport is ready at the right place at the right time. This is a complicated and important job, because royalty has so many appointments, and punctuality is the politeness of queens. The present Crown Equerry is Lieutenant-Colonel Sir John Miller, who can be spotted opening carriage doors at Ascot, and generally making himself useful when the royal caravan is in progress.

Horses are still part of the English way of life, particularly the English royal way of life. But hawks, once the sport of kings, have declined to a minority hobby. There is still, however, a hereditary Grand Falconer of England. The holder used to be responsible for the royal mews at Charing Cross, where the royal hawks were formerly mewed. His privileges used to include the right, shared by the monarch, to drive down Birdcage Walk, the road along the west side of St James's Park, where the Stuart kings kept their exotic birds. The road was opened to the public in 1828, and today the traffic howls down it to Westminster.

The hereditary Grand Falconer of England is the Duke of St Albans, descendant of Charles II's illegitimate son by Nell Gwyn. The present thirteenth Duke of St Albans is a professional man without a ducal estate or a stately home. He had a distinguished career in military intelligence and psychological warfare during the last war, and at the Central Office of Information after the war. He lives in a leasehold house called St Albans in Chelsea, and never goes near a hawk except by accident.

The Keeper of the Privy Purse and Treasurer to the Queen runs the royal finances from his office in Buckingham Palace. Since 1971 this post has been held by Major Sir Rennie Maudslay, a retired soldier, businessman, and member of Lloyd's, who was assistant keeper of the Queen's finances from 1958. He deals with both personal payments from the Queen's private resources, and the salaries and wages of her officers and servants. He administers the Civil List grant for the pay and expenses of the household.

Eighty-eight-year-old Mrs Julia Talbot: a delighted recipient of the Royal Maundy.

OPPOSITE   *The Queen with the former Dean of Westminster, the Very Rev. Eric Abbott, arriving to distribute the Royal Maundy at Westminster Abbey.*

The Royal Almonry, which administers the Queen's gifts to charities, is an ancient division of the department of the Keeper of the Privy Purse and Treasurer to the Queen. There is a High Almoner, at present the Bishop of Rochester, the Right Reverend Richard Say; and a hereditary Grand Almoner, the Marquess of Exeter. The Almonry organizes the Queen's ancient and modern alms and bounties, of which the most famous and curious is Maundy money.

Each year on Maundy Thursday, the Thursday of holy week, the Queen distributes purses of money to as many poor elderly men and as many poor elderly woman as she is years old. The custom was originally an imitation of Jesus washing the feet of his disciples, and is intended as a symbol of humility. The name Maundy is from the Latin *mandatum*, commandment, in the gospel according to St John, chapter thirteen: '*Mandatum novum do vobis*', a new commandment I give to you. These are the first words of the first antiphon at the ceremony of the *pedilavium* or foot-washing.

The kings and queens of England have been practising it since at least the twelfth century, and there are continuous records of the ceremony from the reign of Edward I. Until the eighteenth century the monarch used to wash the feet of the old people, before giving them their bounty of cloth, food, and money. A series of

increasingly important courtiers used to wash the feet several times first, before the monarch came along to give a final symbolic dab of scented water. George II dropped the foot-washing.

As a remembrance of the days when feet were washed the Lord High Almoner and his assistants still wear linen towels tucked around their waists, and carry nosegays of sweet herbs, which were first used during the Plague. Each of the old men and women receives two purses, one in lieu of the original gift of cloth, the other containing the specially minted Maundy coins in silver pennies, twopences, threepences, and fourpences, adding up to as many pennies as the Queen is years old, and much sought after by dealers and collectors.

There are a number of other traditional alms given by the monarch, in addition to gifts to modern charities. An ancient and little known one is the custom for the monarch to present gold, frankincense, and myrrh on Epiphany, January 6, in commemoration of the gifts of Jesus to the Magi. George III was the last monarch to do this in person. Today the Lord Chamberlain or his deputies represents the Queen at a special service at the chapel royal in St James's Palace, and deposits in the alms dish three purses containing £30 for distribution to the poor of the parish.

The Mistress of the Robes is the senior lady in the Queen's household, and usually a duchess. The Duchess of Grafton has been Mistress of the Robes since 1967. It used to be a political appointment, of great influence when a queen was on the throne, because of the daily access it affords to the monarch. In her heyday Sarah Jennings, the great first Duchess of Marlborough, held the double job of Mistress of the Robes and Groom of the Stole, and twisted Queen Anne around her little finger. The job is no longer a political appointment, and the work is not full-time. The Mistress of the Robes arranges the roster for the ladies-in-waiting, and attends and accompanies the Queen on the grandest state occasions, and sometimes on state visits abroad.

Under her come two Ladies of the Bedchamber, usually the wives of earls, who attend the Queen on major public occasions, but not on the regular routine of royal engagements. They sometimes accompany the Queen on visits abroad. At present they are the Marchioness of Abergavenny and the Countess of Airlie, an American. There is an extra Lady of the Bedchamber, who attends upon the Queen less frequently.

Under them in the hierarchy of the court come the Women of the Bedchamber, chaperones and personal assistants of the Queen. There are four of these, who take it in turns for a fortnight at a time to attend the Queen on all public and semi-private engagements. They also deal with some of the Queen's private correspondence, for example replying to the thousands of letters she receives from children, and do other secretarial and administrative jobs. There are three extra Women of the Bedchamber for occasional duties and holiday relief. All these are appointed by the Queen herself. Women of the Bedchamber need not be titled, and half of the present ones are not.

There are two Permanent Lords-in-Waiting, and seven Lords-in-Waiting, five of whom are Government Whips in the House of Lords. The Lords-in-Waiting attend on the Queen at official functions, and represent her on such occasions as meeting important people arriving or departing from the United Kingdom, and at memorial services.

In addition there are more than two hundred Gentlemen Ushers, Aides-de-Camp, Equerries, Extra Gentlemen Ushers, and Extra Equerries. These are part-time, honorary, and unpaid positions, and their holders only turn out for duty on major official or ceremonial occasions, for example, garden parties, diplomatic receptions, and investitures. In his memorandum to the 1971 Select Committee on the Civil List, Sir Rennie Maudslay remarked on the subject of these courtiers: 'The part-time and unpaid appointments are an extremely important section of the royal household,

The ampulla, used at coronations since the fourteenth century; and the annointing spoon, used since the twelfth century.

and the loyal and devoted service given by the holders of these appointments is out of all proportion to the small cost involved'. In reply to Willie Hamilton, who had suggested that so many Lords-in-Waiting, Extra Gentlemen Ushers, and so on, were unnecessary, the Queen's press secretary replied; 'In order to organize the garden parties properly quite a lot of people are needed, and the numbers of Gentlemen Ushers and so on are not excessive'.

Other ancient offices with romantic or odd titles proliferate around the Queen. A woman was appointed Captain of the Honourable Corps of Gentlemen at Arms for the first time after Labour won the general elections of 1974, Baroness Llewelyn-Davies of Hastoe, a life peeress and the wife of the architect and town planner, Baron Llewelyn-Davies, also a life peer. Her sex caused no difficulties with antique military duties, since what the title means today is Government Chief Whip in the House of Lords. But a more feminine uniform of a special badge had to be designed for the Captain to replace the scarlet coat, blue trousers, and gilt metal helmet with white swan feathers sported by her Gentlemen. She still salutes, however. The Gentlemen at Arms also have a Clerk of the Cheque, who would be called an adjutant by a less honorific formation.

Then there are two functionaries called Gold Sticks, alias Field Marshal Sir Gerald Templer and the ubiquitous Admiral of the Fleet, the Earl Mountbatten of Burma. These are the Queen's ceremonial personal bodyguards, though any serious bodyguarding is done by younger, less conspicuous men of the special branch. The order instituting the office of Gold Stick in 1528 decreed 'that he should wait next to His Majesty's person before all others', as he was responsible for the sovereign's personal security. Charles II decreed that the position of Gold Stick should be held by the Colonel of his Life Guard. As a consequence since then the Gold Sticks in England have been the Colonels of the two Household Cavalry Regiments, the Life Guards and the Blues and Royals. In Scotland the post of Gold Stick is held *ex officio* by the Captain General of the Royal Company of Archers. The name Gold Stick is derived, for once straightforwardly, from the stick topped with gold that is carried as a symbol of office.

These are the upper circles of the hierarchies that surround and support the Queen. The lower and outer circles spread in ripples throughout many activities of the nation from the postage to the coinage. The latter is tested annually at the Trial of the Pyx, or treasure chest, a royal ceremony that originated in Saxon times to ensure that the king's coinage was not adulterated or clipped. In

St Edward's Crown, used for the crowning at a coronation, and worn by the sovereign only at the coronation

those early days the Lord Chancellor, the Lord Treasurer, and other Lords of the Council presided at the trial. Today the Queen's Remembrancer and Senior Master of the Supreme Court presides over a jury of goldsmiths in Goldsmiths' Hall to make sure that the coins issued by the Royal Mint in the previous year are of correct size and weight, and are made from metals of the appropriate standard required by law. There is no test or assay yet devised that can ensure that the value of the coinage is not eroded by inflation.

The most notable furnishings of the monarchy are the royal palaces, which lie thick upon the land as working offices, or ancient monuments, or vanished memories. Buckingham Palace is the home and headquarters of the monarchy, from which the royal family conducts its business. It is a working palace with six hundred rooms, a mile and a half of corridors, and a staff of about two hundred. It is also the cynosure of all tourists to London, and the tribal meeting ground for the natives on such a great national occasions as the ending of a war.

It is built on the site of the Mulberry Garden, a disreputable seventeenth-century pleasure garden for refreshment, entertainment, and other pleasures of the night. The last of a series of mansions built in the Mulberry Garden was Buckingham House, the magnificent town house of the Duke of Buckingham and Normanby, a minor poet and zealous Jacobite. George III acquired it as the private family home for himself and Queen Charlotte and their large family. The Prince Regent had it internally rebuilt within the old carapace by John Nash to make a palace fit for the British monarchy and himself. Victoria added a new wing facing the Mall, so completing the square of Buckingham Palace, and blocking the most beautiful part of the palace from public view. It is not the most attractive building, or even the most attractive palace in London. But it is the Queen's office when she is in London, where she is at home and at work on week-days for most of the year. Prince Philip has described living there as 'living over the shop'.

A quarter of a mile down the Mall is St James's Palace, the red-brick turreted hunting-lodge that Henry VIII built for Anne Boleyn. It is still the official palace to which ambassadors to the United Kingdom are accredited. It is the offices of the Lord Chamberlain and the official residence of the Duke of Kent. Clarence House, the Queen Mother's home, is part of St James's.

Other members of the royal family – Princess Margaret, all the Gloucesters, Princess Alice, Countess of Athlone, and the Beauforts – have their residences in Kensington Palace, built by William and Mary to replace Whitehall, and the principal palace of the Georges. The state apartments are run as a museum by the Department of the Environment, and furnished by the Queen from the state collections.

Other historic ancient palaces such as the Tower of London, Hampton Court, and Kew Palace have become almost completely ancient monuments, run by the Department of the Environment to the great profit of the tourist industry. They retain such links with their royal origins as the nightly Ceremony of the Keys at the Tower, and the Grace and Favour apartments for courtiers and retired and distinguished servants of the state or their widows at Hampton Court.

Windsor Castle is the Queen's week-end palace, and conforms to romantic images of what a royal castle ought to look like. In fact the exterior romance is spurious, most of it having been stuck there by that magnificent builder George IV, who had castellation, portcullis-grooves, and machicolations for pouring boiling oil on his many critics inserted as engaging Gothic anachronisms. The castle itself is old, having been planted there by William the Conqueror as one of a ring of strongholds to hold London.

His fortress was wooden on a high mound of earth. Subsequent kings have added curtain walls of shining stone around the round tower. Edward III made it the spiritual home of the Order of the Garter; and Edward IV built St George's Chapel in it, the world's glory of Gothic perpendicular. Windsor is used increasingly for entertaining visiting heads of state, so as to avoid adding to the traffic congestion of central London. The Queen now always spends Christmas and Ascot week there, and uses the castle frequently at Easter and in the summer, and for week-ends throughout the year.

Holyroodhouse on the outskirts of Edinburgh is the Queen's official residence in Scotland. The ancient and sinister palace of the Scottish kings was damaged by Cromwell's troops, and rebuilt by Charles II in its present form incorporating the medieval tower. The Queen spends at least one week a year there, usually early in July, while carrying out her round of Scottish engagements. It is also used by other heads of state who visit Scotland.

Balmoral and Sandringham, although exceedingly grand houses by most standards, are the Queen's private residences, not royal palaces. Balmoral, in Aberdeenshire beside the Dee, was built and decorated by Prince Albert in the 1850s with unimaginable splendours of Victorian Gothic and tartanitis. The Queen and her family spend August and September on Deeside; not on holiday, since her constitutional duties and voluminous state papers follow her everywhere, but showing the same devotion to the Highlands at their most beautiful time of year that her great-great-grandmother Victoria discovered.

Many other strange and romantic objects have become attached to the Crown down the centuries. For example, there is the 'stone of destiny' on which the Scottish kings used to be crowned. Edward I removed it from the Abbey of Scone in Perthshire in 1296, and it is contained in the coronation throne known as 'King Edward's chair' in Westminster Abbey. According to the legend the patriarch Jacob rested his head on this stone when he dreamed that he saw a ladder reaching into heaven. All English sovereigns since the thirteenth century have been crowned seated above this stone. Even Oliver Cromwell made use of its symbolism when he was installed as Lord Protector.

The royal collections of antique furniture, and drawings and paintings by old masters are among the finest in the world. The English regalia, royal insignia, crown jewels, and plate constitute the most remarkable collection of jewelry in the world, encrusted with grotesquely huge precious stones and ancient awe. The original crown and other relics of Edward the Confessor, the only English king to have been consecrated as a saint, and certainly the only one to have deserved consecration, were either lost in the Middle Ages or destroyed after the Civil War. Nevertheless, the crown used at the coronation is still known as St Edward's crown, and new crowns, sceptres, and other regalia have been added from the seventeenth century onwards. The oldest items of the regalia to have remained in continual use are the twelfth-century anointing spoon, and the fourteenth-century ampulla, the golden vessel shaped like an eagle for holding the consecrated oil or chrism. They were renovated and ornamented for the coronation of Charles II, but have been in use for much longer than that, and are still used at coronations. The greatest addition to the crown jewels in this century was the Cullinan diamond, presented to Edward VII in 1907 by the government of the Transvaal. It was so large that it had to be divided into four great diamonds, known as the Stars of Africa, and a number of lesser stones. The principal Star of Africa, the largest diamond in the world, is set in the head of the Sceptre with the Cross. The second largest is in the front of the Crown of State, the Stuart Sapphire having been moved to the back of the crown to make room for it.

The hardware of the monarchy is not only exceedingly valuable, but exceedingly ancient and steeped in reverent tradition and superstitition. An old and strong tradition records that the sapphire in the cross surmounting the Imperial State Crown is the jewel from Edward the Confessor's ring, removed from his finger when his coffin was opened in the twelfth century by an abbot of Westminster. The regalia of the English monarchy, like its other roots and traditions, go back at least a thousand years. The antiquity and endurance of the institution are complemented by its ancient court and trappings.

9 The Future

The English monarchy has survived and evolved by a process of judicious amputation for more than a thousand years. What is the prognostic for its survival into the future? The notion and institution of royalty are peculiar creatures to find flourishing in the second half of the twentieth century. In an age of democracy, it is hierarchic; in an age of egalitarianism, it is elitist; in an age of scepticism, it is mystical. A priori arguments for the monarchy are unpersuasive in the modern tide of ideas. Its justification must be pragmatic in the good old tradition of English empiricism. Does it work?

The prime function of the monarchy today has become negative. It sticks out of the ancient constitution of the United Kingdom as Eddystone lighthouse sticks out of the English Channel south of Plymouth, not active, but at the same time not allowing certain disastrous things to happen. It is a tower of strength in times of constitutional storm, enabling changes to be made without violence, while maintaining the sense of continuity and tradition that is so strong an element in the English idiosyncrasy.

Some convinced republicans would like to pull down the lighthouse; and, in any case, expect it to crumble and disappear before long. Rather more would like to remove the vestigial and potential powers of the monarchy and leave the Queen as an ornamental puppet, an attraction for the tourist industry and the opium of the people. For example, the Home Policy Committee of the Labour Party recommended in the spring of 1976 that the Queen should be taken out of politics by removing the monarchy's power to dissolve Parliament and to call on a party leader to form an administration. It also recommended that Labour should reduce the number of honours awarded by the Crown to very few; abolish hereditary titles; and promote people to the House of Lords without ennobling them. Policy committees propose, but the Prime Minister and the Cabinet dispose what becomes government policy, without necessarily taking account of their proposals.

The motive for abolishing the constitutional powers of the monarchy must be that it is supposed that the monarchy impedes progress: that is, stops politicians from making what they think are desirable changes. There is little evidence for this, though some do suppose it. The monarch has only had a real choice of whom to invite to be Prime Minister in exceptional cases in this century: Lloyd George in 1916, Ramsay MacDonald in 1931, and Winston Churchill in 1940. In none of these crises did the monarch make a personal choice without meticulous soundings of opinion. In at least two of them the man he eventually sent for was not the one he would have chosen personally. And in all of them it can be persuasively argued that the best man for the country was chosen.

The monarch's rare direct interventions into politics this century have generally been imaginative and progressive rather than reactionary. For example, one of the best political initiatives of George VI was to influence Clement Attlee to make Ernest Bevin rather than Hugh Dalton Foreign Secretary. Bevin was an improbable political master for the exquisite mandarins and brilliant, bumptious young men of the Foreign Office. Before he met Bevin for the first time the King asked Jimmy Thomas, the Labour politician and a friend of his, what sort of man Ernie Bevin was. Thomas made the cheerful reply: ''E's a bloody 'ound, your majesty'. George VI and Bevin took to each other immediately; and Bevin made one of the best British Foreign Secretaries, immeasurably better than Dalton would have made.

A more serious argument against the monarchy is that its conservative influence against 'progress' is not direct, but indirect. It is argued that a hazy image of Buckingham Palace lies behind many old-fashioned attitudes that prevent Great Britain from coming to terms with its changed position in the world, and from making the painful transition from imperial splendour to the hard realities of competitive trading. If this were true, it would not be fair to blame Buckingham Palace, which has been notably readier to adapt to Britain's new and doubtful role in the world than much of the rest of the country. A constitutional monarchy actually makes change easier, by lending its authority to the government of the day. Opponents of the government think twice before taking to the barricades against what appears to be the majesty of the Crown.

To abolish the monarchy in order to end its supposedly pernicious social influence would be to cut off our nose to spite our face, because we should lose a priceless constitutional safeguard. The case is altered since Magna Carta. Bureaucrats, politicians, and to some extent trade unionists and multinational companies are the masters now; and the Crown, which has far less practical power than King John's barons or even Simon de Montfort's knights of the shires, is the ultimate guardian of the liberties of the people. The House of Commons in theory, and in particular practice the Cabinet and Whitehall, have become virtually omnipotent. There is wisdom and safety in keeping some lingering constitutional powers in reserve, out of the hands of politicians, and in hands that are above politics and indisputably seen to be so, for the political storms ahead. They would only be needed in extreme crisis: for example, an extremist government, elected on a minority vote, which tried to abolish the monarchy, the House of Lords, and all other constitutional restraints, and perpetuate the existence of the sitting House of Commons. In such improbable circumstances a monarch would be justified in exercising her constitutional powers, which would almost immediately afterwards be approved or repudiated by the people in a general election. No monarch could exercise these powers unadvisedly, lightly, or wantonly because, apart from anything else, she would not get a second chance to exercise them, if a general election did not validate her action.

It would be folly to throw away such a useful constitutional mechanism without getting some corresponding advantage. In any case, there is no need to abolish the monarchy at a stroke. It would divide the country bitterly. Evolution not revolution is the British way of doing things, as well as the civilized way of doing things. If changes are needed, the monarchy has shown itself to be almost infinitely adaptable over the past thousand years.

Although the constitutional role of the monarchy is a pearl of great price and the envy of less orderly, more tyrannical societies, the need for the monarchy and justification of it have deeper roots, going back to the days before Parliaments and politicians. It satisfies some atavistic and prehistoric streak in human nature that needs somebody to look up to. Carlyle touched on it with his theory of heroes, hero-worship, and the heroic in history. Two thirds of the men and women who have been monarchs of England have been blackguards, egomaniacs, idiots, and generally the most unadmirable specimens of the human race. The same can be said of the men who have been popes. Nevertheless, the monarchy and the papacy are still living institutions, because they satisfy this primeval need for a representative, a hieratic symbol, a big daddy. It is expedient for us that one man should be elevated in front of the people. Churchill filled the role in the last war. Film stars and football players fill it in part today. The instinct may be primitive, but it goes deep. If human beings were rational, unselfish animals, they would not need somebody to look up to. But they are not.

Modern urban and industrial society needs its tribal rituals, father figures, scapegoats, and other symbols just as much as primitive societies. It is not the case that ritual and symbols are purely for primitive tribes, used to make the rain fall or the yams grow; and that as a society grows more civilized and rational, it gradually sheds its rituals, and replaces its witch-doctors with weather forecasters and its priests with sociologists. Football and pop music are two obvious examples of modern cultural rituals. They are generally beneficent jujus that help modern man and modern woman to overcome the split between mind and body, and the sterile rationality of their technological society. They soothe existentialist despair by making people feel that they belong to something bigger than themselves. As the man said: 'Man does not live by bread alone'.

The monarchy is the supreme national and unifying symbol for Great Britain, and it is difficult to think of any substitute that would do the job as well. People need symbols to live by, and to give meaning to their random little lives. The Americans have their Declaration of Independence, their founding father figures, and, at least until recently, their national flag. Russians have dreams of world revolution, or older and hazier dreams of Mother Russia. None of these are as symbolically satisfying as the Crown, personified by a real person; and most of these national unifying symbols of other nations are now looking shabby and unconvincing.

The Crown is the validating symbol of British nationhood. That is why it excites such strong reactions in both directions. Those who have roots and established positions in the British way of life tend to see any attack on the Crown as a personal attack on their positions. Conversely, the alienated, rootless, and restless feel the Crown and its associated rituals aggravating their sense of separateness from mainstream society. That is why royal rituals such as Princess Anne's wedding or the Queen's Christmas broadcast excite so much extravagant loyalty on one hand, and so much extravagant derision on the other. Many of the older generation find any criticism of royalty or flippancy about it profoundly shocking and unpatriotic, because it seems an attack on the country and themselves. In all societies the young, the poor, the disaffected, and the unestablished tend to favour change and irreverence; older people prefer continuity and stability. The monarchy is a potent catalyst to crystallize these inveterate feelings. By challenge and criticism the monarchy responds and evolves.

The British are deservedly famous for their excellence at staging such civic and nationalist pageantry as Trooping the Colour on the Queen's official birthday, the state opening of Parliament, and the Remembrance Day parades, which are a modern cult of the dead. It is a chestnut for the British to be overheard congratulating themselves complacently on at least managing such ceremonial better than anybody else in the world, even if they no longer lead the world at anything else. British theatre, cinema, and television are similarly preoccupied with royalty. The most successful films and television series are disproportionately concerned with the wives of King Henry VIII or the private life of Edward VII.

Royalty, and especially royal romance, is for British television what the Western is for American culture: the one original national art form. The Crown and its surrounding rituals, on Horse Guards Parade, or postage stamps, or the television screen, serve to legitimate the political and economic status quo, and to represent national continuity. The monarchy strikes deep ancestral chords in the English breast. It moved Sir Winston Churchill, whose instincts were very English, to refer regularly and with sincere emotion to 'Our Noble King'.

One of the considerable advantages of a constitutional monarchy as opposed to other systems of government is that the armed forces and other public servants are taken out of party politics by being made to serve the supreme, disinterested, and neutral national symbol, the Crown. In theory, at any rate, they cannot be used for partisan purposes by any of the factions of the state. And in practice in the United Kingdom the Army and the Civil Service are impartial and above party politics; although they are not always considered so by those who wish to overthrow the state.

Most periods of history no doubt seem uncertain and volatile to their contemporaries. Even in a period of rapid and radical change such as the world is engaged in at present, the Crown can be used to legitimate almost any new political and economic system that the national will throws up. In constitutional theory the Queen would have to give her royal assent to a Bill to dethrone and decapitate her passed through both Houses of Parliament. In practice, she would find it less painful to abdicate. The Crown has shown itself to be almost infinitely adaptable in its long retreat from absolute rule. Behind the glitter and the silliness of its more blatant partisans and its more exhibitionist enemies, it serves an essential purpose as a symbol of national unity even in a very divisive period. It can be all things to almost all men, from the reactionary monarchist to the radical democrat.

Not only constitutional theorists and sociologists adduce powerful explanations of the usefulness and mystique of royalty. Psychologists also have their explanations, as they have an explanation for everything conscious, and most unconscious things under the sun. One theory explains the primeval emotions aroused by royalty as the result of a father-fixation, or, when appropriate, a mother-fixation on the person of the monarch. The far-flung tribes of the British Empire who called Queen Victoria 'Great White Mother' were more profound in their appellation than was supposed at the time. Harold Nicolson argued persuasively that the ordinary citizens learned to regard King George V both as the father of his people and as the reflection of their own collective virtues. This theory has been enlarged to embrace a whole royal family that is both ideal and idol. Frances Donaldson finds even this inadequate, as being prosaic, and taking no account of the glamour and the glory, the jewels and the uniforms, the limelight on the slim groomed figure gravely receiving homage; or of man's upward strivings, his sense of beauty, his ordinary human failings. She observes that when people who have previously believed themselves to be immune to the attractions of royalty find themselves in its presence, they are often taken by surprise by the ecstasy of pleasure and appreciation they feel.

Other psychological theories dive down deeper into the unconscious and come up muddier. It has been suggested that infant fantasy sees childhood as a royal court, and parents as interchangeable with royalty. The infant ego, that most majestic of incarnations of His Majesty the Ego, experiences growing-up as a dethronement or exile from its former royal state. The myth of King Oedipus, who killed the king and took the queen who was also his mother to wife, may reveal the infantile wish to be king, as well as the more orthodox infantile wish, which is later opposed and repudiated by the barrier against incest.

Other interesting work has been done on the theory that monarchy is the apotheosis of the well-known British penchant for fancy dress. Subjects can only indulge themselves in white tie and tails, tiaras, academic and civic gowns, football supporters' costumes, bogus insignia of King Arthur and his knights of the Round Table, and other absurd dress on special occasions, when sympathetic *cognoscenti* are present, and profane outsiders cannot scoff. But there is something peculiarly satisfying for such a race in having as head of state somebody whose official uniform is a velvet mantle, stars, garters, ribbons or even ribands, crown, orb, and sceptre. That, apparently, is the costume that the subconscious of many true Britons wears in its fantasies.

No doubt most of these theories contain some truth, on the middle-aged view that most theories about any subject have some part of the truth, however infinitesimal. But it is unnecessary to explore such recondite explanations of the monarchy, nor the explanations of it adduced by animists, economists of the school of Milton Friedman, Flat-Earthers, ecologists, and other sects. The main justification for it is that it is there, that it has been there for a thousand years, that it works, and that it can be adapted if necessary. It is an invaluable last line of defence of the constitution, and an invaluable symbol of British nationhood and of unity between the disparate races of the Commonwealth. The present Queen is a woman of great conscientiousness, tact, and character, who has continued the work of her father and mother in preserving and reforming the monarchy, after her uncle had nearly destroyed it. The Prince of Wales has been sensibly educated for his demanding constitutional and symbolic role, and promises extremely well. The monarchy could no longer survive an autocratic monarch like George III, or a dissolute one like George IV; and everybody recognizes this, most of all the Palace.

The hereditary principle for selecting people for jobs is seen to be anomalous and unfair today. But any other way of selecting a monarch would be divisive instead of cohesive, and would break the historic tradition, which is so potent an element of the totemism of monarchy. There is little reason to suppose that Britain's unique, illogical, but functionally useful system of constitutional monarchy will not survive for many more jubilees and reigns, provided that it keeps its head, remembers its place, and does not produce a really bad king of the old-fashioned sort. The finances need to be put right, and to be seen to be put right. And some of the sillier snobberies of the honours system and ceremonial need to be pruned. But no doubt the monarchy will continue to adapt itself to the needs of the time and the people by the infinite flexibilities of the constitution, as it has with wonderful success in the past.

Bibliography

Albert, Harold. *The Queen and the Arts*, 1963.

Attlee, C. R. *As It Happened*, 1954.

Bagehot, Walter. *The English Constitution* Introduction by R. H. S. Crossman, 1963.

Beaton, Cecil. *The Glass of Fashion*, 1954.

Beaverbrook, Lord. *The Abdication of King Edward the Eighth*, edited by A. J. P. Taylor, 1966.

Black, Percy. *The Mystique of Modern Monarchy*, 1952.

Bocock, Robert. *Ritual in Industrial Society*, 1974.

Bolitho, Hector. *George the Sixth*, 1937.

Boothroyd, Basil. *Philip – An Informal Biography*, 1971.

Burke's *Guide to the Royal Family*, 1973.

Campbell, Judith. *Elizabeth and Philip*, 1972.

Carter, Byrnes. *The Office of Prime Minister*, 1956.

Cathcart, Helen. *Her Majesty*, 1962; *The Queen Mother*, 1965.

Churchill, Randolph. *They Serve the Queen*, 1953.

Crawford, Marion. *The Little Princesses*, 1950.

Dimbleby, Richard. *Elizabeth our Queen*, 1953.

Duncan, Andrew. *The Reality of Monarchy*, 1970.

Emden, Paul. *Behind the Throne*, 1934.

Fisher, Graham and Heather. *Elizabeth Queen and Mother*, 1964.

Fletcher, I. H. *The British Court: Its Tradition and Ceremonial*, 1953.

Gore, John. *King George V*, 1941.

Hamilton, Willie. *My Queen and I*, 1975.

Hardie, Frank. *The Political Influence of the British Monarchy 1868–1952*, 1970.

Harris, Leonard M. *Long to Reign over Us*, 1966.

Hibbert, Christopher. *The Court at Windsor – A Domestic History*, 1964.

Hogart, A. M. *Kingship*, 1927.

Holmes, Martin and Sitwell, Major-General H. D. W. *The English Regalia*, 1972.

Inglis, Brian. *Abdication*, 1966.

Jennings, Sir W. Ivor. *The British Constitution*, 1950; *The Law and the Constitution*, 1959; *The Queen's Government*, 1960.

Keith, A. B. *The Constitution of England from Victoria to George VI*, 1940.

Kinross, Lord. *The Windsor Years – The Life of Edward as Prince of Wales, King, and Duke of Windsor*, 1967.

Laird, Dorothy. *How the Queen Reigns*, 1959.

Longford, Elizabeth. *The Royal House of Windsor*, 1974.

Macmillan, Harold. *Riding the Storm*, 1971; *Pointing the Way*, 1972; *The End of the Day*, 1973.

Magnus, Philip. *King Edward the Seventh*, 1964.

Marie Louise, Princess. *My Life in Six Reigns*, 1956.

Martin, Kingsley. *The Crown and the Establishment*, 1962.

Michie, Allan. *The Crown and the People*, 1952.

Morrah, Dermot. *To Be a King*, 1968.

Murray-Brown, Jeremy, editor. *The Monarchy and its Future*, 1969.

Nicolson, Harold. *King George V, his life and reign*, 1952; *Monarchy*, 1962.

Petrie, Sir Charles. *Monarchy in the 20th Century*, 1952.

Philip, Prince, Duke of Edinburgh. *Prince Philip Speaks* – Selected Speeches, 1960; *Birds from Britannia*, 1962.

Ponsonby, Arthur. *Henry Ponsonby, his life from his letters*, 1942.

Ponsonby, Sir Frederick. *Recollections of Three Reigns*, 1951.

Simon, Viscount. *The Crown and the Commonwealth*, 1953.

Stationery Office. *Britain 1976*, an official handbook, 1976.

Wheeler-Bennett, John. *King George VI, his life and reign*, 1958; *A wreath to Clio*, 1967.

Wilson, Harold. *The Labour Government 1964–70 – A Personal Record*, 1971.

Wilson, S. S. *The Cabinet Office to 1945*, 1975.

Windsor, Duchess of. *The Heart has its Reasons*, 1956.

Windsor, Duke of. *A King's Story*, 1951.

Acknowledgments for the Illustrations

The Associated Press Ltd: pp. 2/62/77.
Mansell Collection: p. 10.
Associated Newspapers: p. 12.
Camera Press Ltd: pp. 13/col. III de Lynk/57/61/67 bottom/73/107 right/126/130 left/col. IX Peter Grugeon/col. X Karsh/col. XI Norman Parkinson/col. XII Lord Snowdon/140/150.
Keystone Press Agency Ltd: pp. 21/30/col. I/col. VIII/135/col. XIII/col. XIV/190/191.
Copyright reserved: pp. 23/107 left.
The Times: pp. 27/51/59/81/83/85/88/111 top/160/175 right/182/187.
Poppertoto: pp. 31/col. IV/71/79/95/100/109/123/138/141/145/147.
The Press Association Ltd: col. II/pp. 104 left/111 bottom/130 right.
Courtesy of the Economist Newspaper Ltd: p. 35.

Australian Information Service, London: pp. 46/101 right.
Topix: p. 67 top.
Independent Television Corporation and British Broadcasting Corporation: pp. 78/173.
Spink & Son Ltd, London: col. V/col. VI/pp. 99 left top, left bottom, right bottom/106 bottom row left, right centre, right.
Garrard the Crown Jewellers: p. 99 right top.
New Zealand Ministry of Defence: p. 101 left.
Canadian High Commission, London: p. 101 centre.
By courtesy of Men's Wear: p. 104 right.
Crown copyright; photo the Royal Mint: p. 106 bottom row left centre.

The Sunday Times Colour Library: col. VII.
Punch: p. 118.
Private Eye: p. 119.
Reproduced from *Britannia Bright's Bewilderment in the Wilderness of Westminster* by Clive James, illustrated by Mark Boxer by kind permission of Jonathan Cape Ltd: p. 120.
Crown Copyright Reserved: p. 129.
Reproduced by kind permission of the Treasurer and Master of the Bench of Lincoln's Inn: p. 142.
The Central Press Photos Ltd: p. 175 left.
The Telegraph Colour Library, photos Adam Woolfitt: pp. 179/184.
Crown copyright, reproduced with the permission of the Controller of Her Majesty's Stationery Office: col. XV/col. XVI.